CW01197928

SOPHIE SADLER

GERMAN HOME KITCHEN

Traditional Recipes That Capture the Flavors of Germany

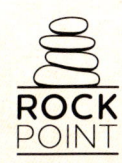

ROCK POINT

Contents

Introduction 4

The German Kitchen 6

FRÜHSTÜCK (*Breakfast*) 15

Weizenbrötchen (*White Rolls*) 16

Kürbiskernbrötchen (*Pumpkin Seed Rolls*) 18

Müslibrötchen (*Granola Rolls*) 20

Berliner (*German Donuts*) 23

Plunderteig (*German Croissant Dough*) 25

Franzbrötchen (*Croissant-Style Cinnamon Rolls*) 28

Laugenecken (*Lye Pastries*) 30

Leberwurst (*Liver Paté*) 32

Pflaumenmus (*Plum Butter*) 34

FÜR ZWISCHENDURCH & BEILAGEN (*Snacks & Sides*) 37

Spargelcremesuppe (*Asparagus Cream Soup*) 39

Obatzda (*Bavarian Beer Cheese Spread*) 41

Brezeln (*Pretzels*) 42

Gebackener Camembert (*Baked Camembert*) 45

Mixed Pickles (*Pickled Veggies*) 46

Gemischter Salat (*German Mixed Salad*) 48

Kartoffelklöße (*Potato Dumplings*) 51

Semmelknödel (*Bread Dumplings*) 52

Spätzle (*German Egg Noodles*) 55

Rotkohl (*Braised Red Cabbage*) 56

Sauerkraut (*Fermented Cabbage*) 59

Bratkartoffeln (*Pan-Fried Potatoes*) 60

HAUPTSPEISEN (*Main Dishes*) 63

Sauerbraten (*Sweet-and-Sour Beef Roast*) 64

Käsespätzle (*Cheese Spätzle Noodles*) 67

Linsensuppe (*Lentil Soup*) 68

Rinderrouladen (*Beef Roulade*) 70

Kohlrouladen (*Stuffed Cabbage Rolls*) 72

Backfisch (*Beer-Battered Cod*) 74

Königsberger Klopse (*German Meatballs*) 76

Jägerschnitzel (*Pork Schnitzel with Creamy Mushroom Sauce*) 78

ABENDBROT (*Traditional Cold Dinner*) 81

Roggenmischbrot (*Rye and Wheat Bread*) 82

Körnerbrot (*Seeded Bread*) 85

Quark Dips 87

Fleischsalat (*Bologna Salad*) 90

Gewürzgurken (*Seasoned Pickles*) 91

SÜßE SPEISEN (*Sweet Meals*) 93

Pfannkuchen (*Pancakes*) 95

Milchreis (*Rice Pudding*) 96

Saure Sahne Waffeln (*Sour Cream Waffles*) 99

Dampfnudeln (*Steamed Dumplings*) 100

IMBISSBUDE (*Street Food*) 103

Döner (*Meat-Stuffed Bread Pockets*) 105

Pommesgewürz (*German Fry Seasoning*) 107

Frikadellen (*German Hamburgers*) 108

Currywurst (*Bratwurst with Curry Ketchup*) 111

Flieten (*Fried Chicken Wings*) 112

AUS OMA SIEGHILDES KÜCHE (*From Oma Sieghilde's Kitchen*) 115

Klößchen (*Mini Potato Dumplings*) 117

Erbsbrei (*Mashed Pea Puree*) 118

Kartoffelpuffer (*Potato Pancakes*) 121

Zwiebelkuchen (*Onion Pie*) 122

Karoffelsalat (*Creamy Potato Salad*) 125

Baumkuchen (*Tree Cake*) 126

KAFFEE & KUCHEN (*Afternoon Coffee & Cake*) 129

Hefezopf (*Yeast Braid*) 130

Blaubeer Quarkstrudel (*Quark and Blueberry Strudel*) 133

Schwarzwälder Kirschtorte (*Black Forest Cherry Cake*) 135

Spaghettieis (*Spaghetti Ice Cream*) 138

Rote Grütze (*Berry Grits*) 141

Käsekuchen im Glas (*Raspberry Cheesecake in a Jar*) 142

Apfelkuchen (*Apple Cake*) 144

Rhabarberstreusel (*Rhubarb Streusel Cake*) 146

Marmorkuchen (*German Marble Cake*) 148

Rotweinbirnenkuchen (*Red Wine Pear Cake*) 150

Tante Heidruns Mandarinen-Schmand-Kuchen (*Mandarin Orange Sour Cream Cake*) 152

Erdbeerrolle (*Sponge Cake with Strawberries and Cream Filling*) 154

WEIHNACHTEN (*Christmas*) 157

Vanillekipferl (*Vanilla Bean Cookies*) 158

Spitzbuben (*Jam-Filled Cookies*) 161

Glühwein (*Mulled Wine*) 162

Raclette (*Tableside Cheese Meal*) 163

Käsefondue (*Cheese Fondue*) 166

Recipe Index by Keyword 168

Index 171

Acknowledgments 174

About the Author 175

Introduction

When I was in first grade, we—very atypical for a German family—were always running late for school. On the way, my mom would ask, "Do you want to stop at the bakery for a belegtes Brötchen (sandwich) or be on time?" The right answer was always take the Brötchen and be late.

I remember the french fries we ate at the public swimming pool on a warm summer day. The homemade spinach-stuffed pasta I attempted making with my cousin when I was eight years old. Blowing out candles on the not-so-super-sweet, chocolate-glazed marble cakes, topped with chocolate candies, for my twin sister Jeanne's and my birthdays.

Those early food memories followed me into my Oma Sieghilde's kitchen when she became our after-school caretaker after we moved to the same little village, tucked between the most stunning vineyard-covered hills.

I remember shredding an endless pile of potatoes for Kartoffelpuffer, eating them fresh out of the pan, and watching and identifying birds from her kitchen window. Picking fresh chives from her garden for herbed Quark to spread on slices of fresh bread from the bakery in town. Making a competition out of finding the smallest, sweetest strawberries in her garden.

Then, one day she had a stroke. Oma was paralyzed from head to toe for what felt like years. But she fought her way back. Growing up, all I saw was her relentless determination to get better. Eventually, she came back so strong that she wasn't just walking again but also back in the kitchen, cooking for us. My sister and I knew we had to step in and help her because there was no way we wanted to live without her meals.

Later, when I moved to the United States, I wanted nothing more than to bring Oma's meals into my life, into this new, unfamiliar world.

But the food at German restaurants here didn't taste like home. And cooking those dishes? Not easy. The ingredients, the ovens, the measurements—everything was just so different. It took trial after trial to make authentic Brötchen for Frühstück. It took years to perfect pretzels that came out of my oven tasting like they had been purchased from the best German bakeries.

Eventually, I felt called to help Americans realize that German food really is so much more than pretzels and bratwurst. German cuisine is

From l–r: My great-grandpa, Ewald; my twin sister, Jeanne; my Oma Ingeborg; me; and my Oma Sieghilde.

German Home Kitchen

vast, diverse, and deeply personal—every region has its own take on tradition and every family has its own way of creating the food experiences that make us feel at home.

I am so grateful that my Oma made a comeback. She gave me so much after. Mostly she inspired me to create my blog and this book. Oma and I always had a special connection—writing letters back and forth, sending me recipes and books. She helped me cope with my homesickness. When I struggled to replicate a recipe, Oma Sieghilde was there with tips and long phone calls. Other family members jumped in to help, too, because Oma didn't write down her recipes, and observing her from five thousand miles (8,047 km) away was a bit of a challenge.

In 2015, I began sharing my German recipes with the world through my German food blog, *Dirndl Kitchen*. The name is a playful nod to the stereotype that Americans think all Germans wear Dirndls and Lederhosen at all times. (Not true, of course, but funny.)

At some point, I discovered that blogging could be my career. It was a no-brainer to focus on blogging during the pandemic, when I found myself at home, cooking and baking more than ever. It helped me to stay connected and comforted when visiting family wasn't possible.

Creating and sharing authentic German recipes feels surreal and fulfilling. And I get to do it while spending so much time with my three little loves—Zoë, Eloïse, and Maximilian—and you, Jason, the great love of my life.

Now, my dream of writing a German cookbook—*this book*—is a reality. Someone pinch me. I hope it inspires you to find your way with German cooking and baking and that your journey goes far beyond pretzels and bratwurst.

Oma Sieghilde guided me in writing this book, even though she passed away shortly after I started my blog. Part of her story and those of many other family members and friends who have inspired me are woven into these pages.

But this book is not meant to honor any one specific person. Its mission is to honor every one of you. Whether you're longing to connect with your German roots, rediscover a family recipe, or simply explore the depth of German cuisine, I want this book to help you bring those flavors home.

So, from my kitchen to yours, allow me to take you by the hand and show you how—from homemade Sauerkraut and Leberwurst to Oma's bite-size potato dumplings, Klößchen.

Mit viel Liebe, with much love,
Sophie

Introduction

The German Kitchen

SPEISEKAMMER *(Pantry)* STAPLES

In Germany, pantry essentials are twofold. Traditionally, each home has a speisekammer (pantry) right by the kitchen and another pantry in the keller (cellar).

Modern homes often do not have a keller anymore, but I think it would be wonderful to bring it back. Since a cellar is underground or partially underground, it's naturally cooler, making it an ideal place for storing backups, wine, and canned goods, such as Gewürzgurken (page 91), Mixed Pickles (page 46), jams, and Pflaumenmus (page 34). Potatoes and onions also keep better in cool, dark spaces.

The speisekammer is where dry goods are stored. It's home to the brotmaschine (bread slicer) and brotbox (bread box), both staples in every German household.

Spices are either found in kitchen cabinets or on a shelf in the pantry, depending on the distance to the cooktop.

If you'd like to stock your pantry with German basics, here are the common spices, jarred items, and dry goods found in my German kitchen:

HERBS

- Dried thyme
- Dried oregano
- Bay leaves
- Fresh and dried chives
- Fresh and dried parsley
- Dried marjoram

SPICES

- Sweet paprika
- Spicy (half-sharp) paprika
- Cinnamon sticks and ground cinnamon
- Whole and ground cloves
- Whole nutmeg (freshly grated—danke, Oma Inge)
- Whole caraway seeds
- Ground white pepper (my Oma preferred it)
- Ground black pepper (I prefer it)
- Mild curry powder
- Cayenne pepper

SPICE BLENDS

Pul Biber: A Turkish chili seasoning blend that adds a kick to Turkish foods, pasta dishes, and more. It's used in my Chicken Döner Kebab recipe (page 105).

Pommesgewürz: An addictive German fry seasoning that's also an amazing all-purpose seasoning (page 107).

Currywurstgewürz: A must-have! Sprinkle it over a ketchup-drenched Bratwurst for an instant Currywurst. (However, my Currywurst recipe on page 111 with homemade curry ketchup sauce is even better!)

Flietengewürz: While not every German keeps this on their spice rack, it's my go-to seasoning

German Home Kitchen

for Trier-style chicken wings (page 112). It's also amazing on grilled chicken.

Schwenkbratengewürz: This specialty pork seasoning from Saarland (used in the Raclette recipe on page 163) is unlike anything you can find in the States. It's great for all grilled meats.

Cinnamon Sugar: It's a simple combination and a great, warming sprinkle of sweetness to Berliner (page 23), Pfannkuchen (page 95), and Milchreis (page 96). To make it, combine 1 part cinnamon and 2 parts granulated sugar in an airtight container. Cinnamon sugar keeps for up to 2 years.

SALT
I like using fine Redmond Real Salt for my cooking and baking, which is a light pink mineral rock salt. A great alternative would be fine sea salt.

JARS
Jam: The most popular jam flavors include apricot, strawberry, cherry, raspberry, quince, plum, rose hip, red currant, and black currant.

Pflaumenmus (plum butter): A must-try! Find the recipe on page 34.

Sauerkraut: Homemade is so much better than store-bought. Let my recipe on page 60 show you why.

Rotkohl (braised red cabbage): It's best homemade. You can jar it or freeze it. Find the recipe on page 59.

Pickles: Sweet-and-sour varieties, such as Gewürzgurken (page 91) and Mixed Pickles (page 46).

FLOURS
All-purpose flour is used in most recipes in this book; it's most comparable to Type 550 wheat flour in Germany. Likewise, dark rye flour is used in this book; it's most comparable to Type 1900 whole grain rye flour in Germany. Other flours are more straightforward.

SUGARS
Sugar in this book will be labeled as either granulated sugar, powdered sugar, or vanilla sugar.

COCOA POWDER AND CHOCOLATE
It's always good to have some of both on hand! If you don't bake often, store chocolate in the freezer. I prefer semisweet chocolate (between 35 and 65% cocoa content) for cakes.

VANILLA
I primarily use vanilla extract in this book, but in Germany, vanilla beans or vanilla sugar are more common. 1 teaspoon of vanilla extract is equal to about 2 teaspoons of vanilla sugar. 1 vanilla bean is equal to about 1 tablespoon of vanilla extract.

To make vanilla sugar: Place scraped vanilla beans in a small jar with granulated sugar. Seal and let it sit undisturbed for a week or so to allow the vanilla to infuse the sugar.

YEAST
Active dry yeast is used in this book, as it's the closest equivalent to the type of yeast most commonly used in Germany. It activates easily in lukewarm (105 to 115°F or 40 to 46°C) liquid—no sugar needed. Store it in an airtight container in the refrigerator to extend shelf life.

RUM
My Oma Sieghilde loved adding spiced rum to baked goods, even waffle batter! It adds great depth of flavor. Oma always used the Austrian Stroh rum, though it's harder to find in the United States. Any spiced rum will work. You can also leave it out.

FRYING OIL

When cooking over high heat, I like to use avocado oil—it's neutral and has a high smoke point, which makes it ideal for high-temperature cooking. To get the most out of it, I reuse my oil after deep frying. I strain the completely cooled, once-used oil back into its original bottle, label it, and typically reuse it twice. (Just don't fry Berliner after frying fish—trust me, it doesn't work out well.)

LYE

Also called Sodium Hydroxide (Natriumhydroxid or Natronlauge in German), lye is what gives Brezeln (page 39) their deep brown color and authentic pretzel flavor. Lye comes in white granules that dissolve in water. In Germany, it's usually purchased from a pharmacy (Apotheke), while in the States, food-grade lye is available online.

LYE SAFETY TIPS

- Never touch the dry or the diluted lye. Wash your hands immediately if contact occurs.
- Always add lye granules to cold water and never the other way around.
- Work in a well-ventilated area. Turn the vent hood to high or step outside when mixing.
- Store lye in a tightly sealed container in a dry, cool place, away from children.
- You are working with a chemical here, but don't be intimidated. Just follow these steps and keep the delicious end results in mind—you can do this!

KELLER (*Cellar*) STAPLES

If you have a keller (or something similar), here are some of the fruits and vegetables to store there:

APPLES

For most recipes in this book, I like to use tart apples that keep their shape well when cooked or baked, like Granny Smith. If you like sweeter apples for baking, Honeycrisp, Gala, Jonagold, Golden Delicious, and Jonathan apples also work well.

ORGANIC LEMON

The zest is often used in German baking, which is why organic is best.

GARLIC

Germans love using fresh garlic, and a garlic press is a common household item. Store garlic in a dark spot.

ONIONS

I could write a romance novel about onions because I (and 90 percent of Germans) love them so much (see my recipe for Zwiebelkuchen (page 122). Yellow onions are my die-hard onion, cooked or raw. Sweet onions are great for serving raw—I love them with Leberwurst (page 32). I also love shallots, which are milder, great raw and cooked, and they add a pop of color. Store onions and shallots away from potatoes and fruit as they will cause potatoes to sprout and fruit to spoil prematurely.

POTATOES

It's no secret that Germans love their potatoes. Both starchy and waxy potatoes are used in the recipes in this book.

Waxy potatoes: These are lower in starch content and tend to keep their shape better. Examples in the USA are red potatoes, fingerling potatoes, baby potatoes, and new potatoes. In Germany, use Cilena, Linda, Nicola, Annabelle, or Belana.

Starchy potatoes: These are higher in starch content and tend to fall apart more easily; they are best used in recipes where you want a thickening effect, such as stews, soups, or dumplings. In America, the most common starchy potatoes are russet/Idaho. In Germany, starchy potatoes are Adria, Augusta, Adretta, Ackersegen, and Karelia.

All-purpose potatoes: Called *vorwiegend festkochende Kartoffeln* in Germany, these fall somewhere in the middle. They tend to keep their shape better than starchy potatoes and are great for pretty much any use. In the USA, Yukon Gold are a great all-purpose potato with a mild, buttery flavor. In Germany, go for Finka, La Bonnotte, Lady Balfour, Laura, and Marabel.

KÜHLSCHRANK *(Fridge)* STAPLES

German fridges tend to be smaller than those in the United States, which is one reason why eggs in Germany are unwashed and can be kept out of the refrigerator, freeing up valuable space for dairy, produce, and beloved condiments.

EGGS
All recipes in this book use large American eggs. One large American egg weighs an average of 2 ounces (57 g). For comparison, a large egg in Germany weighs about 2.4 ounces (67 g).

BUTTER
Germans favor grass-fed, sweet cream butter. All of the recipes in this book use unsalted butter. If you are using salted butter in a baking recipe, omit additional salt.

FRESH MILK
Whole milk is standard in all of my recipes.

HEAVY CREAM
Heavy cream (also called heavy whipping cream) is essential for sauces and homemade whipped cream (a must-have with cakes in Germany!).

To make whipped cream: In a large bowl, whisk 7 ounces (200 ml) of heavy cream, 2 tablespoons of powdered sugar, and 2 teaspoons of vanilla extract until soft peaks form. Store any leftovers in the fridge for up to 3 days. Whipped cream also freezes well for up to 3 months. To thaw, transfer to the fridge for 8 hours before using.

MAYONNAISE
Germans love their mayo, especially with Fritten (french fries), and just about anything else that pairs well with it.

MUSTARD

In Germany, you will find all sorts of mustards ranging from sweet mustard to eat with Weisswurst to some really spicy mustard if you want to kick things up a notch. Our fridge is always stocked with an excessive selection.

CURRY KETCHUP

Store-bought curry ketchup is a staple condiment in Germany. I encourage everyone to make a batch of homemade curry ketchup because it tastes so much better than store-bought versions. Use the Currywurst recipe (page 111) to experience the magic of homemade curry ketchup. If you plan to bottle some, either dice the onions extra fine or strain them out for a smoother texture.

SAMBAL OELEK

This Indonesian chili sauce is popular in Germany and great for kicking things up a notch. I use it in one of my Quark Dips on page 87.

REMOULADE

Remoulade is like a tartar sauce, but upleveled. Once you make it from scratch, you'll mourn the fact that you have been missing out on it for so many years of your life! My recipe for remoulade is found in the Backfisch recipe on page 74. Remoulade is also great with Frikadellen (page 108), on Weizenbrötchen (page 16), or in a belegtes brötchen—a classic German sandwich with deli meat like ham or salami, sliced raw veggies like fresh cucumbers, tomatoes, a leaf of lettuce, and either good butter or remoulade.

PEARS

Pears are at their best when ripe, juicy, and soft, at which point they are best kept in the crisper drawer of your refrigerator. To ripen pears, place them in a paper bag at room temperature with an apple. After 2 to 4 days, they should be juicy and ready to go in your fridge or to be eaten or used in a recipe. Bosc and Anjou pears are best for baking, as they keep their shape well.

STONE FRUITS

Stone fruits, which are commonly used in German baking, spoil faster at room temperature, so keep them in the crisper drawer of your refrigerator.

QUARK

Quark (page 12) is every German's must-have dairy. It's super versatile and has a consistency similar to thick-strained Greek yogurt, but it doesn't taste as tart. In German cooking and baking, it is used to make Käsekuchen (page 142) and Quark Dips (page 87) and is commonly eaten on its own with granola and fruit, or mixed with fruit compotes, just like you would eat yogurt.

KÜCHENGERÄTE (TOOLS)

Most of the tools I use regularly are things you probably already have in your kitchen, but there are a few my German kitchen wouldn't be complete without.

KITCHEN SCALE

I could not live without my kitchen scale! Germans mostly weigh ingredients, so this is an essential tool to have, especially when it comes to baking. It makes everything so easy, more accurate, and less messy.

CANNING JARS

Glass canning jars are essential for storing pickles, jam, quark, sauerkraut, and more. I also use them for serving individual desserts—they're incredibly versatile.

To sterilize and prepare jars for canning: Wash the jars in hot, soapy water. In a pot large enough to fit the canning jars in a single layer, add the jars facing upright, lids, rubber seals, then fill with enough water to cover the jars by at least

1 inch (2.5 cm). Heat to boiling over high heat, and let boil, uncovered, for 10 minutes. Using tongs, carefully transfer the jars to a clean kitchen towel to dry.

DEEP FRYER OR FRYING THERMOMETER

I don't actually own a deep fryer; instead, I use a deep pot, a frying or candy thermometer, and a splatter guard to protect myself from any hot oil splatters. Deep frying may sound intimidating, but it's easier than you might think!

GRATERS

From chocolate to onions, you'll be grating all sorts of ingredients throughout this book, so it's worthwhile to invest in a quality grater or two. I like using a box grater for its variety of grating options. If yours doesn't include a super-fine grater, you may want a Microplane or another rasp-style grater for grating garlic, citrus, and nutmeg. For more extensive grating jobs—like making Kartoffelpuffer (page 121) or Klößchen (page 117)—I recommend using a protective glove.

SPÄTZLE TOOLS

Spätzle are Germany's signature noodle, so having a proper tool for it makes complete sense. A spätzle press is my family's tool of choice, creating long, skinny noodles, while Spätzle graters—also popular in Germany—produce thicker, shorter, drop-like noodles called Knöpfle. Not ready to commit to a new tool? I get it. You can also make Spätzle using the cutting board and knife method (see page 51).

PIPING BAGS

Piping bags have all kinds of uses beyond cake decorating—though they're perfect for piping the whipped cream onto a Schwarzwälder Kirschtorte (page 135; use a large round or a large star tip for this). They also make adding Käsekuchen (page 142) batter to jars and filling Berliner doughnuts (page 23; use a long, skinny filling tip) much easier and less messy.

RACLETTE GRILL

I couldn't imagine the holidays without gathering tableside around a sizzling raclette grill to share a cozy meal with loved ones. Our favorite raclette grill comes with individual pans for cheese and toppings, plus a grill top—either stone or metal—for cooking meats. Learn more about Raclette on page 163.

FONDUE POT

We love Käsefondue (page 166) all winter long, but meat fondue is also popular in Germany. While you could use a small saucepan over a teapot warmer and dip your fondue dippers with regular forks instead of long-handled fondue forks, there's just something extra cozy and special about investing in a quality fondue pot.

> **A NOTE ABOUT OVENS**
>
> For German ovens: All recipes mentioned in this book that don't use convection (umluft) are based on the ober-/unterhitze setting in Germany.

The German Kitchen

Quark

For a homesick German, there is nothing quite as comforting as knowing you can make quark at home. It took me about six years of trial and error—getting frustrated, then trying again—before I finally came up with a method that creates creamy and mild quark that tastes just like the quark I grew up with. This method also keeps the probiotic cultures alive, making it not only delicious but also gut-healthy. You'll need a multi-cooker with a yogurt function, such as an Instant Pot, a yogurt maker, or a proofing box. The rest is as simple as can be. I hope you love this method and make quark over and over again, no matter where you are.

PREP TIME: 10 minutes
COOK TIME: 25 hours
YIELD: 4½ cups (1.1 L)

4¼ cups (1 l) cultured buttermilk

8½ cups (2 l) whole milk (see Note)

NOTES

✦ I prefer to store quark in a glass jar. Always make sure the container is clean and (preferably) sterilized to prevent unwanted bacteria. (For sterilizing instructions, see page 11.)

✦ After using, rinse your cheesecloth thoroughly under hot water to remove residue. Soak it in a mild detergent for a few minutes, rinse it thoroughly, squeeze out excess water, and hang to dry.

✦ If you won't use freshly made quark within 2 weeks, freeze it in a freezer-safe jar (or multiple smaller jars for quicker thawing), leaving space for expansion. To thaw, transfer to the fridge 1 to 2 days before using, depending on portion size.

1. In the bowl of a multi-cooker, or a large bowl that fits into a yogurt maker or proofing box, stir together the cultured buttermilk and the milk. Cover with a bowl cover or a clean large plate and let sit at room temperature until thickened and the mixture smells a bit sour, about 12 hours. This process could take longer, depending on room temperature. The goal is to encourage the buttermilk cultures to multiply, turning the milk into buttermilk as well. Curdling may or may not occur at this stage, depending on how active the cultures are—but don't worry, both outcomes are normal. The key is to give the cultures time to work, just like with sourdough fermentation.

2. Place the bowl in the multi-cooker, yogurt maker, or proofing box. Cover with a clean plate (do not use the lid that comes with the multi-cooker), set the temperature to 110°F (43°C) and incubate for 8 hours. (If using a multi-cooker, set it to the yogurt setting and select a custom temperature.) During this time, the buttermilk should start to separate into whey (a clear liquid) and quark.

3. Line a colander with 4 layers of cheesecloth and set it over a large bowl. Ladle in the curdled buttermilk, cover with a large plate or plastic wrap, and refrigerate. Let it strain until it resembles Greek yogurt in consistency, about 5 hours. Approximately 8 cups (2 L) of whey will have drained off. It's okay if you let it strain for longer, you can add whey back into it if necessary.

4. If the quark weighs less than 2½ pounds (1.1 kg), or measures less than 4½ cups (1.1 L), whisk in more whey. If it weighs more than 2⅔ pounds (1.2 kg), or measures more than 5 cups (1.2 L), strain it further.

5. Transfer the quark to a clean glass jar (see Notes) and store in the fridge for up to 2 weeks.

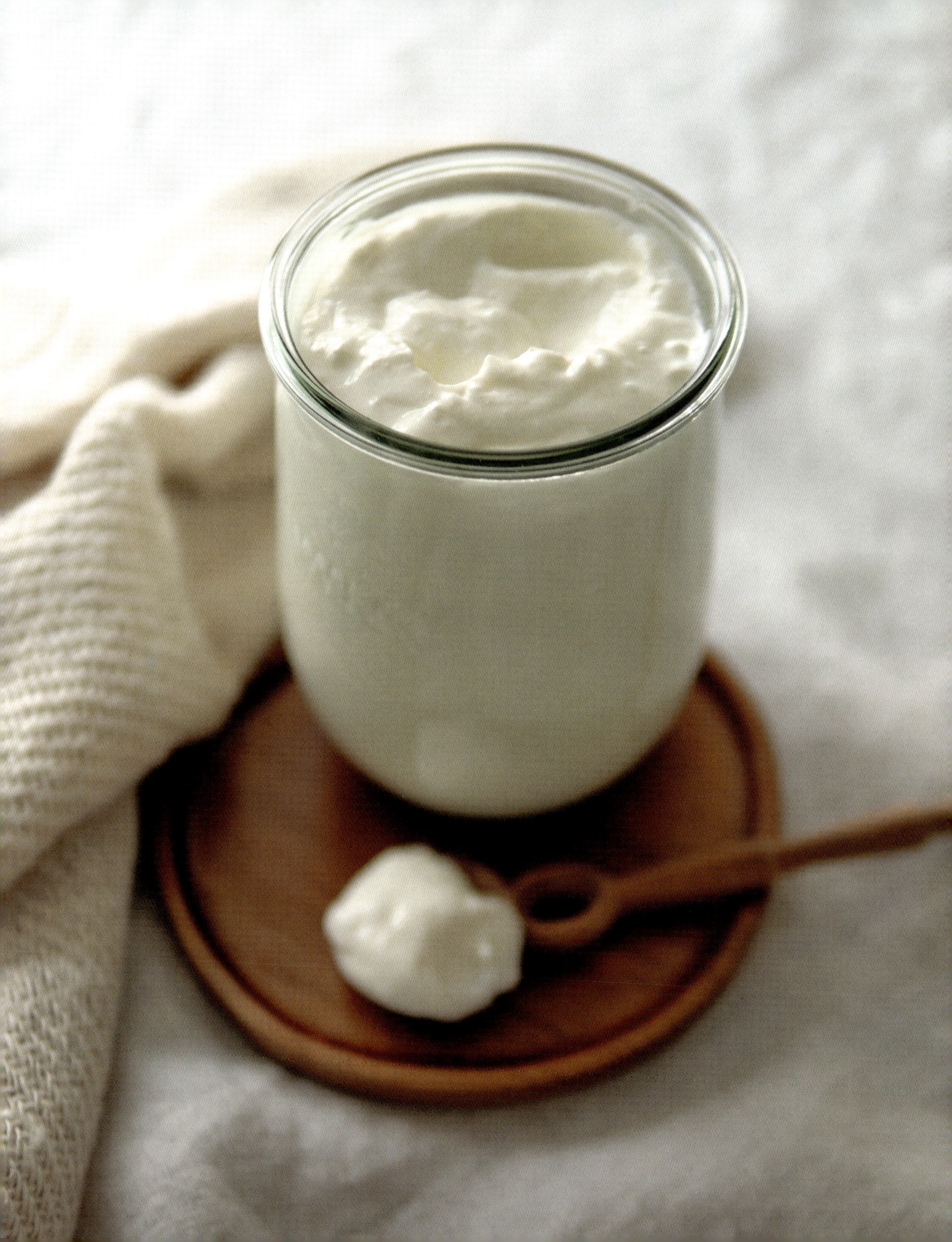

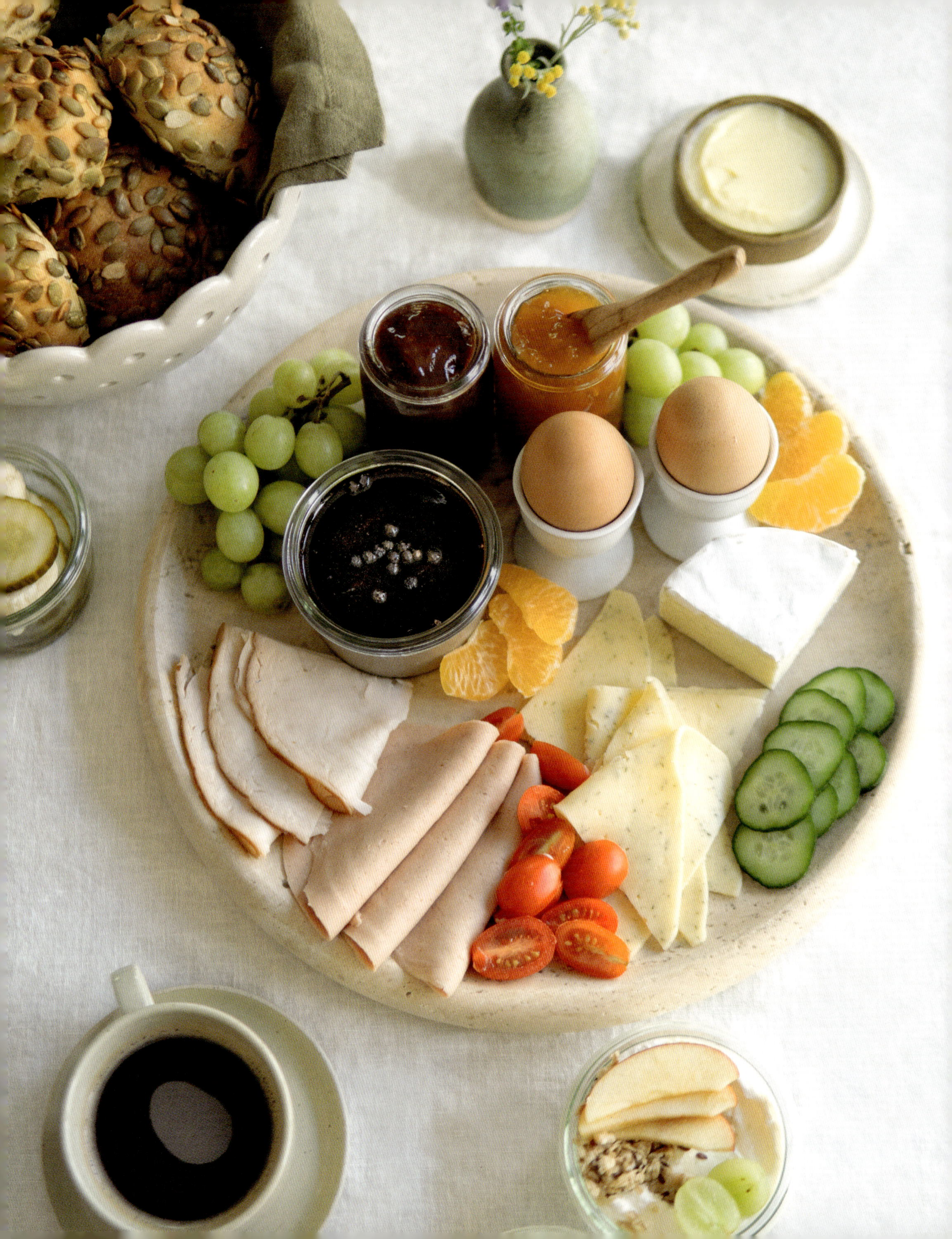

FRÜHSTÜCK

Breakfast

Breakfast in Germany is an art. It's easily my favorite meal of the day. On weekdays, breakfast is often short and simple. But weekend breakfasts are an elaborate brunch-style affair. At my Mama Ute's home, weekend breakfasts always include pretty placemats, candles, and tasteful music. I grew up with a wide assortment of amazing brötchen (rolls) and teilchen (pastries), both essential to the German breakfast table. Other Frühstück essentials include:

Das frühstücksei: A warm, medium-boiled egg with a jammy yolk (see tips right).

Sliced meats and cheeses: I prefer milder cheeses for breakfast, like young Gouda, Emmentaler, Brie, or Camembert. Leberwurst (page 32) is amazing served for breakfast with sweet onions and Gewürzgurken (page 91). Fleischsalat (page 90) is also another Frühstück favorite.

Quark (page 12), müsli (granola), and fruit: A simple and refreshing classic.

Quark Dips (pages 89): These make a fantastic addition.

And sometimes even cake: Because why not?

An extended Frühstück always makes me feel more at home. We also love hosting brunch parties to introduce our American friends to German breakfast foods they might not otherwise get to experience.

THE PERFECT BREAKFAST EGG

Germans take their frühstücksei seriously. A medium-boiled egg with a jammy yolk, served warm in a little egg cup, is necessary for a real German breakfast experience. To make frühstücksei from large, American eggs, fresh out of the fridge:

1. Heat a small pot of water to boiling over high heat. Using a soup spoon, carefully lower the eggs into the water; boil for 6 minutes.

2. Drain and immediately run cold water over the eggs to stop the cooking process. Place them in egg cups and serve with your Frühstück.

3. Using a sharp knife, slice off the top third of the egg, sprinkle with salt, and eat with a spoon. I love mine on a slice of buttered fresh bread.

Weizenbrötchen

White Rolls

These rolls are a bakery staple and an essential part of an authentic German breakfast. They're also perfect for enjoying bratwurst on the go! Weizenbrötchen are super versatile and popular at fast-food trucks, known as Imbissbuden. When ordering and eating bratwurst, Currywurst (page 111), or Frikadellen (page 108), you're almost always served one alongside. But they are just as great with sweet toppings, like chocolate hazelnut spread or butter with Pflaumenmus (page 34).

PREP TIME: 2 hours and 30 minutes, plus 2 days resting

COOK TIME: 20 minutes

YIELD: 8 rolls

PREFERMENT

- 1 cup plus 2 teaspoons (130 g) all-purpose flour
- 3 ounces (90 ml) lukewarm water
- ¼ teaspoon (1 g) active dry yeast
- ½ teaspoon (3 g) salt

DOUGH

- 2½ ounces (75 ml) lukewarm water
- 1½ teaspoons (6 g) granulated sugar
- 1 teaspoon (3 g) active dry yeast (½ packet)
- 2½ cups (300 g) all-purpose flour, plus more for dusting
- 3½ ounces (100 ml) lukewarm whole milk
- 1 teaspoon (6 g) salt
- 2 tablespoons (30 ml) hot water

1. **Make the preferment:** In a small bowl, add the flour, water, yeast, and salt; stir with a fork until a thick dough forms and no lumps remain. Cover the bowl tightly and refrigerate until the dough is nice and bubbly and has doubled in size, 48 to 72 hours.

2. **Make the dough:** In the bowl of a stand mixer fitted with the dough hook attachment, combine the lukewarm water, sugar, and yeast and stir. Let activate, about 5 minutes, or until bubbly. Add the flour, lukewarm milk, salt, and chilled preferment and mix at low speed until a smooth and elastic dough forms, about 5 minutes. Increase the speed to medium-low and knead until the dough is smooth and pulls away from the sides of the bowl, about 8 minutes. Cover the bowl tightly and let the dough rest for 30 minutes.

3. Keeping the dough in the bowl, grab a section of the dough from the bottom, stretch it upward, and fold it over the top. Rotate the bowl slightly and repeat this step all the way around. Cover the bowl tightly and let the dough rest for 30 minutes. Meanwhile, line a baking sheet with parchment paper.

4. On a clean work surface, with lightly floured hands, knead the dough for a few seconds to release the air bubbles. Using a bench scraper or a sharp knife, divide the dough into 8 equal pieces, about 3 ounces (90 grams) each. Roll each piece into a ball. Place the dough balls on the prepared baking sheet, leaving 2 inches (5 cm) between them. Cover with a clean kitchen towel and let rest in a warm spot until doubled in size, about 45 minutes.

5. Meanwhile, fill a large baking dish halfway with water and place it on the bottom rack of the oven; this will create steam. Preheat the oven to 450°F (230°C).

6. Brush the rolls with the hot water. Using a sharp knife, score the top of each roll with a straight cut about ½ inch (12 mm) deep. Bake for 10 minutes, then open the oven door wide for about 5 seconds to release steam. Continue baking for another 5 minutes. Remove the rolls and the baking dish from the oven. Lightly brush the rolls with some of the hot water (about 2 tablespoons) from the baking dish and return only the rolls to the oven. Continue to bake until golden brown, about 5 minutes. (Brushing with water toward the end of baking creates a shiny finish, while removing the water dish at the end helps the rolls crisp up and develop a beautiful color.) Transfer to a cooling rack and let sit until cool enough to handle, about 10 minutes, before enjoying.

NOTE

✤ *To freeze and reheat these rolls, I recommend doubling the batch and slightly reducing the bake time by a couple of minutes, so they don't get too dark when reheated. Let cool completely, then store the rolls in a freezer-safe bag for up to 3 months. When ready to enjoy, preheat the oven to 350°F (180°C) and lightly moisten each brötchen by swiping it under a thin stream of cold running water. Bake until the outside is crisp again, about 8 minutes.*

Kürbiskernbrötchen

Pumpkin Seed Rolls

PREP TIME: 40 minutes, plus 13 hours resting
COOK TIME: 20 minutes
YIELD: 8 rolls

Okay, picking favorites is so hard—but if I had to, these brötchen with pumpkin seeds would be it! Brötchen are the essential part of a German breakfast, and pumpkin seeds are my favorite kind of seeds. The soft interior, the crisp crust, and all those nutty pumpkin seeds make them completely irresistible. And then there's that dreamy bakery smell that fills your entire house as these rolls crisp up in the oven. There's just nothing like it, and I cannot wait for you to experience the magic in your own home.

DOUGH

2¼ teaspoons (8 g) active dry yeast (2 packets)

⅔ cup (160 ml) lukewarm milk

2 cups (240 g) all-purpose flour, plus more for dusting

¾ cup (100 g) semolina flour

½ cup (55 g) dark rye flour

⅔ cup (160 ml) cold water

1½ teaspoons (8 g) salt

2 teaspoons (10 ml) avocado oil

¾ cup (75 g) pumpkin seeds, toasted

TOPPING

½ cup (50 g) pumpkin seeds, not toasted

2 tablespoons (30 ml) hot water

1. **Make the dough:** In a small bowl, combine the yeast and milk and stir well. Let activate, about 5 minutes until bubbly.

2. In the bowl of a stand mixer fitted with the dough hook attachment, mix the flours, cold water, salt, oil, and yeast mixture at low speed until combined, about 10 minutes. Increase the speed to medium-low and continue to mix until the dough is smooth and elastic and pulls away from the sides of the bowl, about 5 minutes. Add the pumpkin seeds and mix at low speed until incorporated, about 1 minute. Cover the bowl tightly and refrigerate until the dough has doubled in size, about 12 hours (overnight is easiest).

3. On a lightly floured work surface, using your hands, roll out the dough into a log, about 2 inches (5 cm) wide, being careful not to overwork it to preserve the air bubbles that help create a more open-crumb structure. Using a bench scraper or a sharp knife, divide the dough into 8 equal pieces. Working with one piece at a time, press down on the dough with the palm of your hand, then stretch it until it is about three times as long as it is wide. Imagine each piece as 3 connected squares. Take one end square of the dough and fold it over the middle square, then fold the other end square over the middle square as well. You should now have a small, square, 3-layer dough package. Lightly press down with your palm to flatten it to half its original height. Finally, use your fingertips to gently press along the seam to seal it.

4. **For the topping:** Line a baking sheet with parchment paper. Place the pumpkin seeds in a small bowl. Brush the rolls with the hot water, then press them into the seeds so that they are coated on all sides. Place seam sides down on the prepared baking sheet, 2 inches (5 cm) apart. Cover with a clean kitchen towel and let rest in a warm spot until doubled in size, about 1 hour.

5. Meanwhile, fill a large baking dish, such as a casserole dish, halfway with water and place it on the bottom rack of the oven; this will create steam. Preheat the oven to 450°F (230°C).

6. Turn the rolls over, seam sides up, then lightly sprinkle them with water. Bake for 10 minutes, then open the oven door wide for about 5 seconds to release steam. Continue baking for another 5 minutes. Remove the rolls and the baking dish from the oven. Lightly brush the rolls with some of the hot water (about 2 tablespoons) from the baking dish and return only the rolls to the oven. Continue to bake until golden brown, about 5 minutes. (This will ensure a nicely browned, crisp surface.) Transfer to a wire rack to cool completely, about 10 minutes, before serving.

Müslibrötchen

Granola Rolls

PREP TIME: 30 minutes, plus 16 hours resting
COOK TIME: 20 minutes
YIELD: 8 rolls

What's a good frühstück without some müsli? But wait—what if we put müsli inside a brötchen for the ultimate German breakfast experience? I just adore these breakfast rolls packed with fruit, seeds, and nuts, especially when topped with Pflaumenmus (page 34). I like using dried cherries, but raisins, dried cranberries, dates, or any other dried fruit work just as well. And you MUST try adding a layer of cream cheese under the Pflaumenmus—it's my absolute favorite way to eat them! Prepare these rolls the night before, and by morning, you're just one hour away from an oven-fresh German breakfast experience. (This really makes all the difference when you're missing Germany.)

---

2 cups (250 g) all-purpose flour, plus more for dusting

⅓ cup (50 g) dark rye flour

1 cup (120 g) whole spelt flour

9½ ounces (280 ml) lukewarm water

1 teaspoon (3 g) active dry yeast (½ packet)

2 teaspoons (10 g) salt

½ tablespoon (8 g) unsalted butter, melted

1 teaspoon (5 g) malt syrup (optional)

⅓ cup plus 1 tablespoon (50 g) pumpkin seeds, toasted

⅓ cup plus 1 tablespoon (50 g) sunflower seeds, toasted

⅓ cup (50 g) chopped hazelnuts (optional), toasted

⅓ cup (50 g) dried fruit, chopped (optional)

⅔ cup (50 g) rolled oats

1. In the bowl of a stand mixer fitted with the dough hook attachment, mix the all-purpose flour, rye flour, spelt flour, water, yeast, salt, butter, and malt syrup at low speed until a smooth, wet dough forms, about 10 minutes. Increase the speed to medium and mix until the dough is smooth and dense and still slightly sticks to the bowl, about 5 minutes. Add the pumpkin seeds, sunflower seeds, and, if using, hazelnuts and dried fruit; mix at low speed until worked in, about 1 minute. Cover the bowl with plastic wrap and let the dough rest at room temperature until bubbly and just starting to rise, about 30 minutes. Refrigerate and let proof until the dough has doubled in size, about 15 hours (overnight is easiest).

2. On a lightly floured work surface, turn out the dough. With flour-coated hands, press the dough into a 1-inch-thick (2.5 cm) circle. Using a bench scraper or a sharp knife, divide the dough into 8 triangular pieces, like a pie.

3. Line a baking sheet with parchment paper. Fill one small bowl with water and another with the oats. Dip one side of a roll into the water, then into the oats. Place it oat-side up on the prepared baking sheet. Repeat with the remaining rolls. Cover the rolls loosely with a clean kitchen towel and let them rest at room temperature until slightly puffed up, about 30 minutes.

4. Meanwhile, fill a large baking dish halfway with water and place it on the bottom rack of the oven; this will create steam. Preheat the oven to 450°F (230°C).

5. Using a sharp knife, score each roll from the pointed tip down to the base, about ¼ inch (6 mm) deep. Bake for 10 minutes. Open the oven door wide for about 5 seconds to release the steam. Continue baking for 5 minutes. Remove the rolls and the baking dish from the oven. Lightly brush the rolls with some of the hot water (about 2 tablespoons) from the baking dish and return only the rolls to the oven until golden, about 5 minutes. (This will help to achieve a nicely browned crust.) Transfer to a cooling rack and let sit until cool enough to handle, about 5 minutes. Enjoy while still warm.

NOTE

✤ *Any leftovers can be refrigerated in an airtight container or plastic bag for up to 1 week. To reheat, preheat the oven to 390°F (200°C), swipe the rolls under a thin stream of cold running water, then bake directly on the oven rack until the crust is crisp again, about 6 minutes.*

Frühstück

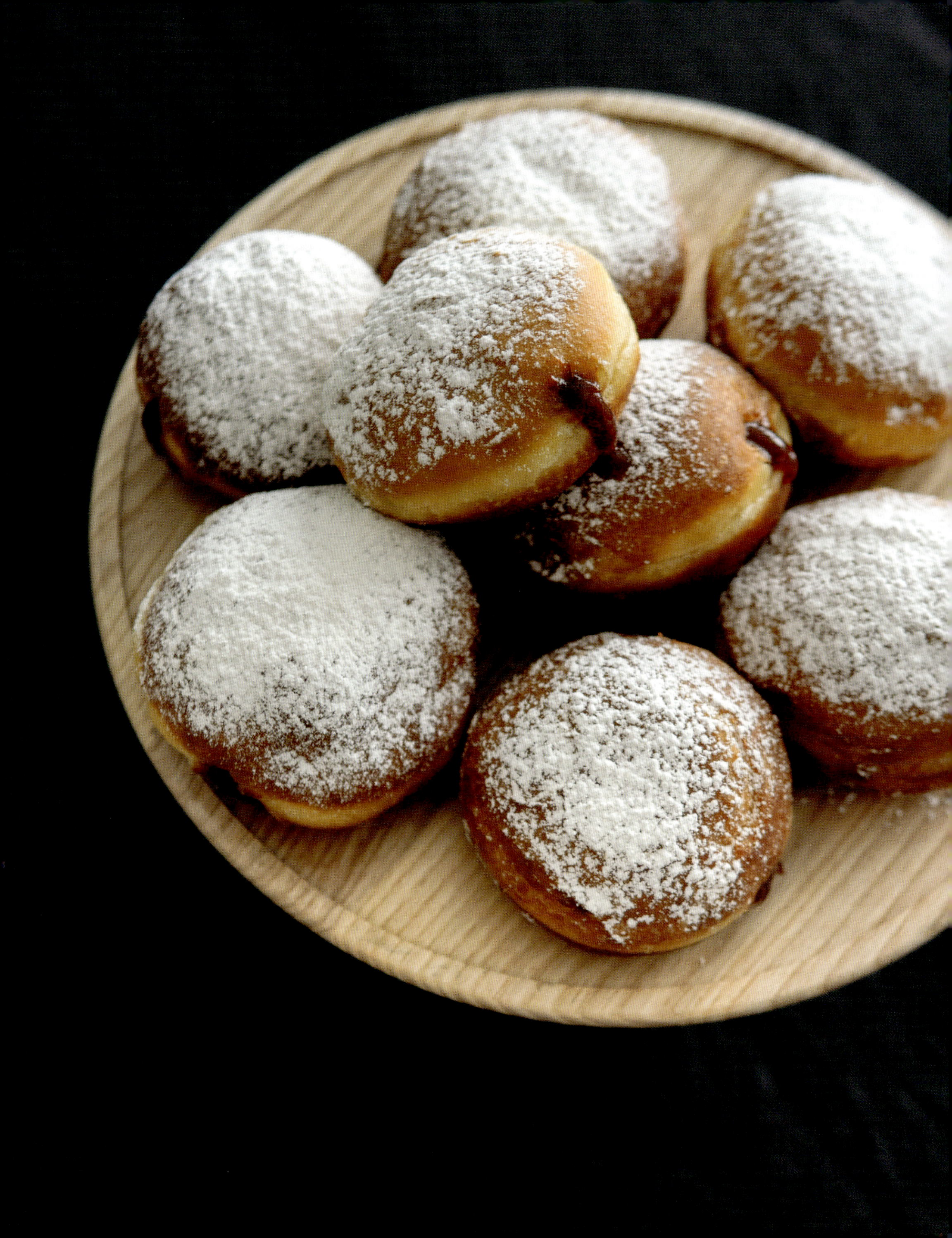

Berliner

German Doughnuts

PREP TIME: 15 minutes, plus 1 hour 30 minutes resting

COOK TIME: 20 minutes

YIELD: 12 doughnuts

The best part (in my opinion) about the German Fastnacht season is that bakeries fill their shelves with Berliner doughnuts! Other words used for Berliner doughnuts are "Krapfen" and "Kreppel." And ironically, in Berlin they are called "Pfannkuchen." Fastnacht is celebrated in Catholic-prominent regions of Germany, including Trier, where I grew up. While the tradition has religious origins, religious and nonreligious people celebrate it alike. It's a six-day-long party ending with the start of the fasting period (Fastenzeit) until Easter (Ostern), when many Germans give up sweets or alcohol. Kids and adults like to dress up, attend carnival parades, and just have the time of their lives. While Berliner are most popular during Fastnacht, Germans love eating them any time of year. I enjoy them the most as part of a relaxed weekend brunch or as a sweet afternoon snack with a cup of coffee.

---

2 teaspoons active dry yeast (1 packet)

8½ ounces (250 ml) lukewarm milk

4 cups (500 g) all-purpose flour, plus more for dusting

4 large egg yolks, at room temperature

⅓ cup (80 g) granulated sugar

4¼ tablespoons (60 g) unsalted butter, at room temperature

1 teaspoon vanilla extract

1 pinch salt (or use salted butter and omit adding extra salt)

7 ounces (200 g) jam of choice (see Notes)

2 quarts to 1 gallon (2 to 4 L) avocado oil or any neutral oil, for frying

Powdered sugar, for topping

1. In a small bowl, add the yeast and lukewarm milk and stir well. Let activate, about 5 minutes until bubbly.

2. In the bowl of a stand mixer fitted with the dough hook attachment, mix the flour, egg yolks, granulated sugar, butter, vanilla, and salt at low speed until the dough is smooth and pulls away from the sides of the bowl, about 10 minutes. Cover the bowl with plastic wrap or a tight-fitting lid and let rest in a warm spot until the dough has doubled in size, about 1 hour.

3. Transfer the dough to a lightly floured surface. Using a bench scraper or a sharp knife, divide the dough into 12 equal pieces. (To do this easily, I shape a log, cut it into quarters, and then cut each quarter into thirds.) With flour-dusted hands, roll the portions into balls, leaving them on the work surface with a little space in between. Cover with a clean kitchen towel and let the dough balls rest until doubled in size, about 30 minutes.

4. Meanwhile, fit a piping bag with a filling tip and add your jam of choice. Line a baking sheet with paper towels and place a wire cooling rack on top; set near the stove.

(CONTINUED)

Frühstück

5. In a large, heavy-bottomed pot, heat the oil over high heat until a frying thermometer reaches 320°F (160°C). Working in batches, place the dough balls, one at a time, on a skimmer and carefully lower into the hot oil. Only fit enough so they have room to float at the surface of the oil, keeping in mind that they will expand quickly during this process. Fry until golden on the bottom side, about 2 minutes and 30 seconds. Keep a close eye on the frying thermometer during this time and adjust the heat level as needed (see Notes). Using the skimmer, flip and fry on the second side until golden brown and cooked through, about 2 minutes and 30 seconds. Transfer to the prepared cooling rack.

6. To fill, place a Berliner on its side, insert the filling tip until you almost do not see it anymore, meaning you should be at the center, and squeeze the bag to add the filling. (Once you have done this a few times, you will get a good feel for how much to squeeze.) In the beginning, hold the Berliner, as you will feel an increase in weight in your hand. (You could also place it on a scale, tare your scale, and then fill in about 17 grams of jam for each one.) Return the filled Berliner to the cooling rack. Dust the tops with loads of powdered sugar, then transfer to a serving platter or stack them on a cake stand.

NOTES

✤ *Raspberry jam is the easiest for filling, as there are no chunks in it. If choosing a different jam, first strain it through a fine-mesh sieve before filling.*

✤ *When the oil is too hot, I either turn off the heat or remove the pot from the burner, as it can retain significant heat. Ideally, you want the temperature to be between 300 to 340°F (150 to 170°C). If the temperature drops too low for too long, increase the cooking time slightly, so the insides of the Berliners are not doughy. Of course, it's easiest to use a deep fryer for a constant temperature.*

✤ *I love making cinnamon plum Berliners: after frying, roll your doughnuts in Cinnamon Sugar (page 7) and fill the Berliners with Pflaumenmus (page 34).*

Plunderteig

German Croissant Dough

Plunderteig is the dough that your flakiest German pastry dreams are made of! Once you learn how to make this dough for teilchen (what pastries are called in German), you may become a bit high maintenance and insist on making your own croissants and pastries at home. The butter-layered "laminated" dough can be morphed into anything from Franzbrötchen (page 28) to Laugenecken (page 30). You will need some patience and time, but I promise that you will be hugely rewarded! Make sure to use a really good butter (I am talking grass-fed). Get inventive and use this amazing, flaky dough to make your own variety of teilchen.

PREP TIME: 1 hour, plus 3 hours and 30 minutes resting

COOK TIME: 12 minutes

YIELD: 2 pounds (1 kg) dough; enough for 12 pastries

PLUNDERTEIG DOUGH

1½ teaspoons (5 g) active dry yeast

1⅓ cups (320 ml) lukewarm milk

4 cups (500 g) all-purpose flour

1½ teaspoons (10 g) salt

3 tablespoons (40 g) granulated sugar

BUTTER PLATE

16 tablespoons (225 g) grass-fed butter, at room temperature

¼ cup (30 g) all-purpose flour

1. **To make the plunderteig dough:** In a small bowl, add the yeast and lukewarm milk and stir well. Let activate, about 5 minutes until bubbly.

2. In the bowl of a stand mixer fitted with the dough hook attachment, mix the yeast mixture with the flour, salt, and sugar at low speed until a smooth, elastic dough forms, about 8 minutes. Cover the bowl and refrigerate for 30 minutes.

3. **To make the butter plate:** Prep two letter-size pieces of parchment paper. In a large bowl, mix the butter and flour until fully combined. Transfer the mixture to a piece of parchment paper and place the other piece on top, making sure both pieces are aligned. Using a rolling pin, roll out the mixture into a rectangle, about 7 by 9 inches (18 by 23 cm) and no more than ¼ inch (6 mm) thick. To achieve the shape, it helps to press the long side of the rolling pin against the sides of the butter plate. Freeze the butter plate until it is just hard enough to pick up without bending, 15 to 20 minutes. Alternatively, you can chill the butter plate in the fridge for 30 minutes.

4. On a lightly floured surface, using a rolling pin, roll out the yeast dough into a rectangle large enough to perfectly envelope the butter plate from all sides. Remove a piece of parchment paper from the butter plate and place the butter plate, parchment side up, in the center of the rolled-out dough. Fold in the dough from all sides. It doesn't matter which sides are on the top or on the bottom; you want the dough to generously overlap on the seams and no butter should be peeking through.

(CONTINUED)

5. Laminate the dough. Start with simple lamination. Roll out the dough lengthwise until it is about two to two-and-a half times as long as it will be wide and ½ inch (12 mm) thick. Imagine that the dough consists of 3 small "notebooks" that are attached to each other. Taking one of the narrow ends of the dough, fold the top notebook down and the bottom notebook up, creating 3 overlapping layers of dough. Wrap in plastic and refrigerate until the dough is completely chilled, about 1 hour (or more if your kitchen is warmer).

6. Proceed with double lamination. Roll out the dough again into an even longer rectangle, about three times as long as it is wide and ½ inch (12 mm) thick. Imagine that the dough consists of 4 "notebooks" this time. Fold the top notebook down and the bottom one up, so there are 2 layers on both sides. Fold in the center, creating 4 overlapping layers of dough. Wrap in plastic and refrigerate until the dough is completely chilled, about 1 hour.

7. Repeat the simple lamination process (step 5); refrigerate until completely chilled, about 1 hour.

8. On a lightly floured surface, using a rolling pin, roll out the dough to approximately 11 by 24 inches (28 by 60 cm) and about ¼ inch thick (6 mm). At this stage you can either freeze it (see Notes) or use it to make the German pastries of your dreams, such as my favorites, the iconic Franzbrötchen (page 28).

NOTES

✤ *When in doubt, chill out—and I mean it. This is not a dough you want to rush. If the butter gets too soft, it likes to tear up the dough and make its way through. Not cool. What's cool is giving the dough some extra time to chill and stay compact.*

✤ *If you witness any kind of tearing of the dough and butter peeking through, STOP and put it back in the refrigerator for another hour.*

✤ *I've made the dough through step 2 the day before, then let it chill overnight and continued the next day. I have also made it through step 6, then chilled the dough overnight so that it's ready to be rolled out. This comes in handy when wanting to make fresh pastries for breakfast the next morning!*

✤ *If freezing your plunderteig, make sure you're rolling it out completely, then dust it with flour, wrap it in plastic, and freeze it on a baking sheet. The day before using it, transfer the dough to the fridge. When ready to use, roll it out a little bit if needed, then shape your pastries of choice.*

Enveloping the butter plate

Ready for lamination

Simple lamination

Double lamination

Franzbrötchen

Croissant-Style Cinnamon Rolls

Franzbrötchen are croissant-style cinnamon-roll pastries that have reached cult status across Germany. Made from German croissant dough called Plunderteig (page 25), they may be the BEST pastry you've ever tasted. Imagine a croissant and a cinnamon roll having a superstar baby. Franzbrötchen have their origin in Hamburg, one of my favorite German cities. If you're lucky, you can find them at bakeries throughout Germany, but they taste even better when you make them at home. Pro tip: In case you're running short on time and don't have room temperature butter, you can microwave it for 5 to 10 seconds, while rotating it in between increments.

PREP TIME: 20 minutes, plus 1 hour resting
COOK TIME: 12 minutes
YIELD: 12 pastries

½ cup (100 g) brown sugar

1½ tablespoons ground cinnamon

½ cup (50 g) almond flour, plus more for dusting

4½ tablespoons butter, at room temperature

1 recipe (2 pounds, or 1 kg) Plunderteig (page 25)

1 large egg, beaten with equal part water

1. In a medium bowl, add the brown sugar, cinnamon, and almond flour and stir to combine.

2. Using your hands (what I do) or a rubber spatula (if you prefer), spread the butter onto the dough. Sprinkle with the brown sugar mixture, making sure to distribute it evenly. From a long side, tightly roll up the dough into a log. Place the roll so that the finishing seam is facing the side (this is totally for looks and will create prettier franzbrötchen). Using a bench scraper or a sharp knife, cut the roll into 10 to 12 pieces at a 45-degree angle, alternating the angle every time so that each piece has a short side and a wide side. Set each roll, wide side down, and dust them with a bit of flour.

3. Using the handle of a small spoon (a chopstick works great for this too), push the narrow top side down, forcing the cut sides to tilt toward the top. Gently slide the spoon out from the side or carefully pull it up.

4. Preheat the oven to 350°F (180°C) on the convection (umluft) setting. Line a baking sheet with parchment paper or a silicone baking mat.

5. Transfer the rolls to the prepared baking sheet, cover with a clean kitchen towel, and let rest in a warm spot until doubled in size, about 1 hour. Give the baking sheet a gentle shake. If the pastries are barely wiggling, they are good to go into the oven; if they are not yet, let them rest and rise some more. (I find that in winter, the rolls sometimes need to rise for up to 3 hours, while in summer it sometimes only takes an hour or so.) Important step: Press down the narrow side one more time after the final rise to make sure they keep their shape.

6. Brush the rolls with the egg-water mixture and bake on the middle rack until golden brown, 13 to 15 minutes, rotating the baking sheets halfway through. The pastries are done baking when you press on the outer pieces and the dough jumps back up. Enjoy either warm or cold, but most definitely the same day!

NOTES

✤ *These pastries taste the absolute best the same day they are baked. The flakiness will wear off the next day, so I do not recommend baking more than you think you will eat the same day.*

✤ *To freeze them, reduce the baking time by 2 minutes, allow to cool completely, and freeze in an airtight container for up to 3 months. When ready to eat, bake for about 8 minutes at 350°F (180°C), no preheating necessary.*

Frühstück **29**

Laugenecken

Lye Pastries

Laugenecken are a wakeup moment if you've never had them before. They are my twin sister Jeanne's and my favorite German breakfast treat and the best part is that they (kind of) count as a brötchen but are technically a pastry. These flaky, pretzel-like croissant corners are so super delicious and the most versatile savory pastry, perfect for topping just like you would a brötchen. You can also eat them plain, of course. I know you will want to plan to make them again as soon as you take a bite of your last one.

PREP TIME: 15 minutes, plus 4 hours resting
COOK TIME: 15 minutes
YIELD: 11 or 12 pastries

Avocado oil, for greasing (optional)

All-purpose flour, for dusting

1 recipe (2 pounds, or 1 kg) Plunderteig (page 25; be sure to leave out the sugar when making the dough)

10 ounces (300 ml) cold water

1½ level teaspoons (12 g) food-grade lye (100% sodium hydroxide granules), be very precise when measuring this (see page 8 for tips on working with lye)

Seeds (I like sesame, pumpkin, and sunflower), for topping (optional)

1. Line two baking sheets with parchment paper rubbed with avocado oil or use silicone baking mats.

2. On a lightly floured work surface, using a lightly floured rolling pin, roll out the plunderteig into a large rectangle, about 10 by 17 inches (25 by 43 cm). Fold the dough in half to make it 5 by 17 inches (12 by 43 cm). Roll out gently, mainly to combine the seams. Using a bench scraper or a sharp knife, cut the dough into 11 or 12 elongated triangles (see photo opposite). Transfer the triangles to the prepared baking sheets, cover with a clean kitchen towel, and let rest in a warm spot until the rolls have doubled in size, about 1 hour.

3. Give the baking sheet a gentle shake. If the rolls are barely wiggling, they are good to go into the oven; if they are not yet, let them rest and rise some more. (I find that in winter, the rolls sometimes need to rise for up to 3 hours, while in summer it sometimes only takes an hour or so.) Refrigerate to cool the butter back down, about 1 hour.

4. Meanwhile, in a well-ventilated area (such as outside or under your stove vent hood turned to high), prepare the lye solution: In a medium metal or glass bowl, add the cold water, then the lye granules. It is important to do it in this order. At this point, I like to step to the side for about 20 seconds to let potential fumes evaporate. Then carefully whisk the solution until it is clear. Set aside until you are ready to dip your Laugenecken.

5. Preheat the oven to 350°F (180°C) on the convection (umluft) setting.

German Home Kitchen

6. Working one at a time, using a skimmer or two large, slotted spoons, carefully dip the triangles in the lye solution until they are sufficiently coated and have a slight yellow tint, 8 to 10 seconds, making sure not to touch the solution. Immediately place them on the prepared baking sheets, about 1½ inches (4 cm) apart. Discard the lye solution in the kitchen sink drain, followed by running water for just a few seconds.

7. Bake for 8 minutes, then rotate the baking sheets and continue baking until medium brown in color, 7 to 8 minutes. Transfer to a wire rack to cool for 10 minutes before eating.

NOTE

✤ *Laugenecken are best eaten the same day, but if you have leftovers, you can either store them in a bread box or wrap them airtight and freeze them. I highly recommend swiping them under a thin stream of cold running water before baking. Bake at 350°F (180°C) for 6 minutes if they were stored at room temperature or 8 minutes if they were frozen. If you know you won't finish all the laugenecken when you're making them, you can reduce the baking time by 2 minutes, let cool completely, and freeze to finish baking at a later time.*

Frühstück

Leberwurst

Liver Paté

I do not eat liver, UNLESS it's in leberwurst. This smooth, spiced German liver spread is the perfect savory Abendbrot (page 81) companion, and I am sure you will agree. Spread it thick on freshly baked Roggenmischbrot (page 82) or baguette slices and garnish with thinly sliced onion or shallot and Gewürzgurken (page 91). Depending on what size ramekins or jars you use, you may have extra jelly leftover. You could pour it into another small ramekin or jar as backup jelly to eat with your leberwurst or even with cheese or on buttered bread.

PREP TIME: 10 minutes, plus 3 hours resting

COOK TIME: 20 minutes

YIELD: About 20 ounces (570 g) (see Notes)

LEBERWURST

2 teaspoons avocado oil

4 ounces (120 g) chicken livers, cleaned, patted dry, and cut into bite-size pieces

3 ounces (100 g) pork chop meat, cut into bite-size pieces

1 ounce (30 g) bacon, cut into small cubes

1 small shallot, minced

Grated zest of ½ lemon

1 teaspoon dried thyme or 1 tablespoon fresh thyme leaves

¼ teaspoon dried marjoram

1 pinch ground allspice

1 pinch ground nutmeg

¾ teaspoon salt

½ teaspoon ground black pepper

1 tablespoon brandy

½ cup (120 ml) heavy cream

½ cup (115 g) cold unsalted butter

2 teaspoons dried or 2 tablespoons finely chopped fresh chives

1. Wash and rinse some ramekins or jars for storing.

2. **To make the leberwurst:** In a small saucepan over medium-high, heat the oil until hot, about 1 minute. Add the chicken livers, pork, and bacon and sear lightly, 1½ to 2 minutes. Add the shallot, lemon zest, thyme, marjoram, allspice, nutmeg, salt, and pepper. Turn over the pieces of meat and sear until they are firm, but still pink in the center, just under 2 minutes. Reduce the heat to low and add the brandy. Cook until the liquid has evaporated, about 1 minute. Add the cream and heat until warm, about 1 minute.

3. Remove from the heat and transfer to a blender or food processor. Add the butter and process until completely smooth, about 2 minutes. Stir in the chives. Transfer the mixture into the ramekins/jars and refrigerate for at least 1 hour.

4. **Meanwhile, make the red wine jelly:** In a small saucepan over medium-high heat, add the sugar and, without stirring, let it melt and cook until it turns a caramel color, 1 to 2 minutes (keep a close eye on it, so your sugar doesn't burn). Remove the pan from the heat. Pour in 7 ounces (210 ml) of the wine and the brandy and heat over low heat to a gentle simmer until the liquid is reduced by half, about 10 minutes. Remove from the heat.

5. In a small bowl, add the remaining 1 ounce (30 ml) wine and the gelatin and whisk until the gelatin is dissolved. Add the mixture to the wine reduction and whisk until just combined and no chunks are visible. Pour directly over the top of the leberwurst into the ramekins/jars. Garnish the jelly with some whole peppercorns (if using). Refrigerate until set, about 2 hours.

RED WINE JELLY

1 tablespoon sugar

8 ounces (240 ml) red wine, divided

3 tablespoons brandy

1 teaspoon unflavored gelatin

Whole black or rainbow peppercorns, for garnishing (optional)

NOTES

✢ *I like using canning jars for this, as they already come with a lid for storing. I prefer 2- to 4-ounce (60 to 120 ml) jars that are squattier, so there is more surface area for the delicious wine jelly, but whichever smallish jars or ramekins you have will work.*

✢ *You can make extra leberwust and freeze individual ramekins for up to 3 months, as it will keep in the refrigerator for only about 1 week.*

Frühstück

Pflaumenmus

Plum Butter

While I haven't had much luck growing plum trees in our backyard (two failed attempts so far), I have succeeded in creating the most delicious plum butter made from both farmers' market and store-bought plums. Plum butter is one of my favorite German jam alternatives; there's just something about the tart and sweet combo, mixed with hints of spice. And since it's nearly impossible to find in the US, I created my own. When plum season rolls around, buy all the plums and make a big batch and enjoy it spread on freshly baked Müslibrötchen (page 20) with a layer of cream cheese or as a filling for Berliner (page 23). Pflaumenmus also makes a lovely gift, especially when paired with a fresh loaf of Hefezopf (page 130).

PREP TIME: 15 minutes

COOK TIME: 4 hours and 10 minutes

YIELD: 32 ounces (900 g) or enough to fill 4 half-pint (240 ml each) glass canning jars (see Note)

4½ pounds (2 kg) plums

¼ cup (60 ml) lemon juice (about 2 large lemons)

1½ cups (300 g) granulated sugar

1 cinnamon stick (3 inches, or 7.5 cm), broken in half

4 whole cloves

1 whole cardamom pod

NOTE

❖ I prefer canning my pflaumenmus in small jars so I can enjoy it throughout the colder months until plum season comes around again.

1. Preheat the oven to 320°F (160°C).
2. Wash the plums, then halve them. Remove the pits from half of the plums (leaving in some of the pits adds a subtle almond note).
3. In a large, oven-safe dish (a lid is not needed), add the plums, lemon juice, sugar, cinnamon, cloves, and cardamom and toss to combine.
4. Bake for about 4 hours, carefully stirring once every hour, until the plum butter is thick and holds its shape when you drag a spoon through it (the time may vary depending on how juicy your plums are).
5. Set a fine-mesh sieve over a large bowl. While the plum butter is still hot, transfer it to the sieve and, using a rubber spatula to press it through, strain it to remove any pits or whole spices.
6. Wash and sterilize the jars, lids, and seals (see page 11).
7. While the jars are still hot, immediately fill them with the hot plum butter, leaving ¼-inch (6 mm) headspace. Wipe the jar rims with a clean, damp cloth to ensure a good seal. Seal with a rubber seal and lid. Turn the jars upside down and let them sit for about 5 minutes, until the lids are sealed. Turn the jars right side up and let them cool completely, about 2 hours. Store in a cool, dark place for several months or up to a year. Once opened, refrigerate and use within 1 month.

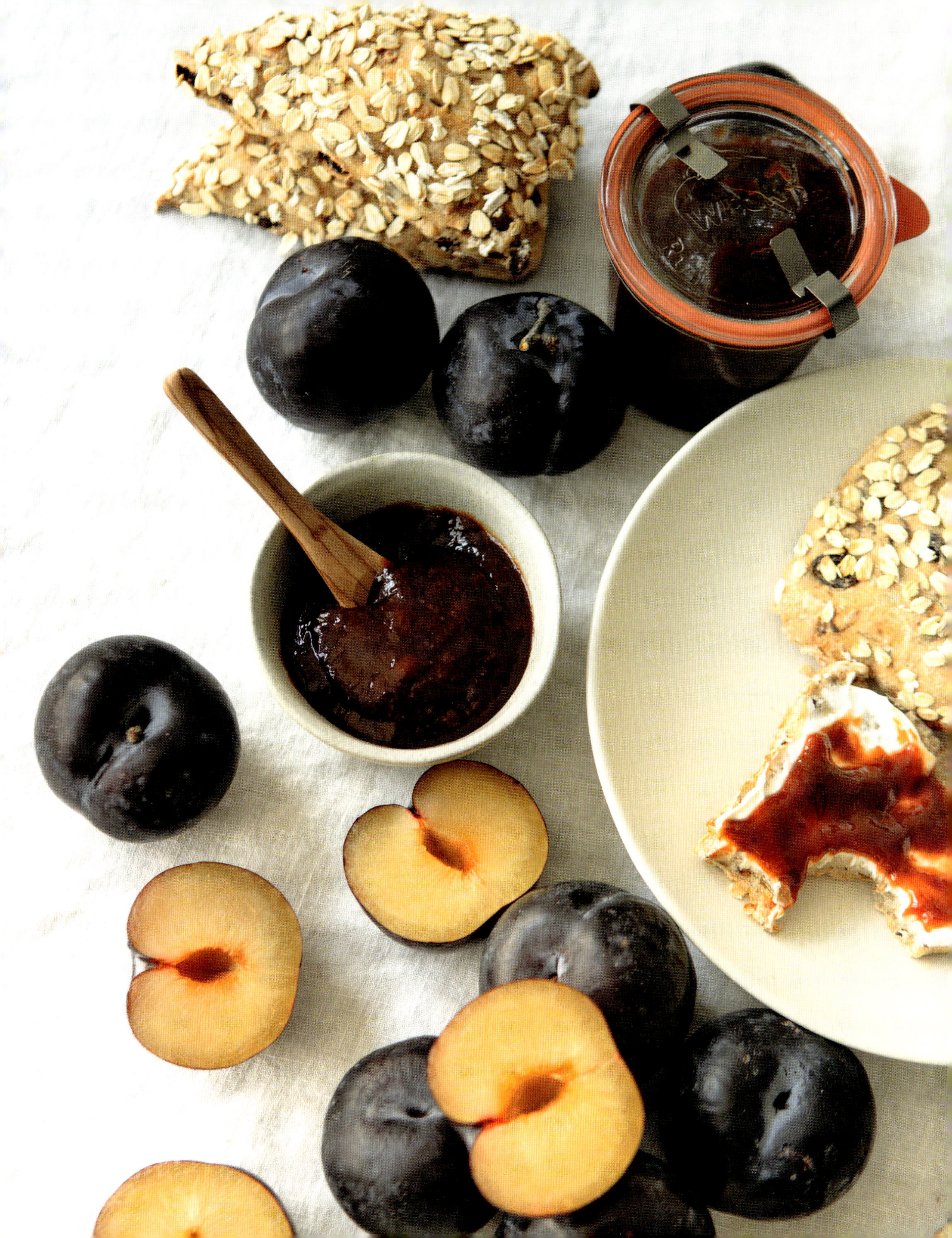

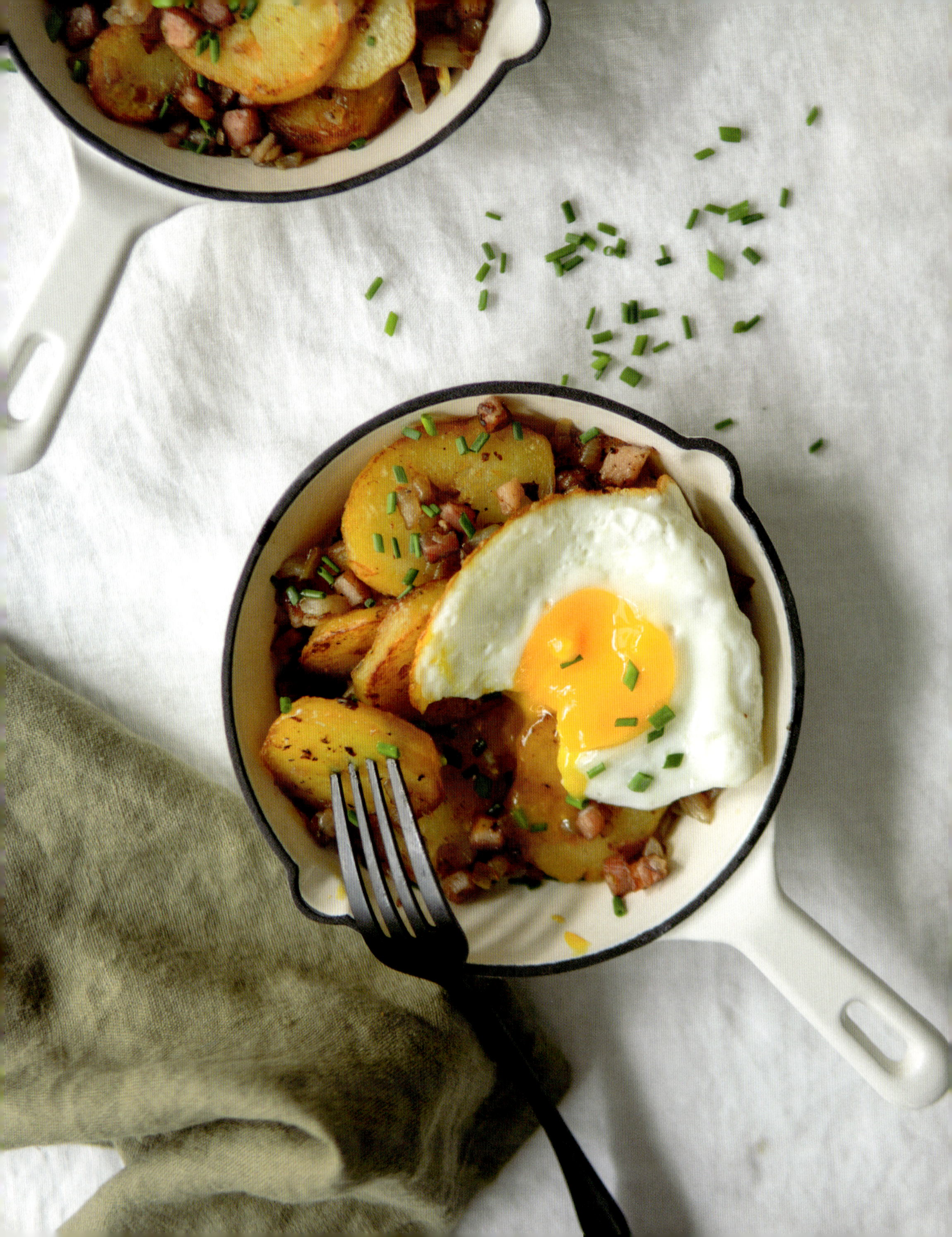

FÜR ZWISCHENDURCH & BEILAGEN

≫ *Snacks & Sides* ≪

Germans aren't big snackers—except during game nights and major soccer matches (cue Brezeln and Obatzda). Most of the time, grabbing a quick bite means stopping at a bakery nearby. For you, that likely means turning on the oven and baking something yourself! I've also included a few less carb-y, fun, and more substantial in-between meals to keep you going.

German sides are never just an afterthought—though they're often cleverly made from leftovers (like Semmelknödel from stale bread). Dumplings and cabbage are staples, and many Beilagen are so hearty that they can double as main dishes, making them a pretty versatile bunch.

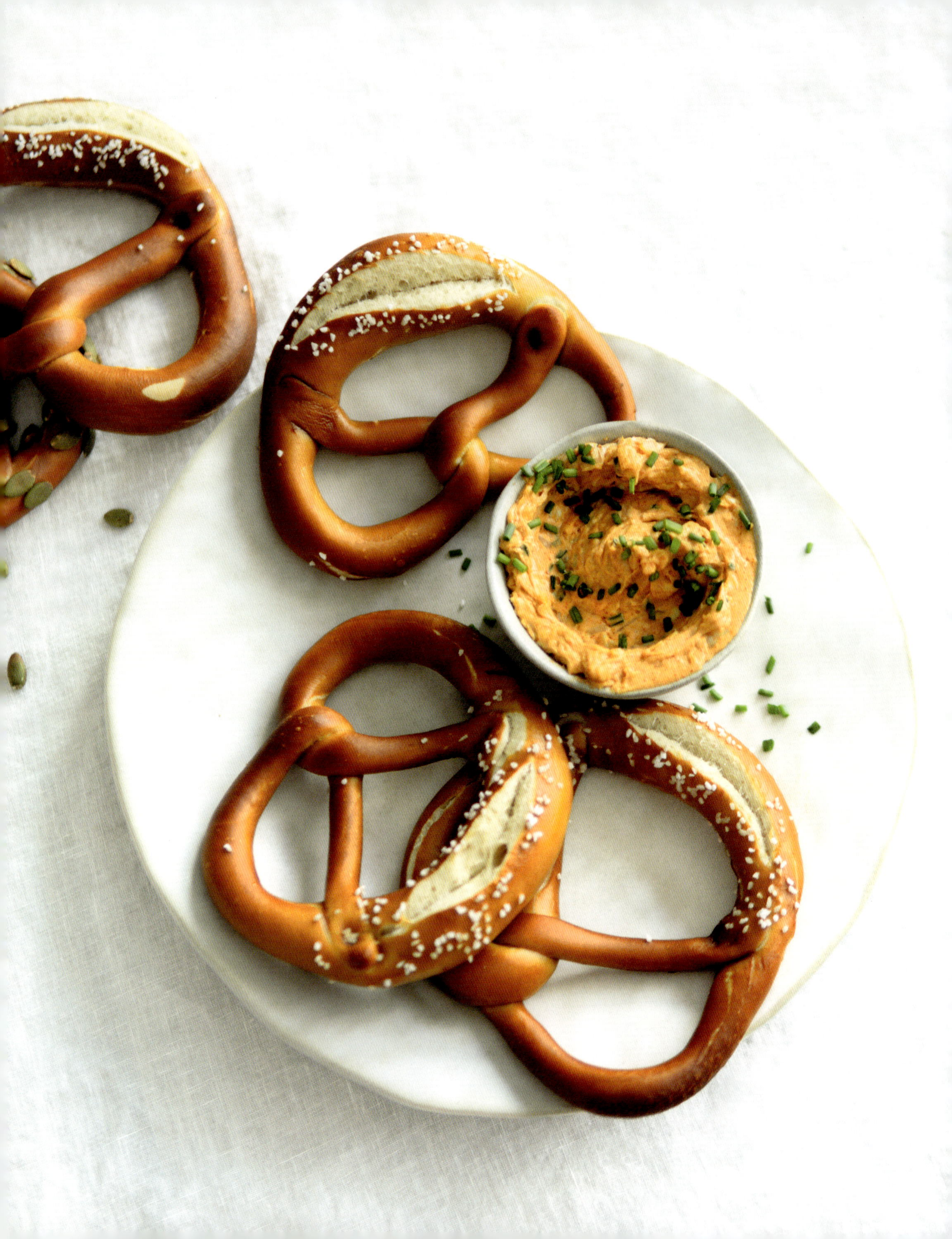

Brezeln

Pretzels

It took me years to figure out the perfect brezel recipe, and this is it. I cried a few happy tears when I took my first bite because they taste just like home. Brezeln are an instant hug from Germany. In fact, I even founded German Pretzel School, where I teach pretzel enthusiasts how to master authentic German Brezeln. That's how transformative real brezeln are, and I can't wait for you to experience that transformation too. This recipe uses lye, which makes all the difference, and is nothing to be afraid of. To save yourself time, especially if you're making a large batch for a party (like I do!), you can make these ahead of time, stopping before baking (see Notes). Enjoy them with butter, cream cheese, or Obatzda (page 41). They are also amazing dipped in Käsefondue (page 166)—but never with mustard (Germans would never!).

PREP TIME: 30 minutes, plus 1 hour resting
COOK TIME: 12 minutes
YIELD: 10 pretzels

DOUGH

- 10 ounces (300 ml) lukewarm water
- 1 teaspoon (3 g) active dry yeast (½ packet)
- 3½ teaspoons brown sugar
- 4 cups (500 g) all-purpose flour, plus more for dusting
- 2 tablespoons unsalted butter, at room temperature
- 1½ teaspoons salt
- Avocado oil, for greasing

LYE SOLUTION

- 10 ounces (300 ml) cold water
- 1½ level teaspoons (12 g) food-grade lye (100% sodium hydroxide granules), be very precise when measuring this

TOPPINGS

- Pretzel salt
- Seeds, such as sesame, pumpkin, or sunflower seeds (optional)
- Shredded cheese of choice, such as Gruyère or Cheddar (optional)

1. **To make the dough:** In the bowl of a stand mixer fitted with the dough hook attachment, combine the water, yeast, and sugar and stir. Set aside to activate, about 5 minutes until bubbly. Add the flour, butter, and salt; mix at low speed until smooth and elastic, 8 to 10 minutes. Cover the bowl with a clean kitchen towel and let the dough rest for about 5 minutes.

2. Line two baking sheets with parchment paper greased with a thin layer of avocado oil to prevent sticking. (Skipping this step will result in sticking—trust me.)

3. On a lightly floured work surface, roll out the dough into a long log of even thickness (this step is just for dividing the dough evenly). Using a bench scraper or a sharp knife, divide the dough into 10 equal pieces, each weighing 2.8 ounces (80 g) if you want them to be exact. Line up the pieces so they're cuddling each other and cover with a clean kitchen towel to prevent a skin from forming.

4. To shape the pretzels, keep a small bowl of avocado oil close by to grease your hands as needed. On a clean surface, working one at a time, use your hands to roll each piece into a log with a thicker middle ("the belly"), about 22 inches (55 cm) long. Taper the ends ("the legs") slightly by rolling them at an angle, using a back-and-forth motion. With the belly in the middle, cross the legs over twice, then attach them to the left and right of the belly to form the classic pretzel shape.

5. Transfer the pretzels to the prepared baking sheets. Cover with a clean kitchen towel and set aside until doubled in size, about 30 minutes.

(CONTINUED)

Für Zwischendurch & Beilagen

6. Stretch each pretzel slightly to open the three peek holes. Transfer to the fridge or freezer, wherever you can fit them (I freeze mine), until they are stiff and barely pliable, 15 to 30 minutes.

7. Preheat the oven to 355°F (180° C) on convection (umluft) or to 380°F (195° C) for a non-convection oven.

8. **In a well-ventilated area (such as outside or under a vent hood on high), prepare the lye solution:** In a medium metal or glass bowl, add the cold water, then the lye granules; always add lye to water, never the reverse (for more lye safety tips, see page 8). Step back for about 20 seconds to let any fumes dissipate. With a wire whisk, carefully whisk the solution until clear.

9. Using a steel skimmer, two pairs of tongs, or two forks, dip each pretzel into the lye solution until coated, 5 to 10 seconds. Transfer back to the prepared baking sheets.

10. You can score the belly, or the fat part of the pretzel, to control where it expands. To make your cut, take a small, sharp knife and cut along the belly to encourage expansion in that spot while baking. If you want to make Bavarian-style pretzels, don't make any cuts and let your pretzels crack open wherever they wish. Lightly sprinkle the pretzel salt over the bellies (or, if you prefer, the whole pretzel). Add any other toppings you like.

11. Bake until medium brown, about 12 minutes, rotating the baking sheets halfway through to ensure even browning. If you like darker pretzels, bake for an extra 1 to 2 minutes. Transfer the baking sheets to cooling racks and let the pretzels cool for about 10 minutes.

NOTES

✣ *If you have leftovers, you probably did something wrong. Joking aside, German pretzels are best enjoyed within a couple of hours of baking. However, if you must store them, place them in an airtight container for up to 2 days. (The salt will dissolve into the pretzels, and they won't look as pretty, but they'll still taste great.) That said, if you anticipate not eating them all, freeze some before baking to bake fresh later.*

✣ *To make pretzels ahead of time, after dipping them in the lye solution (and, if desired, scoring the bellies), arrange them on a baking sheet and freeze for one hour. Once frozen, transfer them to a freezer-safe bag or container. When ready to bake, arrange the desired number of frozen pretzels on a baking sheet, prepared as instructed, and let them thaw for 15 minutes. This will help the exteriors to get sticky again. Then you can add the toppings and bake as directed in the recipe.*

Obatzda

Bavarian Beer Cheese Spread

PREP TIME: 10 minutes

YIELD: 10 to 15 servings

Don't do that thing where you take your pretzel and dip it in mustard . . . or nacho cheese. That's not how Germans do it. Instead, Obatzda is here to teach you a lesson about cheese dips to eat with pretzels. It's the most addictive beer and cheese dip (or spread) and I know you'll agree. Bonus: It's so quick and easy to make! Serve with Brezeln (page 39) or even those little hard, snacking pretzels. Other traditional garnishes and dippers are sliced raw onion and radish.

---

9 ounces (250 g) Camembert or Brie cheese, at room temperature (see Note)

4 ounces (115 g) cream cheese, at room temperature

1 tablespoon unsalted butter, at room temperature

2 tablespoons finely chopped yellow onion

2 tablespoons finely chopped chives, plus more for garnishing

1 teaspoon sweet paprika, plus more for sprinkling

Cayenne pepper (optional)

3½ ounces (100 ml) beer, such as hefeweizen, lager, or pilsner

1. In a small bowl, use a fork to mash together the Camembert, cream cheese, and butter until the mixture forms a chunky, paste-like consistency.

2. Stir in the onion, chives, and paprika until fully combined. If you like your obatzda to have a little kick, add cayenne pepper to taste.

3. Stir in the beer, a little at a time, until the mixture reaches a spreadable consistency (you may not need all of it). For a thinner, dippable consistency, simply add more beer as needed.

4. Transfer to a serving bowl. Sprinkle with paprika and garnish with chives. Obatzda will keep in an airtight container in the refrigerator for up to 3 days.

NOTE

❖ *I prefer young Camembert or Brie and typically choose ones with the farthest expiration date for a milder flavor. However, if you prefer a riper, more intense flavor, feel free to use a cheese closer to its expiration date.*

Gebackener Camembert

Baked Camembert

PREP TIME: 10 minutes

COOK TIME: 10 to 15 minutes

YIELD: 2 to 4 servings

This was one of my all-time favorite foods growing up. It's so popular that even McDonald's Germany features it on their menu sometimes. The Camembert is coated in a double layer of breading and pan-fried (even though we call it baked Camembert), creating the perfect crispy, golden crust. I typically make this using a small wheel of Camembert, but you can also use a larger one and cut it up after frying. Make sure to let the cheese come to room temperature; otherwise, the exterior will finish cooking before the interior has a chance to get perfectly melty. Germans eat baked Camembert cheese with a fork and knife, with a side of lingonberry jam and a green salad, such as the Gemischter Salat (page 48).

---

2 large eggs

¼ teaspoon salt

Ground black pepper

⅔ cup (80 g) all-purpose flour

½ cup (75 g) fine bread crumbs

1 small wheel (8 ounces, or 225 g) Camembert cheese (see Note), at room temperature

5 tablespoons avocado oil

NOTE

✤ *If you have trouble finding Camembert, Brie makes a great substitute. Avoid using an overly ripe cheese, as the rind may be more fragile and prone to tearing—the closer the cheese is to its expiration date, the riper it will be.*

1. In a small bowl, whisk together the eggs, salt, and pepper.

2. Place the flour and bread crumbs in two separate wide, shallow bowls or on two plates. Coat all sides of the cheese wheel with the flour, shaking off any excess. Next, dip it into the eggs, letting any excess drip off. Finally, press it into the bread crumbs, ensuring an even coating. Repeat the process for a second layer of breading.

3. Line a baking sheet with paper towels and place a wire rack on top; set it next to the stove.

4. In a small skillet or saucepan just large enough to fit the cheese, heat the oil over medium heat until it sizzles when dropping in a pinch of bread crumbs, 1 to 2 minutes. Add the cheese (the oil should come up to about half the height of the cheese) and cook until the bottom is golden brown, about 5 minutes. Using tongs or two spatulas, flip the cheese and cook the other side until golden, about 5 minutes. If the oil gets too hot and the cheese is browning too quickly, remove the pan from heat to help cool it down faster; adding a bit more oil can also bring down the temperature. If the sides remain pale, turn the cheese on its side and rotate it until evenly browned.

5. Set the cheese on the prepared cooling rack and let the excess oil drip off, about 1 minute. (Avoid placing it directly on paper towels, as the cheese will stick to the paper.) Transfer to a plate and serve immediately.

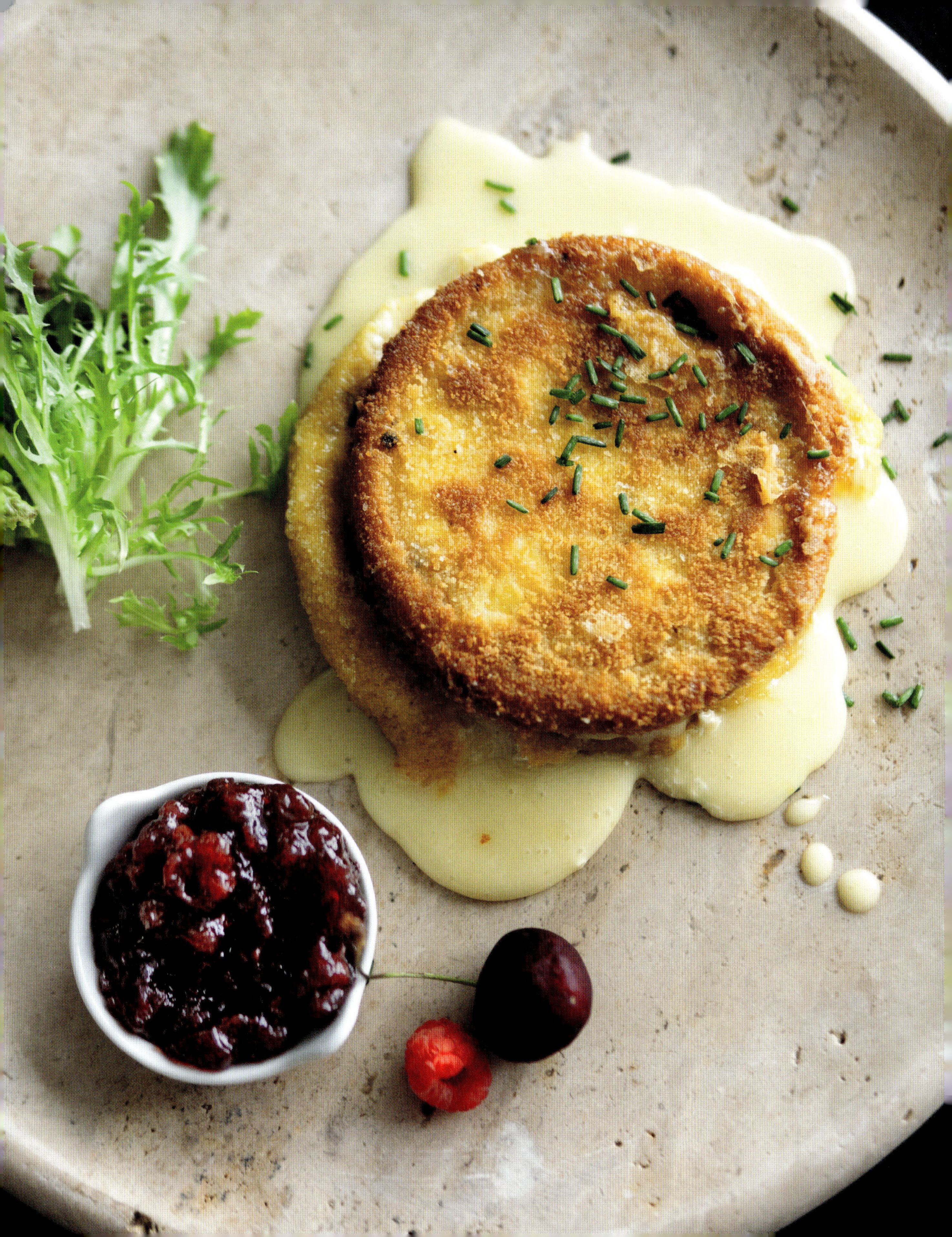

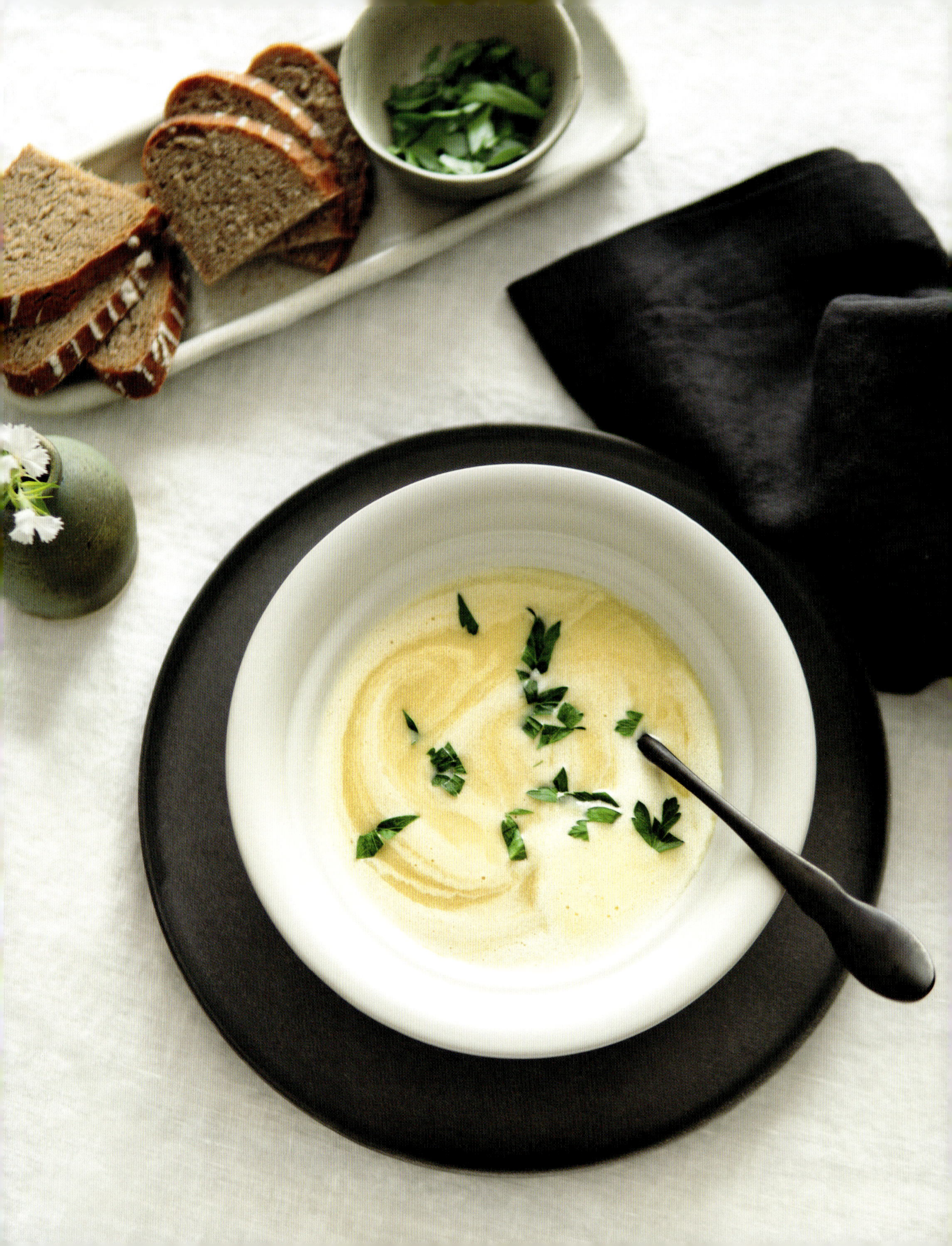

Spargelsuppe

White Asparagus Cream Soup

PREP TIME: 20 minutes
COOK TIME: 40 minutes
YIELD: 4 servings

Spargelzeit is white asparagus season in Germany—it kicks off in April and lasts for about 2 months. White asparagus has a delicate flavor profile and is often described as "white gold." It grows underground and is harvested before it reaches daylight, and from April to June, it fills markets, grocery stores, and restaurant menus across the country. While the word spargel refers to asparagus of any color, when people say spargel, they almost always mean white asparagus. The most classic way to eat it is with hollandaise sauce, cooked ham, and boiled potatoes. However, this creamy spargelsuppe is my favorite way. I hope you love it too. Enjoy with some buttered bread and more sparkling wine!

1 pound (500 g) white asparagus (see Note)

17 ounces (500 ml) vegetable broth

1 teaspoon salt

1 pinch granulated sugar

2 tablespoons unsalted butter

2 tablespoons all-purpose flour or cornstarch

3½ ounces (100 ml) sparkling white wine

1 large egg yolk

7 ounces (200 ml) heavy cream, divided

Salt and black pepper

Freshly grated nutmeg

Juice of ½ lemon

NOTE

✧ *Can't find fresh white asparagus? You can use either jarred white asparagus (though I know it can be pricey) or fresh green asparagus to make a green asparagus soup instead. Either way, no peeling is required!*

1. Peel the asparagus, trim the ends, and cut off the tips. Reserve the tips, as they are the most delicate part, for adding to the soup toward the end of cooking. Using a sharp knife, cut the remaining asparagus into ½-inch (12 mm) pieces.

2. In a small saucepan, heat the broth to boiling over medium heat. Stir in the salt and sugar. Add the asparagus pieces (not the tips). Reduce the heat to medium-low, cover, and simmer until tender, about 15 minutes. Remove from the heat. Using an immersion blender, puree the soup until smooth, 1 to 2 minutes.

3. In a medium saucepan, melt the butter over medium-low heat. Add the flour and cook, stirring constantly, until golden, about 2 minutes. Gradually stir in the wine, then the pureed asparagus. Heat to boiling over medium heat, then add the reserved asparagus tips. Reduce the heat to medium-low, cover, and simmer until the tips are soft, about 12 minutes.

4. Meanwhile, in a medium bowl, whisk the yolk and 3½ ounces (100 ml) of the heavy cream until combined. In a separate medium bowl or a tall measuring pitcher (I like to use this to prevent splattering), use an electric hand mixer with the whisk attachments to beat the remaining 3½ ounces (100 ml) of the cream until stiff peaks form.

5. Carefully stir the yolk mixture and half of the whipped cream into the soup. Season with salt, pepper, and nutmeg to taste. Add the lemon juice, then ladle into soup bowls and garnish with the remaining 3½ ounces (100 ml) whipped cream.

Für Zwischendurch & Beilagen

Mixed Pickles

Pickled Veggies

Some of my favorite dinners are spent cozied up around a pot of Käsefondue (page 166), and these crunchy mixed pickles are always my favorite dipper. But they're not just great with fondue! Their tangy crunch adds the perfect touch to Abendbrot (page 81), Raclette (page 163), or as a quick snack between meals. These fermented pickles are ready to eat in just a couple of days and can be stored in the fridge for several months.

PREP TIME: 30 minutes, plus 3 days fermenting at room temperature and 1 week fermenting in the fridge

YIELD: About 5 pint-size (480 ml each) jars

---

1 cup (240 ml) white wine vinegar

2 tablespoons granulated sugar

1 tablespoon plus 1 teaspoon salt

1 large English cucumber, ends trimmed and cut into ½-inch-thick (12 mm) slices

2 large carrots, cut into ½-inch-thick (12 mm) slices

2 large bell peppers, cores and seeds removed and cut into thin strips

1 medium head cauliflower, core removed and cut into small florets

4 small shallots, thinly sliced

8 cloves garlic, peeled

5 teaspoons mustard seeds

5 teaspoons whole black peppercorns

15 bay leaves

1 large handful fresh dill

1. In a medium saucepan, heat the vinegar, sugar, salt, and 4 cups (960 ml) of water to boiling over high heat, stirring until the sugar dissolves, about 5 minutes.

2. Wash and sterilize the jars, lids, and seals (see page 11).

3. Divide the cucumbers, carrots, bell peppers, cauliflower, shallots, garlic, mustard seeds, peppercorns, bay leaves, and dill evenly between the jars, reserving a few of the cucumber slices. Leave enough headspace to add the reserved slices on top (to help keep everything submerged in the pickling liquid).

4. Pour the hot pickling liquid over the veggies, ensuring they're fully submerged. Place the lids loosely on top; don't seal the jars. Place the jars on a rimmed baking sheet; let them ferment at room temperature, about 70°F (21°C), for 3 days.

5. After 3 days, transfer the jars to the fridge, leaving them unsealed for 1 week. After that, seal the jars and store in the fridge for several months.

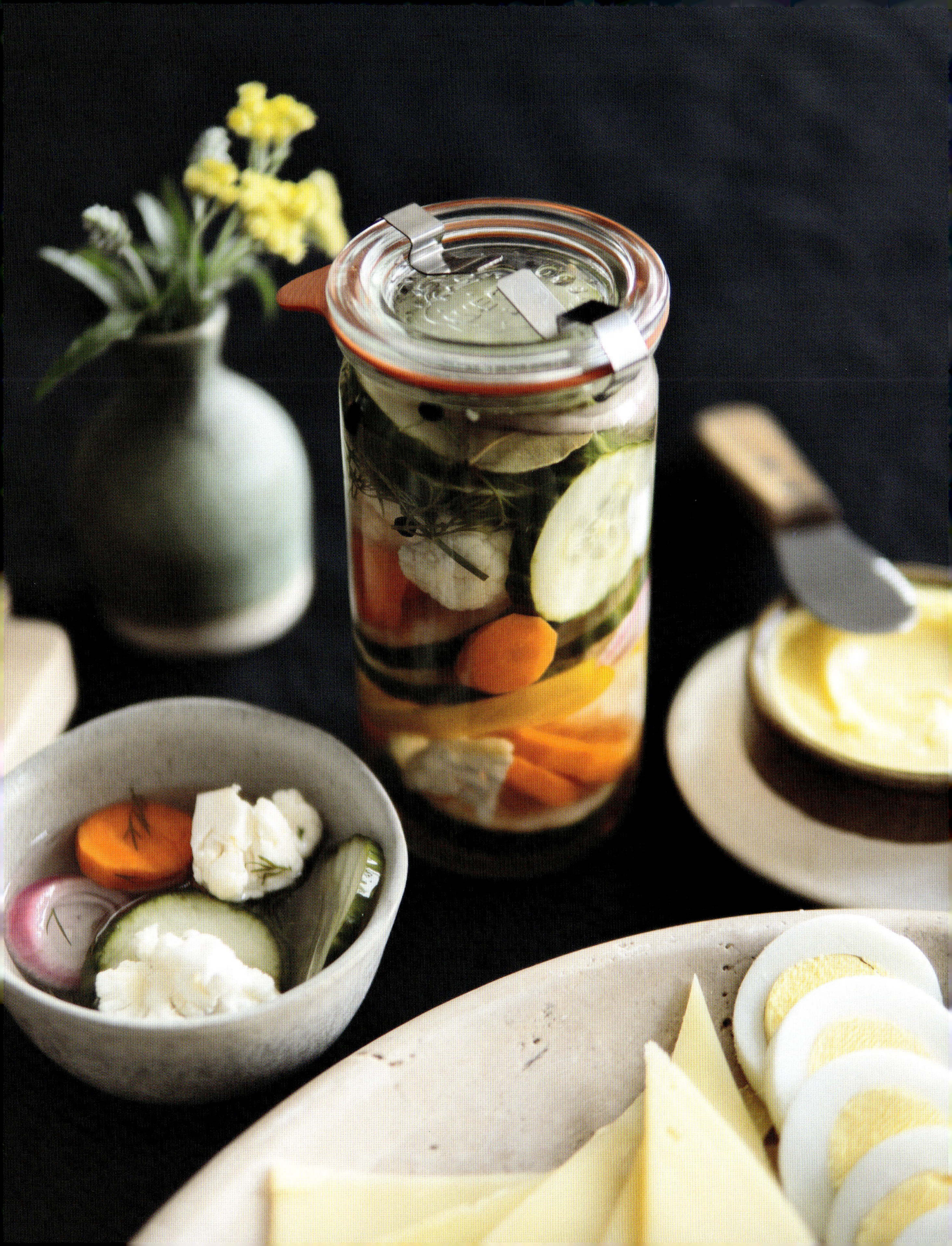

Gemischter Salat

German Mixed Salad

PREP TIME: 30 minutes, plus 30 minutes marinating

YIELD: 6 servings

This classic mixed salad combines fresh lettuce with a variety of delicious raw vegetable salads, such as carrot salad, beet salad, cucumber salad, and a German-style coleslaw. I love it so much that I sometimes make a large portion and call it dinner. For the greens, I like using a mix of butter lettuce and frisée, but any lettuce you like to use will work. Top it with some Schnitzel cut into strips (page 78) or serve with a slice of Zwiebelkuchen (page 122).

KRAUTSALAT (COLESLAW)

- ½ firm, medium head white, green, or red cabbage, thinly sliced
- 1 teaspoon salt, plus more to taste
- ½ cup (120 ml) heavy cream
- ½ cup (120 ml) sour cream
- 2 teaspoons honey

ROHKOSTSALATE
(Raw Veggie Salad)

- 6 tablespoons olive oil
- 2 tablespoons fresh lemon juice
- 1 tablespoon apple cider vinegar
- 1 teaspoon honey
- ¼ teaspoon salt
- ¼ teaspoon ground black pepper
- 2 large carrots, shredded
- 1 large English cucumber, thinly sliced
- 1 cup (130 g) canned/pre-cooked beets, cut into ¼-inch thick (6 mm) slices

KRÄUTER VINAIGRETTE
(Herbed Vinaigrette)

- 6 tablespoons olive oil
- 2 tablespoons fresh lemon juice
- 1 tablespoon apple cider vinegar
- 1 teaspoon Dijon mustard
- 1 teaspoon honey
- 1 tablespoon chopped fresh parsley, or 1 teaspoon dried parsley
- 1 tablespoon chopped fresh dill, or 1 teaspoon dried dill
- 1 tablespoon chopped fresh chives, or 1 teaspoon dried chives
- ¼ teaspoon salt
- ¼ teaspoon ground black pepper

GEMISCHTER SALAT *(Mixed Salad)*

- 1 small head butter lettuce, torn into bite-size pieces
- 1 small head frisée, torn into bite-size pieces
- Kräuter Vinaigrette
- Krautsalat
- Rohkostsalate
- Halved cherry tomatoes, for garnishing
- Chopped fresh chives, for garnishing (optional)
- Chopped fresh parsley, for garnishing (optional)
- Chopped fresh dill, for garnishing (optional)

1. **Make the coleslaw:** In a large bowl, add the cabbage and salt. Using your hands, knead until softened, about 2 minutes. Add the heavy cream, sour cream, and honey and toss to coat evenly. Season with salt to taste. Cover and refrigerate until tender, about 30 minutes.

2. **Make the veggie salad:** In a small bowl, whisk together the oil, lemon juice, vinegar, honey, salt, and pepper until smooth, about 1 minute. Place the carrots, cucumber, and beets in separate bowls, and divide the dressing evenly among them. Stir to coat evenly and let marinate at room temperature for 30 minutes.

3. **Make the herbed vinaigrette:** In a small bowl, whisk together the oil, lemon juice, vinegar, mustard, honey, parsley, dill, chives, salt, and pepper until smooth, about 1 minute.

4. **Make the mixed salad:** In a large bowl, add the lettuce, frisée, and herbed vinaigrette. Using your hands, toss until evenly coated.

5. Divide the dressed mixed salad among individual salad bowls. Top each with portions of the coleslaw, carrots, cucumber, and beets. Garnish with cherry tomatoes and fresh herbs as desired.

Für Zwischendurch & Beilagen

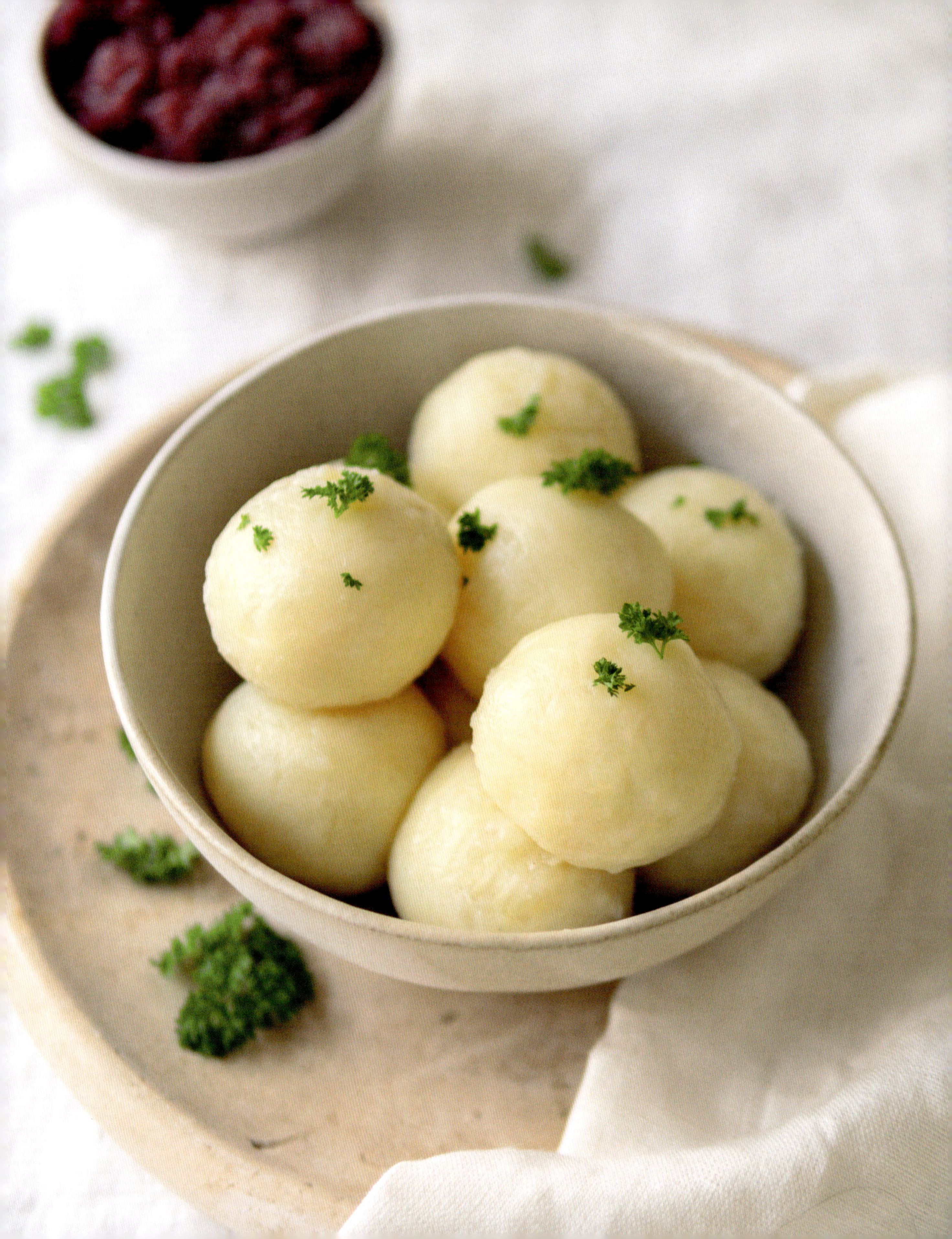

Kartoffelklöße

Potato Dumplings

PREP TIME: 15 minutes
COOK TIME: 25 minutes
YIELD: 10 dumplings

Potato dumplings are a beloved side dish in Germany, and there's nothing better than soaking up sauces with these pillowy-soft bites. If you haven't tried Kartoffelklöße, you're in for a treat, especially when homemade. There are several ways to make them, but my recipe uses a simple combination of boiled potatoes, potato starch (not to be confused with potato flour), and egg—a method that's easy and foolproof, especially if you follow my Oma's no-measurement trick. It may seem imprecise, but it actually reduces the margin of error and ensures the perfect ratio every time. Serve with Sauerbraten (page 64), Rinderrouladen (page 70), or your family's favorite roast. Add some Rotkohl (page 59) to round out the perfect German meal.

---

2 pounds (1 kg) starchy potatoes, such as russet, peeled and cubed

1¼ to 1½ cups (160 g to 195 g) potato starch or cornstarch

1 large egg

1 teaspoon salt, plus more for boiling

NOTE

✤ *Reheat leftover potato dumplings by gently warming them in simmering water (or, when applicable, sauce) to prevent drying out. Another delicious way to eat klöße as leftovers is to cut them into slices and cook them in the skillet with some butter.*

1. Heat a large pot of unsalted water to boiling over high heat. Add the potatoes and boil until fork-tender, 10 to 15 minutes.

2. Drain the potatoes and transfer them to a large bowl; rinse the pan and keep it handy. Using a potato masher or a spätzle press, mash the potatoes until completely smooth with no lumps.

3. Press the mashed potatoes evenly into the bowl. Using a knife or a spatula, divide them into 4 equal sections, ensuring clean, distinct lines. Carefully scoop out 1 section and set it on the remaining 3 sections. Fill the empty section with potato starch, making sure it stays within the lines and comes up flush with the level of the remaining sections. Add the egg, and 1 teaspoon of salt; mix everything with a fork until cool enough to handle, about 3 minutes. Knead by hand until the dough is smooth, about 2 minutes.

4. Refill the pot with fresh water, add a large pinch of salt, and heat to boiling over high heat.

5. Meanwhile, on a clean work surface, using a bench scraper or sharp knife, divide the dough into 10 pieces. Roll the pieces into smooth balls.

6. Reduce the heat to low; the water should be hot but just below simmering. Gently lower the dumplings into the hot water and cook until they float to the surface, about 10 minutes. Transfer to a serving bowl, being careful not to smoosh them.

Für Zwischendurch & Beilagen

Semmelknödel

Bread Dumplings

Semmelknödel are an amazingly delicious way to use leftover bread and soak up some sauce! They are a staple food in Germany. I can feel my Oma applauding me from heaven because I know how much she appreciated not throwing away food. Serve with Jägersoße (page 78) or as a side with Rinderrouladen (page 70) or Sauerbraten (page 64). For a fun twist, try serving Semmelknödel at Thanksgiving as a stuffing alternative!

PREP TIME: 30 minutes
COOK TIME: 20 minutes
YIELD: 6 dumplings

10½ ounces (300 g) stale bread, divided

7 ounces (150 ml) whole milk

½ teaspoon salt, plus more for boiling

¼ teaspoon ground black pepper

¼ teaspoon freshly grated nutmeg

1 tablespoon (15 g) unsalted butter

1 medium yellow onion, finely diced

1 handful chopped fresh parsley

1 large egg

NOTE

✤ The best way to reheat these dumplings is in simmering water. You could also cut the dumplings, cold right out of the refrigerator, into slices, about ½ inch (12 mm) thick, fry them in butter until golden, and top them with Jägersoße (page 78) or serve them with Sauerkraut (page 60) or a Gemischter Salat (page 48).

1. In a food processor with the knife blade attached, process 3½ ounces (100 g) of the bread into coarse crumbs.

2. Cut the remaining 7 ounces (200 g) bread into small cubes and transfer to a medium bowl. Add the milk, salt, pepper, and nutmeg and let soak, stirring occasionally, until soft, about 20 minutes.

3. Meanwhile, in a large skillet over medium-high heat, melt the butter until foamy, about 1 minute. Add the onion and cook, stirring occasionally, until lightly browned, about 2 minutes. Add the parsley and stir until wilted, about 30 seconds. Remove from the heat.

4. To the milk-soaked bread, add the onion and the egg and knead with your hands until just combined. Knead in half of the bread crumbs until combined. Gradually add the remaining half of the bread crumbs, kneading in between, just until the dough holds its shape (you may not use all of the bread crumbs).

5. Heat a large pot of salted water to boiling over high heat, then reduce the heat to low so the water is hot but still—this will allow the dumplings to poach gently without breaking apart.

6. To test the dough, roll a small test dumpling, about the size of a walnut. Gently add it to the pot and poach for a couple of minutes. If it holds together, proceed with shaping and cooking the rest; if it falls apart, knead more bread crumbs into the dough.

7. With wet hands, divide the dough into 6 equal pieces and shape each into a round, smooth ball. Gently add them to the pot and poach until they float to the surface—the sign they're fully cooked—about 20 minutes. Turn off the heat and keep the dumplings warm in the water until ready to serve. Drain just before serving.

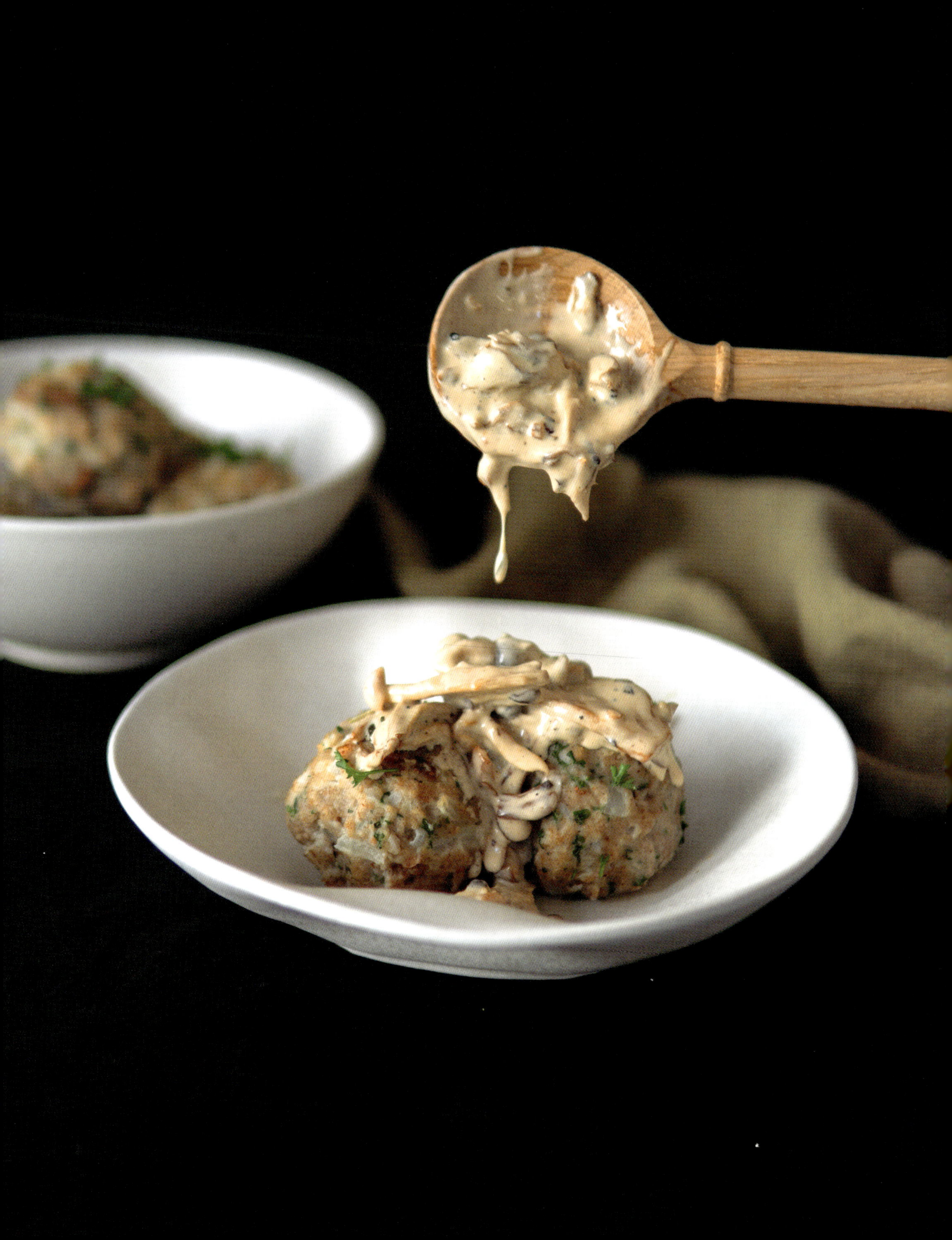

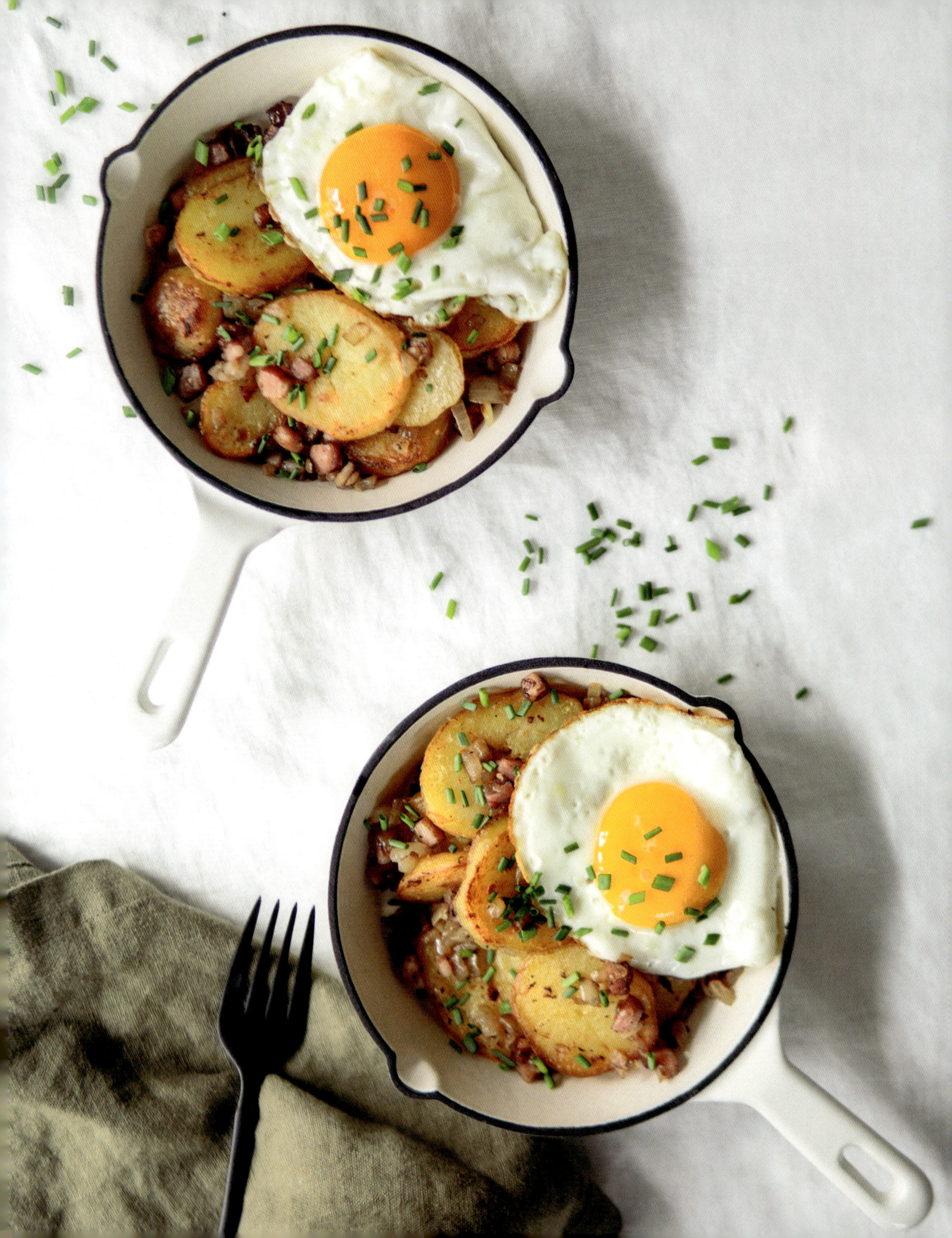

Bratkartoffeln

Pan-Fried Potatoes

PREP TIME: 30 minutes
COOK TIME: 30 minutes
YIELD: 4 servings

Bratkartoffeln is a popular dish in Germany and just one of the seemingly endless ways Germans love to eat potatoes (on average, over 100 pounds, or 45 kg, per person each year!). These pan-fried potatoes are irresistably crispy on the outside and so addictive, especially when you make them my way with onion and bacon, then finish with fresh chives. The key to getting getting them perfectly golden and crispy, with delicious butter flavor without burning them, is to cook them at medium heat and to combine butter (and, in this case, bacon) with a neutral cooking oil with a high smoke point, like avocado oil. Serve as a side with Jägerschnitzel (page 78), Frikadellen (page 108), Currywurst (page 111), or Backfisch (page 74). To serve as a main dish, top with sunny-side-up eggs—just like my Oma always did—and pair with a salad, such as Gemischter Salat (page 48).

---

2 pounds (1 kg) waxy potatoes, scrubbed clean

1 teaspoon salt, plus more to taste

4 slices thick-cut bacon, finely diced (see Note)

1 large yellow onion, finely diced

2 tablespoons unsalted butter

2 tablespoons avocado oil

4 sunny-side-up eggs, for serving (optional)

Chopped fresh chives or parsley, for garnishing

1. Place the potatoes in a large pot and cover with water. Add the salt and heat to boiling over high heat. Reduce the heat to low, cover, and simmer until the potatoes are easily pierced with a knife, about 20 minutes. Drain and let cool for about 10 minutes.

2. Using a paring knife, peel the potatoes. Cut them crosswise into slices, about ½ inch (12 mm) thick.

3. In a large skillet over medium heat, cook the bacon, stirring occasionally, until it just starts to brown, about 2 minutes. Add the onion and cook, stirring occasionally, until the bacon is crisp and the onion starts to brown, about 2 minutes. Using a slotted spoon, transfer the bacon and onion to a small bowl.

4. Melt the butter in the skillet, then add the oil. Working in batches, add the potatoes, arranging them in a single layer; season with more salt. Cook without stirring until browned, about 2 minutes, then flip and brown the other side, about 2 minutes.

5. Return the bacon and onion to the skillet, stirring to reheat, about 1 minute; remove from the heat. Serve directly from the skillet or plate individually with the eggs (if using). Garnish with chives or parsley as desired.

NOTE

✤ *If desired, you can omit the bacon. Instead, cook the onion in 1 tablespoon butter over medium heat, then remove from the pan. Add a little more butter and oil before proceeding to the next step.*

Für Zwischendurch & Beilagen

Spätzle

German Egg Noodles

PREP TIME: 10 minutes
COOK TIME: 5 minutes
YIELD: 4 servings

Originating from Schwabenland (Swabia) in southwestern Germany, spätzle has become a staple in our German-American household. These tender egg noodles are a classic side dish for Beef Rouladen (page 70), Jägerschnitzel (page 78), or even your family's favorite stew. If you haven't tried Käsespätzle (page 67)—spätzle layered with melty cheese and topped with crispy onions—you're in for a treat! That said, give me a bowl of plain, buttered spätzle and I'll be the happiest girl. If you're just starting out on your spätzle journey, and are not yet ready to invest in a Spätzle press (what my family uses) or a spätzle grater (what my Swiss friend uses), you can shape the noodles using a cutting board and knife. See the Notes for details on all these options.

---

2 large eggs

1⅔ cups (200 g) all-purpose flour

5 ounces (150 ml) whole milk, divided

1 tablespoon unsalted butter, melted, plus shaved butter (see Notes) for topping

Freshly ground nutmeg (optional)

Salt, for boiling (see Notes)

1. In a large bowl, add the eggs, flour, 4 ounces (120 ml) of the milk, the butter, and, if using, nutmeg. Whisk until a thick, glue-like batter forms (it should not drip off the whisk). Add the remaining 1 ounce (30 ml) milk as necessary to achieve the perfect batter consistency.

2. Fill a large pot with water, stir in salt, and give it a taste—it should be quite salty, like the ocean, so it can adequately flavor the noodles; heat to boiling over high heat.

3. Working in batches, use a rubber spatula to transfer the batter to a spätzle press and press it through the holes directly into the boiling water. Stir to keep the noodles from clumping. The water temperature will drop slightly after adding the noodles; let it return to a boil, then reduce the heat to medium-low to maintain a gentle simmer. Simmer until the spätzle float to the surface—the sign they are fully cooked—about 2 minutes. Using a skimmer, transfer the spätzle to a serving bowl.

4. Scatter some shaved butter over the hot spätzle, letting it melt into the noodles. (The butter adds flavor to the noodles and keeps them from sticking.)

NOTES

✤ To shave the butter, scrape a butter knife across the surface of a stick of room-temperature butter to create ribbons and flakes that melt evenly over the hot noodles.

✤ For boiling, my salt-to-water ratio is 1 teaspoon for every 4 cups (1 L) of water. The results, of course, depend on the type of salt you use. I use a mineral rock salt or sea salt.

✤ If you don't have a spätzle press or grater, you can shape your noodles using a cutting board and knife. Simply spread a thin layer of batter onto a wet wooden cutting board. Using the back of a chef's knife or a metal bench scraper, quickly fling thin strips of batter into the boiling water. (Use enough speed to cut clean pieces but not so much that you risk injury.)

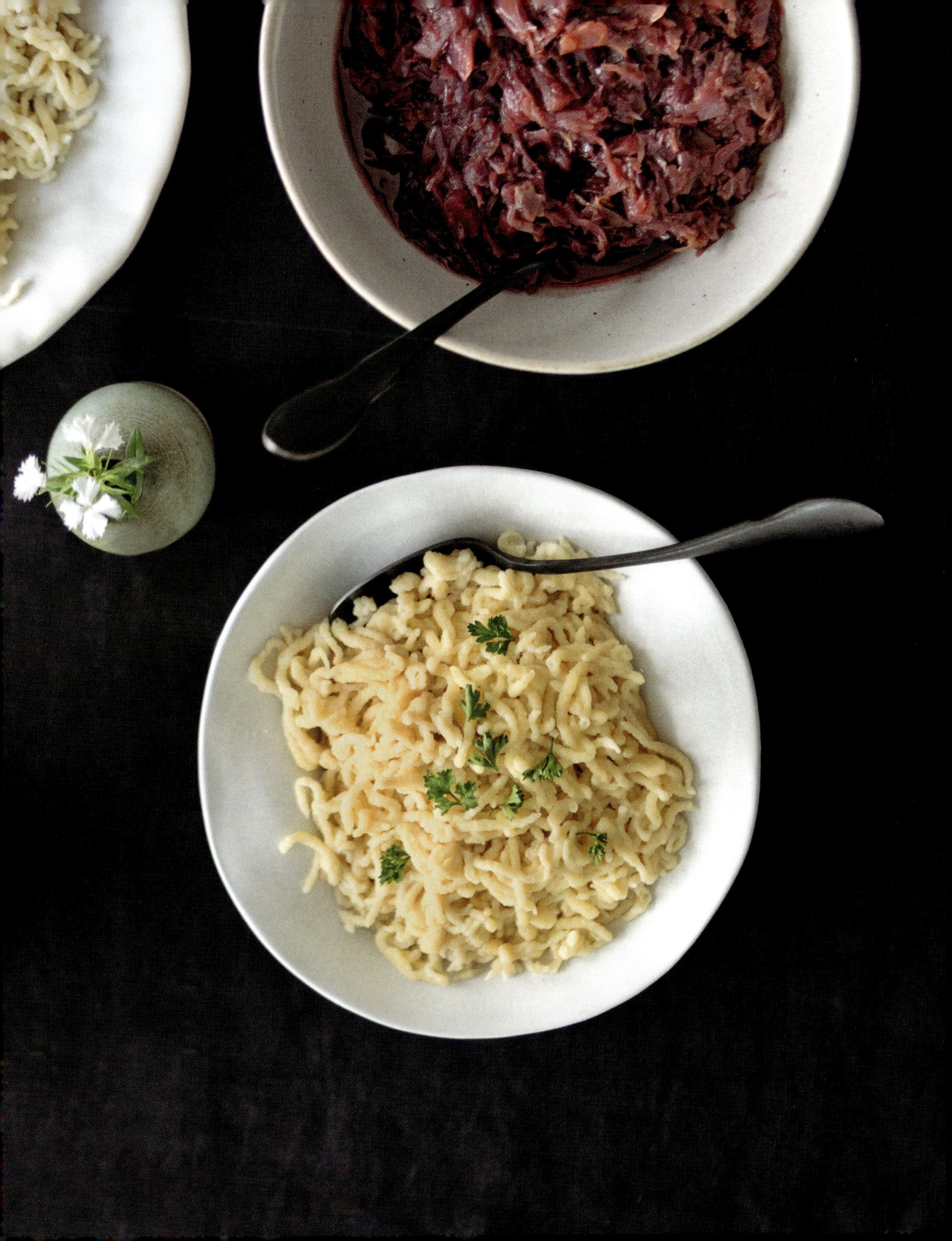

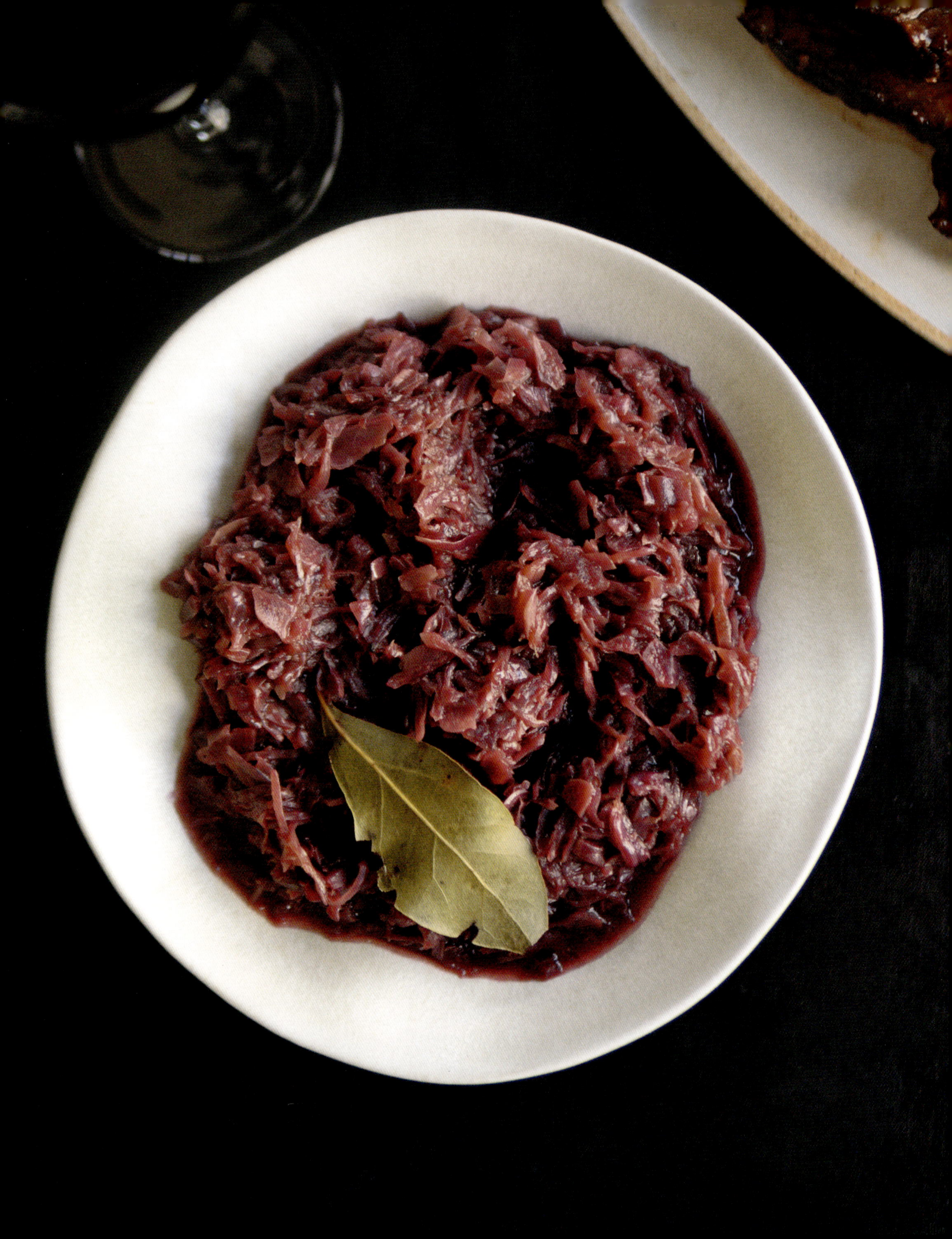

Rotkohl

Braised Red Cabbage

PREP TIME: 30 minutes

COOK TIME: 2 hours and 30 minutes

YIELD: 8 servings

When I think of the most traditional German vegetable side to serve with a roast—Sauerbraten (page 64) or Rinderrouladen (page 70)—it most definitely is rotkohl (or rotkraut or blaukraut, depending on the region). It has the perfect balance of sweet and sour (yin and yang on a plate!). The warming spices in this braised red cabbage bring out its rich depth of flavor. My Oma always used leftover bacon grease to cook rotkohl, which adds another layer of flavor, but if you're one of my vegetarian friends, butter or a neutral oil work just as well.

---

1 firm, large head red cabbage (2 pounds, or 910 g)

2 tablespoons bacon grease, unsalted butter, or avocado oil

1 medium yellow onion, medium diced

3 medium tart apples, such as Granny Smith, peeled, cored, and medium diced

1 bay leaf

4 whole cloves

2 tablespoons brown sugar, plus more to taste

2 tablespoons red wine vinegar, plus more to taste

2 tablespoons lingonberry jam

1 tablespoon cornstarch

2 tablespoons cold water

Salt and ground black pepper

1. Remove and discard the tough outer leaves, then rinse the cabbage and pat it dry. On a large cutting board, use a sharp, sturdy knife to halve the cabbage lengthwise. Place the halves cut side down and cut each into three wedges. Remove and discard the cores.

2. Using a mandoline slicer set to the second thinnest setting, or a sharp knife, thinly slice the cabbage into uniform pieces.

3. In a large pot with a lid, heat the bacon grease over medium-high heat until melted and clear, about 1 minute. Add the onion and cook, stirring occasionally, until it starts to brown, about 2 minutes. Stir in the cabbage and cook until wilted, 3 to 5 minutes.

4. Add the apple, bay leaf, cloves, brown sugar, vinegar, jam, and ½ cup (120 ml) of water; stir to combine. Reduce the heat to low, cover, and simmer, stirring occasionally and adding water as necessary, until the cabbage is super soft and ultra fragrant, about 2 hours.

5. In a small bowl, whisk the cornstarch and water until no lumps remain. Stir into the cabbage mixture and cook for a few minutes until the sauce thickens slightly, giving the Rotkohl a velvety texture.

6. Season with salt, pepper, brown sugar, and vinegar as desired. Remove from the heat and serve hot.

NOTE

✤ *Leftovers keep in an airtight container in the refrigerator for up to 5 days. They can also be frozen in a freezer-safe bag or container for up to 3 months.*

Für Zwischendurch & Beilagen

Sauerkraut

Fermented Cabbage

PREP TIME: 20 minutes, plus 7 days fermenting

YIELD: 1-quart (1 L) jar

Rumors are true—Germans love their cabbage (okay, most of them do). However, few actually make sauerkraut from scratch, even though it's incredibly easy. That said, it's a bit of an arm workout. This homemade sauerkraut has the perfect balance of crunch, tang, and saltiness, plus it's packed with probiotics and vitamin C. Feel free to be creative with add-ins, kneading spices into the cabbage for extra flavor. Caraway seeds are a traditional German addition; I also love adding roasted garlic. You can also replace some of the cabbage with the same amount of shredded carrots or kohlrabi. Fermenting is fun! Eat the sauerkraut raw to preserve its probiotics and vitamins (my favorite way, though not common in Germany), or cook it with butter, bacon, onion and/or garlic and serve with bratwurst and mashed potatoes or Erbsbrei (page 118).

---

1 firm, large head white, green, or red cabbage (2 pounds, or 910 g)

2 teaspoons (10 g) salt

1. Wash the jar with hot water and mild soap and let it air-dry completely. (It the jar is not brand new, sterilize it (see instructions on page 11 before proceeding).

2. Remove and discard the tough outer leaves, then rinse the cabbage and pat it dry with clean paper towels. On a large cutting board, using a sharp, sturdy knife, halve the cabbage lengthwise. Place the halves cut side down and cut each into three wedges. Remove and discard the cores. Using a mandoline slicer, set to the second thinnest setting, or a sharp knife, thinly slice the cabbage into uniform pieces; place in a large, clean bowl and add the salt.

3. Now it's time to roll up your sleeves and, with very clean hands, knead the cabbage until it softens and releases its juices, 5 to 6 minutes. You'll know that you have kneaded your cabbage enough when you press it down and the juices cover it.

4. Transfer the cabbage and the juices to the prepared jar, pressing down firmly to ensure the cabbage is entirely submerged in the juices. Leave about 1 inch (2.5 cm) of headspace, then secure the jar tightly with its lid. Place the jar on a rimmed plate or tray and wrap the bottom in a clean kitchen towel to soak up any juices that may bubble up and escape during the fermentation. Let the jar sit at room temperature until the bubbling stops, about 1 week.

5. Loosely seal the jar and store it in a cool, dark spot—like a cellar—or in the fridge for up to 1 year. The sauerkraut will continue to ferment and the taste will change over time; placing it in the fridge will slow this process.

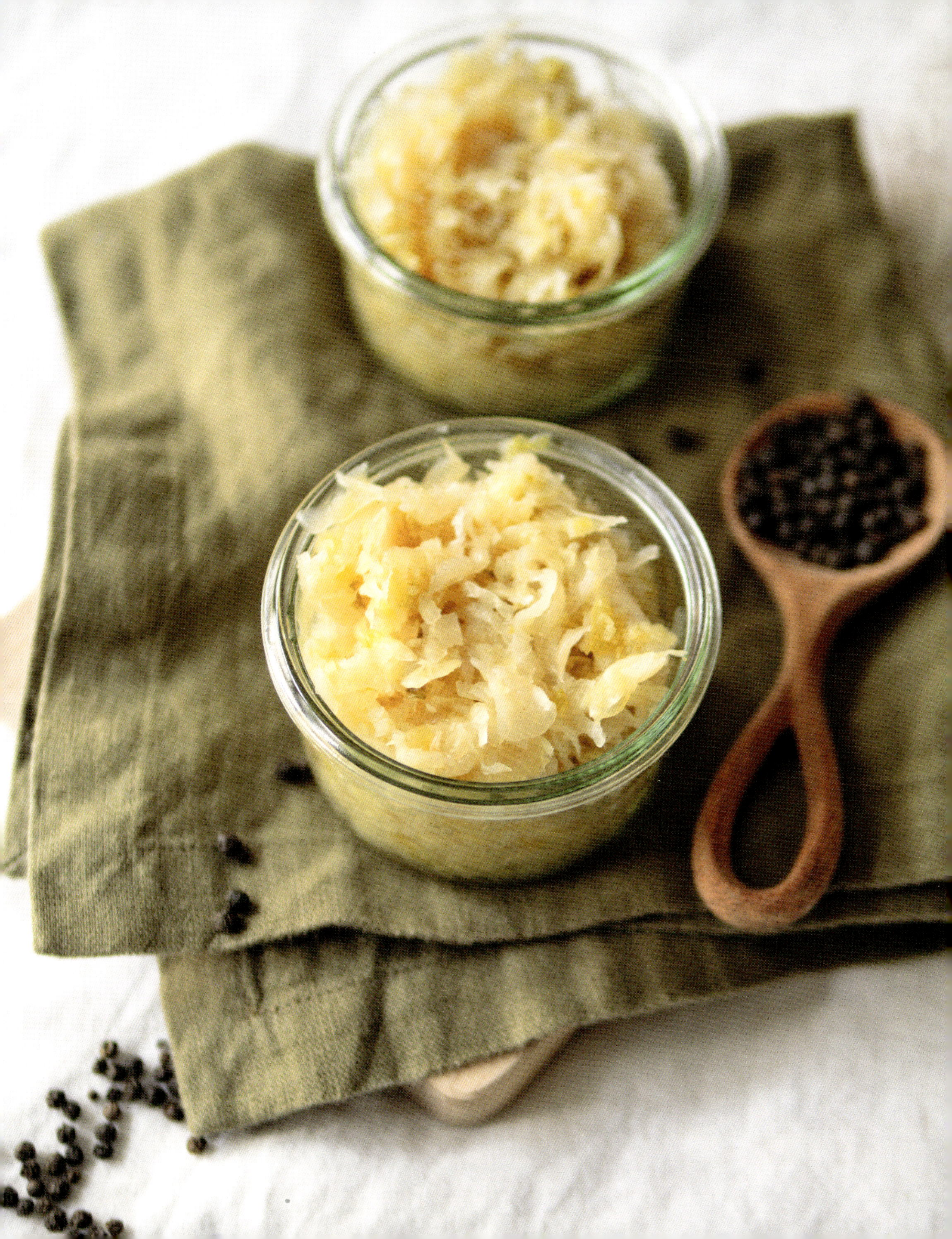

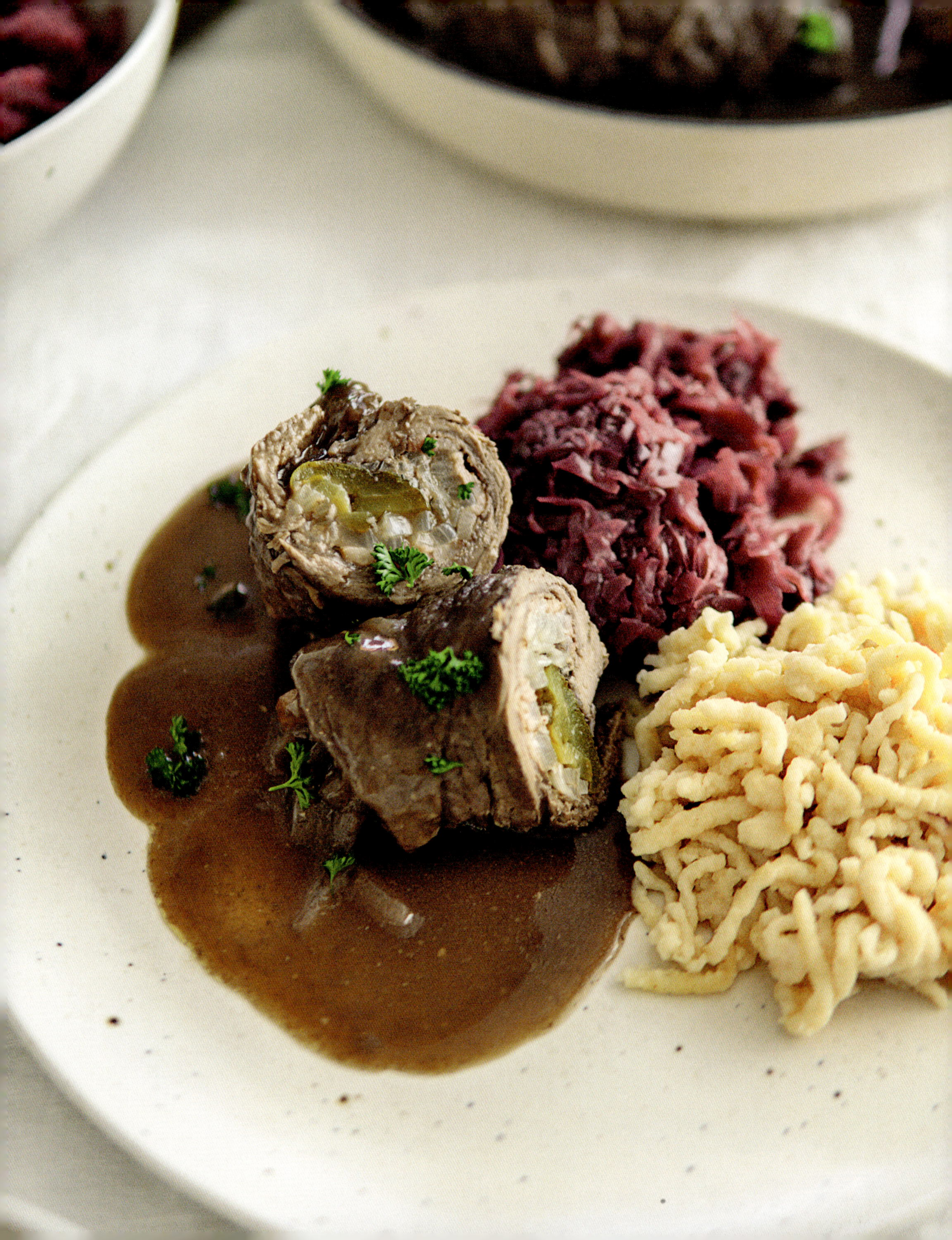

HAUPTSPEISEN

>> *Main Dishes* <<

I hope you'll try something new from this chapter—and then share it to help spread the word that German main dishes go far beyond Schnitzel (though you'll most definitely find my favorite Jägerschnitzel recipe here, complete with the creamiest mushroom sauce!).

Sauerbraten

Sweet-and-Sour Beef Roast

PREP TIME: 30 minutes, plus 3 to 5 days marinating

COOK TIME: 2½ hours

YIELD: 4 servings

This is the most famous German roast in the world. Naturally, it had to find its way into this book. Marinating the meat for 3 to 5 days helps to develop deep, complex flavors, but the process can also be sped up (see Notes). It's hard to beat the sweet-and-sour combination in this roast and there really isn't anything like it! Sauerbraten is totally appropriate as a fun weekend dinner project, but fancy enough to dish up as a holiday meal or for any special occasion. Serve with Semmelknödel (page 52), Kartoffelklöße (page 51), or Spätzle (page 56) and Rotkohl (page 59).

- 4 whole allspice berries
- 6 whole juniper berries
- 4 whole cloves
- 8 whole black peppercorns
- 2 pounds (1 kg) lean beef roast, such as bottom round (rump) roast (see Notes)
- 2 cloves garlic, minced
- 2 medium carrots, medium diced
- 1 large onion, medium diced
- 2 celery stalks, medium diced
- 1 large leek, white and light green parts halved lengthwise, rinsed, and thinly sliced
- 2 bay leaves
- 1 teaspoon dried thyme or 1 tablespoon chopped fresh thyme
- 2 cups (480 ml) red wine, such as Pinot Noir
- 2 cups (480 ml) red wine vinegar
- 3 tablespoons plus 2 teaspoons brown sugar, plus more to taste

1. Using a mortar and pestle or spice grinder, grind the allspice, juniper, cloves, and peppercorns. Rinse the beef and pat it dry with paper towels.

2. In a gallon-size zip-top plastic bag, add the meat, ground spices, garlic, carrots, onion, celery, leek, bay leaves, thyme, wine, vinegar, and brown sugar; press out as much air as possible and seal the bag. Place the bag in a bowl just big enough to hold it (to prevent leaks and keep it upright). Marinate in the refrigerator for 3 to 5 days (longer marinating results in more tender, flavorful meat; if short on time, see the Notes).

3. Preheat the oven to 320°F (160°C). Remove the meat from the bag and pat it dry with paper towels. Set a fine mesh sieve over a large bowl and strain the marinade. Reserve the liquid and the marinated veggies.

4. In a large oven-safe pot with a lid, heat the butter and oil over medium-high heat until foamy, about 1 minute. Add the meat and sear on all sides, 1 to 2 minutes per side. Transfer to a large plate. Add the strained vegetables and cook, stirring occasionally, until softened, about 5 minutes. Add the tomato paste and cook, stirring until fragrant, about 1 minute. Return the meat to the pot. Add the bread, then pour in enough broth and reserved marinade (equal parts) to cover the roast two-thirds of the way. Cover the pot and place in the oven; braise until the meat is tender but not falling apart, about 2 hours. (If the meat is extra lean, extend the cooking time by 30 to 60 minutes.) Rotate the meat halfway through cooking, adding more broth and marinade as needed.

1 tablespoon unsalted butter

1 tablespoon avocado oil

1 tablespoon (15 g) tomato paste

1 heel of stale bread

4 cups (1 L) beef broth, plus more if needed

¼ cup (40 g) dark seedless raisins

1 teaspoon cornstarch

Salt and ground black pepper

5. Transfer the pot to the stove. Using tongs, transfer the meat to a carving board, cover it with foil, and let it rest for 15 minutes. With a carving knife, slice the meat, against the grain, ½ inch (12 mm) thick.

6. Set a fine mesh sieve over a large bowl and strain the liquid. Return the liquid to the pot and add the raisins; simmer over low heat until the raisins have softened and added sweetness, about 15 minutes.

7. In a small bowl, whisk the cornstarch and 1 tablespoon of water until no lumps remain. Stir into the sauce and cook, whisking occasionally, until thickened, 1 to 2 minutes. (For a thicker sauce, cook it slightly longer.) Season with salt, pepper, and brown sugar to taste. Return the sliced meat to the pot, or arrange it on a warmed platter and spoon the sauce over the top.

NOTES

✣ *For quicker marinating, separate out the wine and vinegar and heat them in a small saucepan over medium-high heat until a thermometer reaches 200°F (93°C) before adding to the zip-top bag along with the other marinade ingredients. This helps cut down the marinating time to 2 days in the fridge.*

✣ *You can also use top round or arm roast. It's best to call your butcher ahead of time for this one, as lean beef roasts aren't common everywhere outside of Germany.*

Hauptspeisen

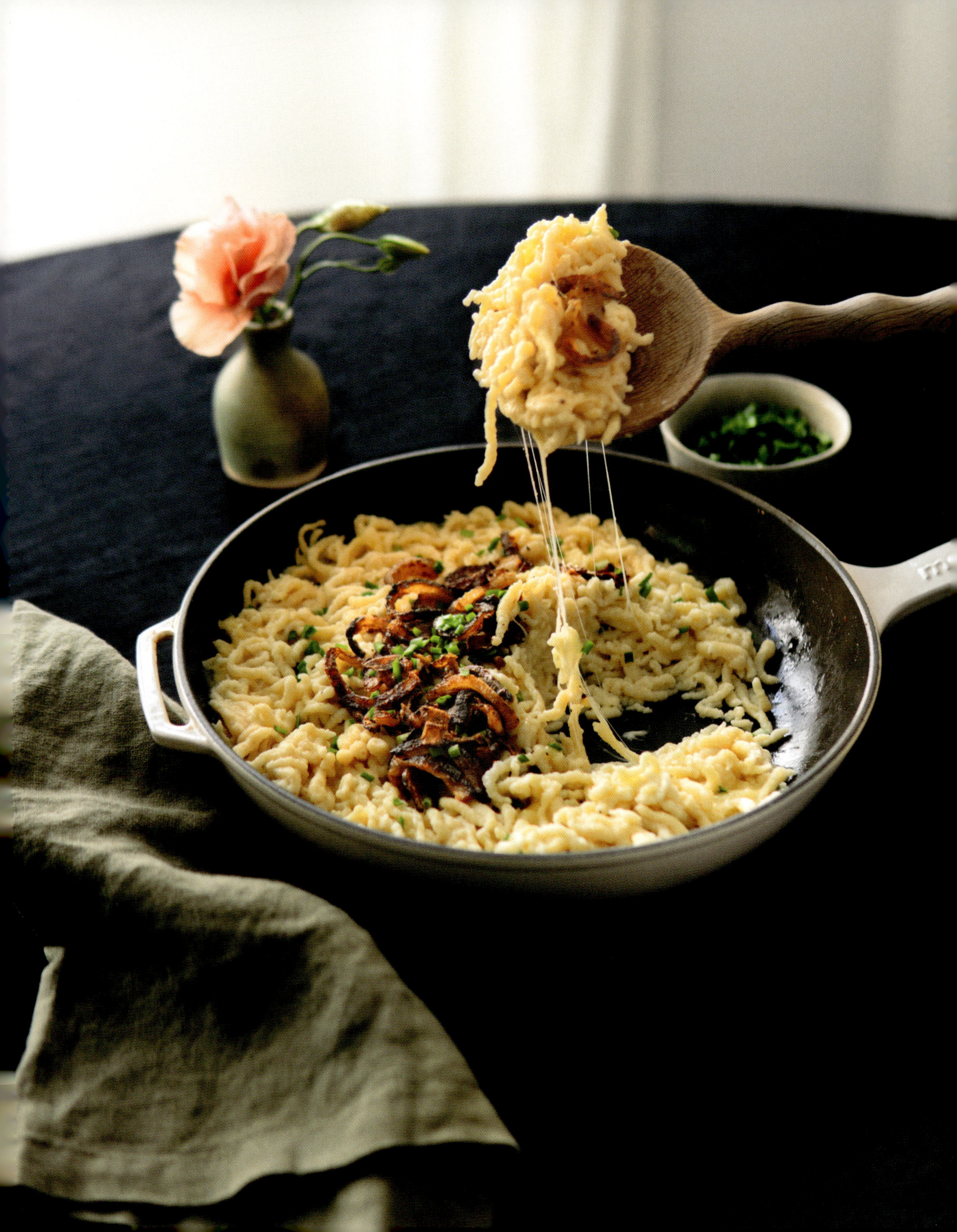

Käsespätzle

Cheese Spätzle Noodles

PREP TIME: 10 minutes
COOK TIME: 10 minutes
YIELD: 4 servings

Käsespätzle is that cozy, comforting meal waiting for you at the end of the Alpine ski run. These are the cheesiest of noodles topped with crispy onions—totally addictive. Originally from Germany's southwestern Swabia region, Käsespätzle has gained popularity across the country. At our wedding reception in Kansas City, we had a Käsespätzle bar with a bunch of topping options—a German twist on mac and cheese—and everyone loved it! For the best flavor, use a mix of Emmentaler and Bergkäse or Gruyère. If you're making this for small kids who might be pickier about strong cheeses, try half young Gouda and half aged Gouda for a milder version. And if you want to take your Käsespätzle to the next level, try making it with homemade Spätzle (page 56).

Salt, for boiling

7 ounces (200 g) uncooked Spätzle noodles, or homemade (page 56)

1 large yellow onion, cut into thin rings or half-moons

1 tablespoon all-purpose flour

5 tablespoons unsalted butter, divided

½ cup (75 g) shredded Emmentaler cheese

½ cup (75 g) shredded Bergkäse or Gruyère cheese

Finely chopped fresh chives, for garnishing

1. Heat a large pot of salted water to boiling over high heat. Add the Spätzle and cook according to the package instructions.

2. Meanwhile, in a small bowl, add the onion and the flour; toss until evenly coated.

3. Line a large plate with paper towels. In a large skillet over medium heat, heat 3 tablespoons of the butter until foamy, about 1 minute. Add the onion and cook, stirring occasionally, until golden brown and crispy, 5 to 10 minutes. Transfer the prepared plate.

4. Drain the Spätzle and return it to the pot. While the noodles are still hot, immediately stir in the remaining 2 tablespoons butter.

5. Layer half of the hot Spätzle in a serving bowl, top with the cheeses, and finish with the remaining Spätzle. Top with the crispy onions and garnish with chives.

6. Serve on its own, with a green salad, or as a side dish.

NOTE

✤ *Store leftovers in an airtight container for up to 3 days in the refrigerator. To reheat, put in an oven-safe dish, cover with foil, and bake at 350°F (180°C) until heated through, 10 to 20 minutes.*

Linsensuppe

Lentil Soup

PREP TIME: 15 minutes
COOK TIME: 40 minutes
YIELD: 6 servings

Linsensuppe is one of those recipes my German soul craves when cooler weather hits. Lentils always remind me of my Oma Sieghilde. This nutrient-dense soup is warming, filling, and—bonus—feeds a crowd on a budget. We often make it for gatherings with our German kids' group, as both adults and kids love it. It's also a quick-to-make eintopf (one-pot meal), so cleanup is a breeze. For a vegetarian version, omit the Wiener sausages at the end. Serve with some good bread (I like the Roggenmischbrot on page 82).

- 2 tablespoons unsalted butter or avocado oil
- 4 cups (600 g) medium diced waxy potatoes (about 5 medium potatoes)
- 1½ cups (200 g) small diced carrots (about 3 large carrots)
- 1 cup (200 g) small diced celery (about 3 celery ribs)
- 1¼ cups (200 g) small diced onion (about 1 large onion)
- 2½ cups (450 g) dried lentils (see Note), rinsed
- 10½ cups (2.5 L) vegetable broth
- 1 bay leaf
- 6 tablespoons red wine vinegar
- 1 tablespoon tomato paste
- 2 tablespoons granulated sugar
- Salt and ground black pepper
- 6 Wiener sausages, sliced or whole (optional)
- Chopped fresh parsley, for garnishing

1. In a large stock pot with a lid, melt the butter over medium heat until foaming, about 1 minute. Add the potatoes, carrots, celery, and onion; cook, stirring occasionally, until softened, about 5 minutes.

2. Add the lentils, broth, and bay leaf and heat to boiling over high heat. Reduce the heat to low, cover the pot, and simmer until softened, about 30 minutes.

3. Stir in the vinegar, tomato paste, and sugar. Season with salt and pepper to taste.

4. Add the Wiener sausages, if using, and heat through without boiling. Alternatively, you can warm the sausages separately in a small saucepan of water over medium-low heat (do not boil or they will split) and add them to individual serving bowls. Remove from the heat.

5. Ladle into soup bowls and garnish with parsley.

NOTE

Black, green, or brown lentils work best in this recipe, as they hold their shape better. Red and yellow lentils fall apart more easily and are not as suitable for this soup.

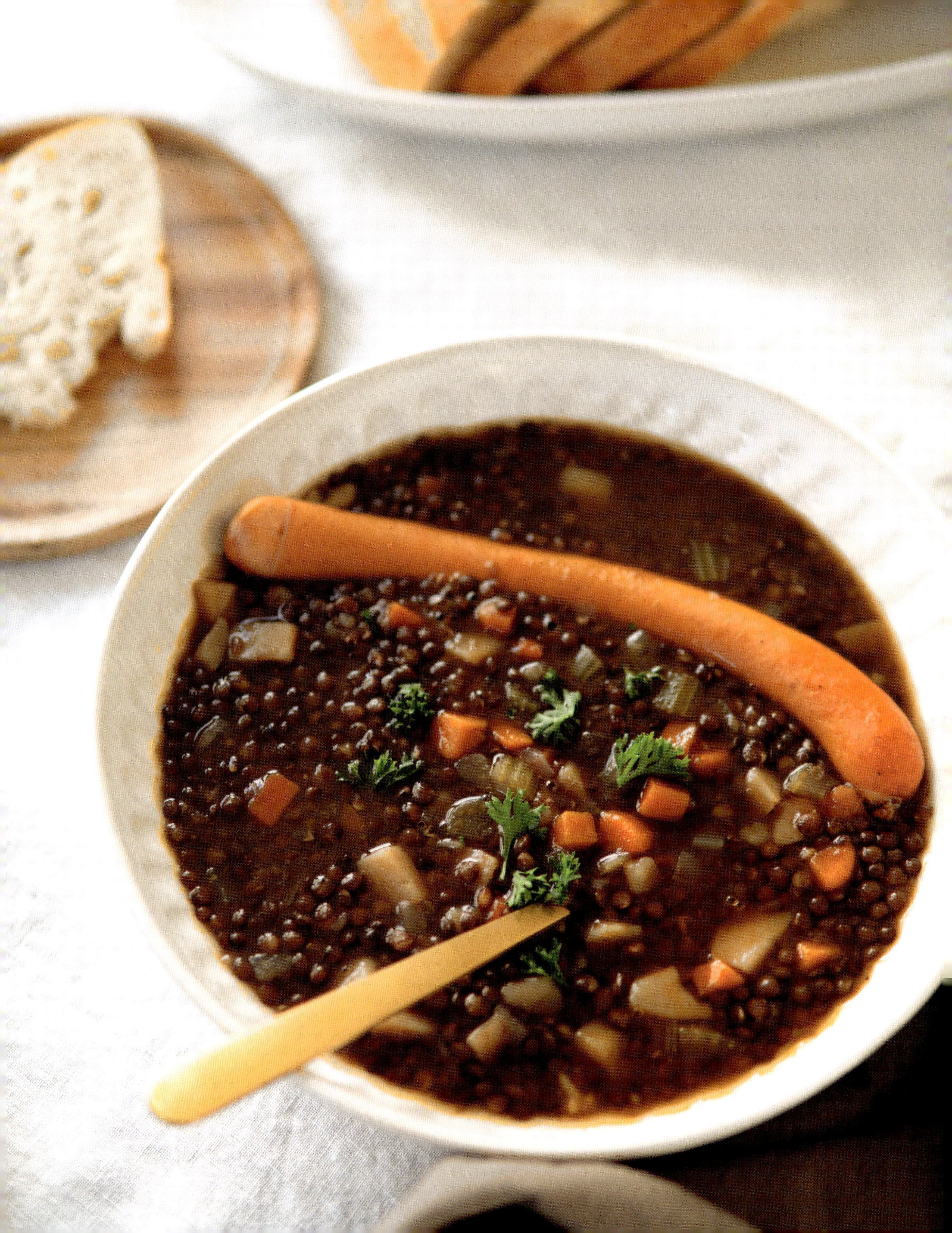

Rinderrouladen

Beef Roulade

This is the meal of meals that could turn any German food skeptic into a German food lover. Tender beef is rolled up with smoky bacon, tangy pickles, onions, and mustard, then braised in a velvety red wine sauce—pure magic. Yes, these take a bit of time, but most of it is hands-off while the oven does the work. Serve your rinderrouladen with plenty of Spätzle (page 56), Semmelknödel (page 52), or Kartoffelklöße (page 51) to soak up all that delicious sauce. Rotkohl (page 59) makes for a perfect vegetable side, but roasted Brussels sprouts or root vegetables are also great options.

PREP TIME: 40 minutes

COOK TIME: 2 hours

YIELD: 4 servings

ROULADEN

1½ pounds beef steak (see Note), cut into 8 strips, about ½ inch (12 mm) thick

Salt and ground black pepper

8 teaspoons Dijon mustard

2 large yellow onions, thinly sliced

40 slices Gewürzgurken (page 91)

8 slices bacon, halved crosswise

SAUCE

2 tablespoons (30 g) unsalted butter

1 rib celery, medium diced

1 small yellow onion, medium diced

1 large carrot, medium diced

1 large leek, white and light green parts halved lengthwise, rinsed, and thinly sliced

1½ cups (360 ml) red wine, plus more as desired

2 cups (480 ml) beef broth, plus more for simmering

1. Preheat the oven to 320°F (160°C). Have some kitchen twine or toothpicks ready.

2. **Make the rouladen:** Rinse the steak and pat it dry with paper towels. With a meat mallet, pound each piece to ¼-inch (6 mm) thickness. Season each piece with salt and pepper and spread 1 teaspoon of mustard on top. Top with the onions, 5 pickle slices, and 2 pieces of bacon. Roll tightly and secure with kitchen twine or toothpicks.

3. **Make the sauce:** In a large skillet, melt the butter over medium-high heat until foamy, about 1 minute. Add the beef rolls and sear on all sides, 2 to 3 minutes per side. Reduce the heat to medium-low; transfer the beef rolls to a large oven-safe pot with a lid. To the skillet, add the celery, onion, carrot, and leek; cook, stirring occasionally, until they begin to brown, about 5 minutes. Add ½ cup (120 ml) of the wine and cook, stirring occasionally, until it evaporates, 5 to 10 minutes. Repeat with the remaining wine, ½ cup (120 ml) at a time. Add the broth and pickle juice, stir occasionally until boiling.

4. Pour the mixture over the beef rolls; they should be covered halfway. Cover the pot. Braise in the oven until the rolls are tender and have some give when pressed, about 90 minutes, checking every 30 minutes and adding more broth as needed. Remove from the oven and turn it off. Carefully transfer the beef rolls to a serving platter, cover with foil, and keep warm in the oven.

5. Set a fine mesh sieve over a large bowl. Strain the sauce and return it to the pot; heat to boiling over high heat. Reduce the heat to medium. In a small bowl, whisk together the mustard, cornstarch, and 2 tablespoons of water; add to the sauce and

German Home Kitchen

5 tablespoons Gewürzgurken juice (page 91), plus more as desired

1 tablespoon Dijon mustard

1 tablespoon cornstarch

Salt and ground black pepper

Chopped fresh parsley, for garnishing (optional)

cook, whisking occasionally, until thickened, 1 to 2 minutes. Season with salt, pepper, a splash of red wine, if desired, and pickle juice (if adding wine, simmer for 5 minutes to cook off the alcohol). Remove from the heat.

6. Spoon some sauce over the beef rolls and serve with extra sauce on the side. If desired, garnish with chopped parsley.

NOTES

✦ *I suggest flank steak or top-round steak. If using top-round steak, you may have to cook your rouladen a little bit longer than the 90 minutes in the recipe, but the end result will be just as delicious.*

✦ *Rouladen are perfect for making ahead of time. They keep in an airtight container in the refrigerator for up to 3 days. To freeze leftovers or the finished dish, store in a freezer-safe container for up to 3 months and thaw in the fridge a day before reheating.*

Hauptspeisen

Kohlrouladen

Stuffed Cabbage Rolls

PREP TIME: 30 minutes

COOK TIME: 40 minutes

YIELD: 4 servings

This is probably the meal that reminds me most of Germany. This staple recipe—cabbage leaves stuffed with the most deliciously seasoned meat filling—is one of the many recipes that my Oma Sieghilde made as I was growing up. You will find a few variations across Germany—some like to serve it in a dark sauce, but this is my favorite version: Tender cabbage rolls in the most luxurious, creamy sauce with smoky bacon. It's heavenly. Serve with boiled or mashed potatoes or Spätzle (page 56) to soak up the sauce. For a beautiful, edible alternative to kitchen twine, try tying up your cabbage rolls with chives or green onion blades.

---

1 crusty white roll, such as Weizenbrötchen (page 16)

1 large head green cabbage

1 pound (450 g) 85% lean ground beef

1 small yellow onion, medium diced

1 large egg

1 teaspoon salt, plus more to taste

½ teaspoon ground black pepper, plus more to taste

1 teaspoon sweet or hot paprika, or a mixture of both, plus more to taste

1 teaspoon dried marjoram

1 tablespoon avocado oil

3½ ounces (100 g) thick-cut bacon, medium-diced

2 cups (480 ml) beef broth

¾ cup (180 ml) heavy cream

1 teaspoon cornstarch, plus more as needed

Chopped fresh parsley, for garnishing

1. In a large bowl, soak the roll in water until completely softened, 10 to 15 minutes. Discard the water, squeeze the roll dry, tear it into small pieces, and return them to the bowl.

2. Remove and discard the tough outer leaves, then rinse the cabbage and pat it dry with clean paper towels. Stab a serving fork through the core. Pour enough water into a large, deep saucepan to reach approximately the height of the cabbage; heat to boiling over high heat. Fill a large bowl with ice water. When the water boils, reduce the heat to low for a gentle simmer, then submerge the cabbage, keeping the fork upright. Simmer until the outer cabbage leaves start loosening, about 2 minutes. Holding the fork in one hand and using tongs, carefully remove 8 large cabbage leaves as they loosen, then transfer them to the bowl of ice water. (Keep the remaining cabbage for other uses; see Notes.)

3. To the bowl with the soaked bread, add the ground beef, onion, egg, salt, pepper, paprika, and marjoram. Knead by hand until well combined and smooth. Divide the filling evenly among the cabbage leaves. Roll each one by folding in the stem end first, then tucking in the left and right sides before rolling up tightly, like a burrito. Secure with kitchen twine and set aside.

4. In a large oven-safe pot with a lid, heat the avocado oil over medium-high heat until it moves around the pan quickly when you tilt it, about 1 minute. Add the cabbage rolls, seam sides down, and the bacon and cook, stirring the bacon occasionally and browning the cabbage rolls on all sides, about 2 minutes per side. Add the broth, cover the pot, and reduce the heat to medium-low. Simmer until the meat is fully cooked, about 30 minutes. Transfer the cabbage rolls to a serving platter and cover with foil to keep warm. Reduce the heat to low to maintain a gentle simmer, then stir in the cream.

5. In a small bowl, whisk the cornstarch and 1 tablespoon of water until no lumps remain and whisk the mixture into the pot. Cook, stirring occasionally, until the sauce thickens, 1 to 2 minutes (for a thicker sauce, cook it for a little longer or repeat this step with more cornstarch and water). Season with salt, pepper, and paprika to taste.

6. Serve family-style, in the pot with the sauce or on a warmed serving platter with sauce spooned over the top. (Alternatively, plate individually with plenty of sauce.) Garnish with chopped fresh parsley.

NOTES

✤ *Cut up the remaining cabbage and cook it separately in a skillet with some oil and bacon, or simply steam it once you're getting closer to eating.*

✤ *Make ahead of time and keep in an airtight container in the fridge for up to 3 days. To freeze leftovers or the finished dish, store in a freezer-safe container for up to 3 months and thaw in the fridge a day before reheating.*

Hauptspeisen

Backfisch

Beer-Battered Cod

PREP TIME: 20 minutes
COOK TIME: 20 minutes
YIELD: 4 servings

When I was in first grade, I found a fish bone in a fish stick at lunch—and I didn't eat fish again until I was twenty-two (and I've loved it ever since). This recipe is a nod to Hamburg, one of my favorite German cities, which is nestled along the Nordsee with easy access to the best fish. This fluffy-crisp pilsner-battered cod recipe is just perfection (and don't worry if you're new to deep-frying at home—it's not hard or scary!). The pickle-forward remoulade sauce is an absolute must—a match made in heaven with this fish. Just be sure to use super fresh eggs, as the yolks will be used raw. Serve with Salzkartoffeln (peeled waxy potatoes cooked in salted water) or some fries tossed in Pommesgewürz (page 107). A refreshing cucumber salad gives the perfect finishing touch (use the herb vinaigrette from the Gemischter Salat on page 48).

REMOULADE

2 large egg yolks

1¼ cups (300 ml) avocado oil

1 teaspoon Dijon mustard

2 teaspoons fresh lemon juice

½ cup (100 g) Gewürzgurken pickles (page 91), finely diced

2 boiled eggs, finely diced

1 tablespoon chopped fresh parsley

⅓ cup (50 g) finely chopped chives

Salt and black pepper

BACKFISCH

1 cup (120 g) all-purpose flour

1 teaspoon salt

½ teaspoon ground black pepper

1 pinch cayenne pepper

½ cup (120 ml) pilsner beer

2 large eggs, whites and yolks separated

1. **Make the remoulade:** In a food processor fitted with the knife blade, process the egg yolks until creamy, about 30 seconds. With the machine running, slowly add the oil through the feed tube—first a few drops, then in a thin, steady stream—until fully incorporated and thickened into mayonnaise. Transfer to a medium bowl. Stir in the mustard, lemon juice, pickles, boiled eggs, parsley, and chives. Season with salt and pepper to taste.

2. **Make the backfisch:** In a large bowl, add the flour, salt, black pepper, cayenne pepper, beer, egg yolks, and butter; stir until smooth. Let the batter rest for 15 minutes.

3. In a large bowl and using a wire whisk, beat the egg whites until stiff peaks form. Gently fold into the batter.

4. Preheat the oven to 150°F (65°C). Line a large plate with paper towels and have a baking sheet handy.

5. In a medium pot, heat about 2 inches (5 cm) of oil over medium heat until a frying thermometer reaches 355°F (180°C). Working in batches, use two spoons to lift one piece of cod at a time, coat it in the batter, and carefully drop it into the oil. (Be sure to adjust the heat along the way to keep the temperature constant to prevent the fish from absorbing excess oil and turning soggy. Do not overcrowd the pan.) Fry, turning occasionally, until golden on all sides, about 5 minutes. Transfer the fried fish to the prepared plate. Keep it warm in the oven until ready to eat (see Note).

6. Serve with fresh lemon wedges

German Home Kitchen

3 tablespoons unsalted butter, melted

Avocado oil, for deep frying

2 pounds (1 kg) wild-caught cod, cut into bite-size pieces

Lemon wedges, for serving

NOTE

✦ *Since you're cooking the fish in batches, you can either have your people pile up in the kitchen for a fish fry party and eat the Backfisch as it comes out of the fryer or keep your fish warm in the oven (this way, everyone can eat together at the table at the same time).*

Hauptspeisen

Königsberger Klopse

German Meatballs

PREP TIME: 40 minutes

COOK TIME: 30 minutes

YIELD: 4 servings

This beloved German classic is often reserved for special occasions—but it's easy enough to serve anytime. Beef and pork meatballs are gently simmered in broth before being finished in a creamy sauce with capers and lemon. As you scan the ingredient list, you might be surprised by the anchovy paste. Don't worry—it doesn't make the meatballs fishy; instead, it adds depth to the flavor of the meatballs, so I would not skip it. Serve with Spätzle (page 56) and steamed mixed veggies or any veggie of your choice.

MEATBALLS (KLOPSE)

1 crusty white roll, such as Weizenbrötchen (page 16)

½ pound (250 g) ground beef

½ pound (250 g) ground pork

1 medium yellow onion, finely diced

2 large eggs

2 tablespoons bread crumbs

1 tablespoon anchovy paste (optional, but strongly recommended)

1 teaspoon salt

1 teaspoon ground black pepper

SIMMERING BROTH

4 cups (1 L) beef broth

1 medium yellow onion, finely diced

1 bay leaf

3 whole black peppercorns

CAPER CREAM SAUCE

3 tablespoons (40 g) unsalted butter

1. **Make the meatballs:** Place the roll in a large bowl and cover with water; soak until softened, 10 to 15 minutes. Discard the water, squeeze the roll dry, tear it into small pieces, and return them to the bowl. Add the beef, pork, onion, eggs, bread crumbs, anchovy paste, salt, and pepper and knead by hand until well combined and smooth. Using your hands or a cookie scoop, shape the mixture into 20 to 24 meatballs.

2. **Make the simmering broth:** In a large pot with a lid, add the broth, onion, bay leaf, and peppercorns; heat to boiling over high heat. Using tongs, gently lower the meatballs into the broth. Reduce the heat to low, cover, and simmer until fully cooked, about 20 minutes. Using a skimmer, transfer the meatballs to a large plate.

3. Set a fine mesh sieve over a large bowl and strain the broth into it. Reserve for later. Return the meatballs to the pot and cover to keep them warm.

4. **Make the caper cream sauce:** In a medium saucepan over medium-high heat, melt the butter until foamy, about 1 minute. Sprinkle in the flour and whisk to combine. Cook, whisking occasionally, until bubbly and golden, 1 to 2 minutes. Reduce the heat to medium-low. Whisk in ½ cup (120 ml) of the reserved broth, allowing it to thicken while whisking away like there is no tomorrow. Whisk in the remaining broth, a little at a time, ensuring a smooth consistency (adding the broth too quickly may result in lumps). Stir in the capers and the heavy cream, whisking until just combined. Don't let the sauce come back to a boil, as this may cause it to separate. The sauce should be smooth, creamy, and pourable. Season with the lemon juice, sugar, and salt and pepper to taste.

2 tablespoons all-purpose flour

1½ cups (360 ml) simmering broth

⅓ cup (50 g) capers

½ cup (120 ml) heavy cream

Juice of ½ lemon

Granulated sugar

Salt and ground black pepper

Chopped fresh parsley, for garnishing

Lemon slices or wedges, for garnishing

5. Gently pour the sauce over the meatballs. Garnish with parsley and lemon slices or wedges and serve family-style from the pot.

NOTE

❖ *To reheat, place leftovers in a skillet over medium heat and bring back to temperature gradually, stirring occasionally. Be careful to not let the sauce boil or it may break.*

Hauptspeisen

Jägerschnitzel

Pork Schnitzel with Creamy Mushroom Sauce

No German restaurant menu is complete without crisp-fried schnitzel, usually made with pork and always served with lemon wedges—a must!—for squeezing over as you eat. This is my favorite version—super thin and crispy, topped with a dreamy, creamy mushroom sauce. This schnitzel is also delicious without the sauce. Either way, don't forget the lemon. Enjoy it with some fries tossed in Pommesgewürz (page 107), which is the most common side with schnitzel in Germany, or Bratkartoffeln (page 55) or Spätzle (page 56) and a Gemischter Salat (page 48).

PREP TIME: 30 minutes
COOK TIME: 30 minutes
YIELD: 2 servings

SCHNITZEL

2 boneless pork loin chops, about 1 inch (2.5 cm) thick, butterflied or cut in half to make 4 pieces

Salt and ground black pepper

½ cup (60 g) all-purpose flour

2 large eggs, beaten

½ cup (60 g) bread crumbs

6 tablespoons avocado oil

6 tablespoons unsalted butter

JÄGERSOßE
(Creamy Mushroom Sauce)

1 tablespoon avocado oil

1 tablespoon unsalted butter

1 cup (100 g) mushrooms, thinly sliced (see Notes)

1 tablespoon chopped fresh or 1 teaspoon dried thyme, plus more for garnishing (optional)

Salt and ground black pepper

2 cloves garlic, minced (see Notes)

3 tablespoons brandy

1. **Make the schnitzel:** With a meat mallet or between two sheets of plastic wrap with a rolling pin, pound each pork chop to an even thickness of ¼ inch (6 mm). Season both sides with salt and pepper.

2. Set out three shallow bowls. Fill one with the flour, one with the beaten eggs, and one with the bread crumbs. One piece at a time, dredge the pork in the flour; shake off any excess. Then, dip it into the egg; let any excess drip off. Finally, coat evenly with the bread crumbs.

3. **Make the sauce:** In a large skillet, heat the 1 tablespoon each oil and butter over medium-high heat until foamy, about 1 minute. Add the mushrooms and thyme (if using). Cook, stirring occasionally, until browned, about 10 minutes. Season with salt and pepper to taste. Add the garlic and cook, stirring occasionally, for about 1 minute. Add the brandy and let cook until evaporated, about 1 minute. Stir in the cream. Reduce the heat to medium and simmer gently, stirring occasionally, until the sauce thickens, 1 to 2 minutes. Season with salt and pepper to taste. Keep warm until ready to serve.

4. Preheat the oven to 150°F (65°C). Line a large plate with paper towels and have a baking sheet handy.

5. In another large skillet, heat the 6 tablespoons each oil and butter over medium-high heat until foamy, or a thermometer reaches 330°F (165°C), 1 to 2 minutes. The mixture should be about ¼ inch (6 mm) deep. Cook one schnitzel at a time until golden and crisp on both sides, about 2 minutes per side. Transfer to the prepared plate to drain, then to the baking sheet. Keep warm in the oven.

7 ounces (200 ml) heavy cream

Chopped fresh parsley, for garnishing (optional)

Lemon wedges, for serving

6. Serve on a platter, topped with the sauce. If desired, garnish with parsley or more thyme. Serve with lemon wedges.

NOTES

✤ Use any mushrooms that you like or are easily available. At our local farmers' market, I love picking up oyster, pioppini, trumpet, and chanterelle mushrooms, but white button or cremini mushrooms work well too.

✤ For a milder sauce, swap the garlic for one small shallot.

✤ You can bread the meat ahead of time (up to 1 day before cooking) and keep it in an airtight container in the fridge until ready to fry. This is especially helpful if you're making the sauce as well or are cooking for a crowd.

Hauptspeisen

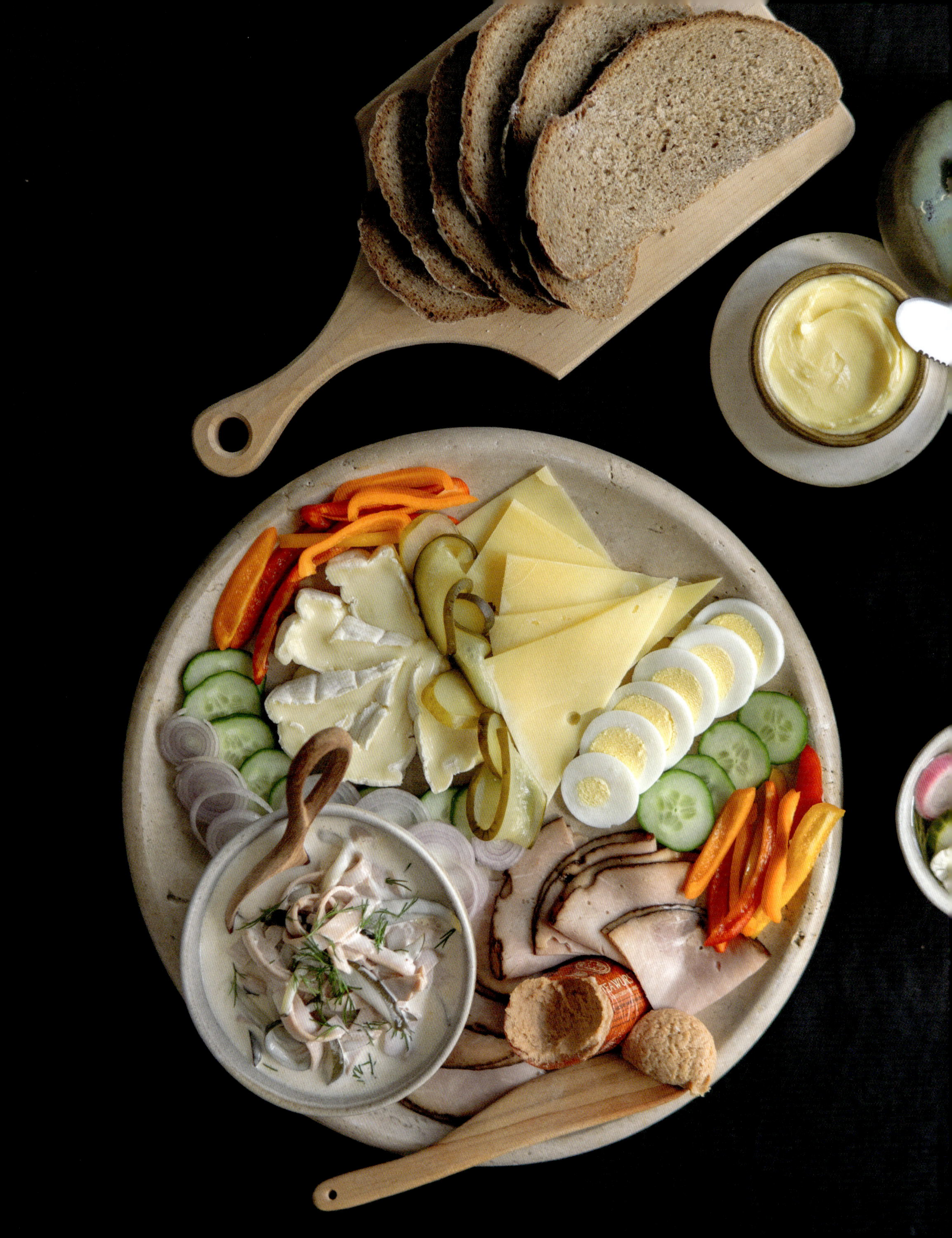

ABENDBROT

Traditional Cold Dinner

Germans love bread so much that they've named an entire meal after it. Abendbrot literally translates to "evening bread" and, more loosely, "dinner." This is the traditional version—a cold meal centered around bread. For families with young kids, the idea of sharing a cold meal at the dinner table *together* feels revolutionary, and with the wide variety of toppings, Abendbrot is likely to make at least 95 percent of kids happy. In our home, it's our go-to dinner on days when I've baked fresh bread. While I am perfectly content eating bread with butter, Abendbrot gives you a few more fun choices to mix things up.

Now, let's break it down. My favorite Abendbrot includes:

Brot (bread): Similar to a German Frühstück (breakfast), bread is the star here. But instead of brötchen, we focus on sliced bread. Brezeln (page 39) and Obatzda (page 41) also make excellent additions.

Sliced meats and cheeses: This, too, is very similar to Frühstück, but with the addition of Fleischsalat (page 90)—a must try! I love serving Leberwurst (page 32) for Abendbrot alongside Gewürzgurken (page 91) and thinly sliced sweet onions. I also like to bring out more pungent cheeses.

Fresh veggies: Abendbrot gets a refreshing touch with some sliced cucumbers, tomatoes, bell peppers, and radishes to serve as toppings for your open-faced sandwiches. It helps this meal to feel less bread-y and more balanced.

Cold hard-cooked eggs: I like to slice and layer them on my bread with other toppings.

Mixed Pickles (page 46): These are great for snacking on the side.

Gemischter Salat (page 48): I love serving mixed salad with Abendbrot. I also like taking just a portion of it, for example the carrot salad, to serve as part of the meal.

A pot of tea: It's common to serve hot, herbal, or fruit teas with Abendbrot, and I love this warming touch, especially since the meal itself is cold.

Roggenmischbrot

Rye and Wheat Bread

Roggenmischbrot is one of Germany's most popular breads—versatile, hearty, and full of flavor. The rustic, malty notes in this bread pair well with savory and sweet toppings alike. You'll need a proofing basket for this. If you don't have one, line a large bowl with a clean, well-floured linen towel to use as a makeshift proofing basket for a round loaf. I prefer a long loaf shape for smaller, more even slices, so I use an oval proofing basket.

PREP TIME: 30 minutes, plus 4 hours resting

COOK TIME: 45 minutes

YIELD: About 20 slices (long loaf) or 15 slices (round loaf)

PREFERMENT

1¼ cups (150 g) dark rye flour

¼ teaspoon (1 g) active dry yeast

5 ounces (150 ml) lukewarm water

DOUGH

1 teaspoon (3 g) active dry yeast (½ packet)

2 teaspoons (15 g) honey (See Note)

9½ ounces (280 ml) lukewarm water

2½ tablespoons (35 g) dark balsamic vinegar

2 cups plus 1 tablespoon (250 g) dark rye flour

2¼ cups (270 g) all-purpose flour, plus more for dusting

2½ teaspoons (15 g) salt

1. **Make the preferment:** In a small bowl, add the flour, yeast, and water. Stir with a fork until no lumps remain. Cover the bowl tightly and let the dough rest at room temperature until it is nice and bubbly, 10 to 12 hours (overnight is easiest).

2. **Make the dough:** In a large bowl, stir together the yeast, honey, and water. Let the mixture activate until bubbly, about 5 minutes. Add the preferment, vinegar, rye flour, all-purpose flour, and salt. Knead until smooth. Cover the bowl tightly and let the dough rest at room temperature until doubled in size, about 1 hour.

3. Fill a large baking dish halfway with water and place it on the bottom rack of the oven. Preheat the oven to 480°F (250°C). Line a baking sheet with parchment paper.

4. On a lightly floured surface, with flour-dusted hands, shape the dough into a 9-inch (23 cm) round or long loaf, about 9 inches (23 cm) long and 4 inches (10 cm) thick. Place the dough, seam side up, in the proofing basket. Cover with a clean linen towel and let rest for 30 minutes.

5. Turn the dough out, seam side down, onto the prepared baking sheet. For a long loaf, make either 1 deep slash down the center along the length of the loaf or 2 smaller diagonal cuts using a sharp knife. For a round loaf, make a cross in the center with each cut about ½ inch (1 cm) deep.

6. Ensure the baking dish is about one-third full; add boiling water if needed. Bake on the middle rack for 45 minutes. After the first 10 minutes, adjust the oven control to 430°F (220°C). Transfer the loaf to a wire rack to cool for 2 hours before slicing.

NOTE

✤ *This recipe can easily be doubled if your mixer can handle kneading a larger quantity or if you knead the dough by hand. I often bake two long loaves side by side on a parchment-lined baking sheet without needing to adjust the baking time. (We frequently freeze the second loaf for later, then thaw it, covered, at room temperature for about 3 hours.)*

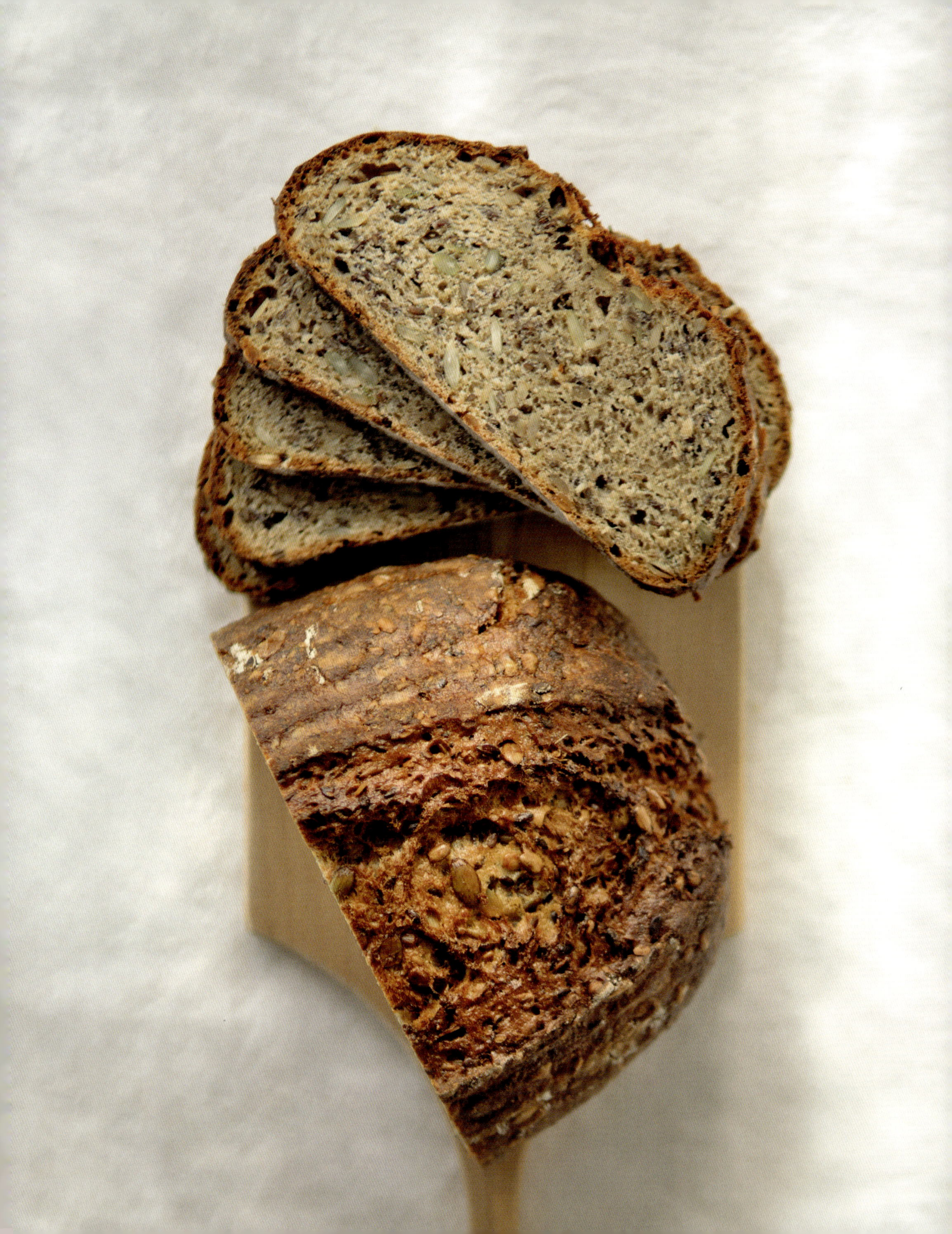

Körnerbrot

Seeded Bread

It's really hard to find seeded breads in the United States that taste anything like the breads I grew up with. This körnerbrot is satisfying and wholesome and delivers the hearty, nutty flavor I love. It's my go-to for sandwiches or simply smeared with some good butter or Leberwurst (page 32). Note: I typically toast and soak the seeds the day before baking. This extra step makes a huge difference—unsoaked seeds pull a lot of moisture from the dough, leading to dry bread (see the Suggested Timeline on page 86). I use an oval proofing basket, to make a long loaf. If you don't have one, line a large bowl with a clean, well-floured linen towel to use as a makeshift proofing basket for a round loaf.

PREP TIME: 15 minutes, plus 19 hours resting

COOK TIME: 50 minutes

YIELD: About 20 slices (long loaf) or 15 slices (round loaf) (see Note)

½ cup (80 g) sunflower seeds, toasted

½ cup (80 g) pumpkin seeds, toasted)

¼ cup (30 g) sesame seeds, toasted

½ cup (70 g) flaxseeds

2 teaspoons (10 g) salt

1 teaspoon (3 g) active dry yeast (½ packet)

3 ounces (90 g) lukewarm water

1⅓ cup (160 g) all-purpose flour

¾ cup (100 g) whole wheat flour

¾ cup (100 g) dark rye flour

1 large egg

1 tablespoon plus 1 teaspoon (20 ml) avocado oil

1. In a medium bowl, add the sunflower seeds, pumpkin seeds, sesame seeds, flaxseeds, salt, and 9½ ounces (280 ml) of water. Cover the bowl tightly and refrigerate until most of the water is absorbed, about 8 hours. Do not drain the excess water.

2. In a small bowl, add the yeast and lukewarm water and let activate, about 5 minutes. It should look bubbly and happy.

3. In the bowl of a stand mixer fitted with the dough hook attachment, mix the yeast mixture, flours, egg, oil, and soaked seeds (along with any liquid in the bowl) at low speed until a wet dough forms, about 8 minutes. Increase the speed to medium and mix until all the dry ingredients are entirely incorporated, about 3 minutes. The dough will still be very sticky at this point. Cover the bowl tightly and refrigerate until the dough has absorbed more water and is less sticky, 10 to 12 hours or overnight.

4. Lightly flour one hand. Keeping the dough in the bowl, use the floured hand to grab a section of the dough from the bottom, stretch it upward, and fold it over the top. Rotate the bowl slightly and repeat this step all the way around. Cover the bowl with a clean kitchen towel and let the dough rest at room temperature for 30 minutes. Generously dust the proofing basket with all-purpose flour.

(CONTINUED)

Abendbrot

5. On a generously floured work surface, knead the dough by folding the bottom of the dough over the top, rotating slightly each time, until you've worked your way around twice. Shape it into a 9-inch (23 cm) round or long loaf, about 9 inches (23 cm) long and 4 inches (10 cm) thick. Place the dough, seam side up, in the proofing basket, cover with a clean kitchen towel, and let it rest at room temperature until increased in size by 50 percent, about 30 minutes.

6. Meanwhile, fill a large baking dish halfway with hot water and place it on the bottom rack of the oven. Preheat the oven to 480°F (250°C). Line a baking sheet with parchment paper.

7. Carefully turn the dough out, seam side down, onto the prepared sheet. Using a sharp knife, make a ½-inch-deep (12 mm) cut lengthwise down the middle, leaving about 1 inch (2.5 cm) on either end uncut. For a round loaf, score a cross in the center, about ½ inch (12 mm) deep.

8. Bake on the middle rack for 10 minutes. Open the oven door wide to release steam, then adjust the oven control to 430°F (220°C). Continue baking until medium to dark brown, about 40 minutes, removing the baking dish for the last 10 minutes to aid browning. Transfer the loaf to a wire rack to cool for at least 2 hours before slicing.

SUGGESTED TIMELINE

1. The day before baking (around noon): Soak the seeds according to step 1.

2. The evening before baking: Mix and knead the dough according to steps 2 and 3.

3. The day of baking: Shape and bake the loaf according to steps 4 through 9.

Quark Dips

So you went through the steps of making Quark (page 12), and now you're ready for some fun ways to use it! Here are three extremely easy and very delicious dips to pair with freshly baked Körnerbrot (page 85), cut-up veggies, Brezeln (page 39), baked or boiled potatoes, potato chips and fries, grilled meats for Raclette (page 163), Backfisch (page 74), and more. You get it. They are good with just about anything. They're a welcome snack for parties, game nights, or just because.

DATTEL CURRY DIP (DATE AND CURRY QUARK DIP)

This date and curry dip isn't just for bread and veggies—it's amazing with pork, chicken, and duck.

PREP TIME: 15 minutes, plus 1 hour chilling

YIELD: About 12 ounces (340 g)

2 tablespoons (30 g) chopped shallot

1 teaspooon extra-virgin olive oil

⅓ cup (75 g) pitted dates

⅔ cup (160 ml) Quark (page 12)

½ cup (100 g) cream cheese, at room temperature

1 teaspoon mild curry powder

½ teaspoon salt

½ teaspoon ground black pepper

Cayenne pepper (optional)

1. In a small saucepan over medium heat, cook the shallot in the olive oil, stirring occasionally, until translucent, 2 minutes. Add the dates and ¼ cup (60 ml) of water and reduce the heat to medium-low; cook until the dates are super soft, 3 to 5 minutes. Remove from the heat. Using a fork, mash the mixture into a paste.

2. In a food processor fitted with the knife blade, add the date mixture, quark, cream cheese, curry powder, salt, pepper and, if using, a pinch of cayenne pepper; puree, stopping to scrape down the sides as needed, until smooth, 1 to 2 minutes. Transfer to a small bowl, cover, and refrigerate until set, about 1 hour, before serving.

(CONTINUED)

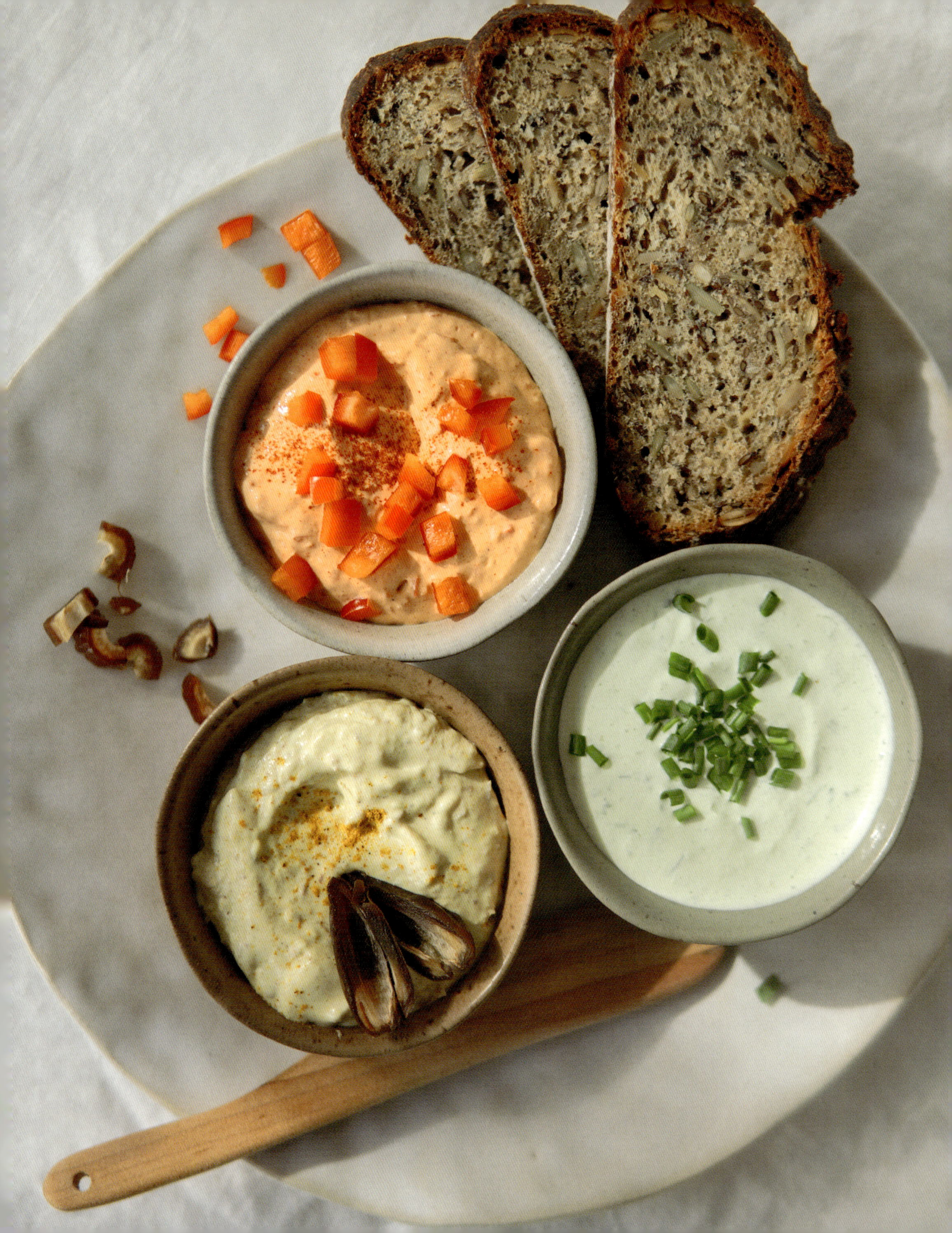

SCHNITTLAUCHQUARK (CHIVE QUARK DIP)

This dip takes me straight back to my Oma's garden, where we would often pick fresh chives to make this dip in her small kitchen. My kids love picking chives to make it, too.

PREP TIME: 10 minutes, plus 1 hour chilling

YIELD: About 9 ounces (250 g)

⅔ cup (160 ml) Quark (page 12)

½ cup (100 g) cream cheese, at room temperature

6 tablespoons finely chopped fresh chives

Salt and ground black pepper

In a small bowl, whisk the quark and cream cheese until smooth. Stir in the chives and season with salt and pepper to taste. Cover and refrigerate until set, about 1 hour, before serving.

PAPRIKA QUARK DIP (QUARK DIP WITH BELL PEPPER)

This dip is refreshing, a tad bit sweet and spicy. It's just perfect. While German food isn't typically spicy, some Germans love adding sambal oelek, an Indonesian chile paste, to foods to kick things up a notch!

PREP TIME: 10 minutes, plus 1 hour chilling

YIELD: About 7 ounces (200 g)

½ cup (120 ml) Quark (page 12)

½ cup (100 g) cream cheese, at room temperature

1 small clove garlic, minced

1 teaspoon sweet paprika

1 tablespoon sambal oelek, plus 1 teaspoon for garnishing (optional)

1 medium red bell pepper, cored and finely diced, plus 1 tablespoon reserved for garnishing (optional)

Salt and ground black pepper

In a small bowl, whisk the quark, cream cheese, garlic, paprika, and sambal oelek until smooth. Stir in the bell pepper and season with salt and black pepper to taste. Garnish with the reserved bell pepper and/or an extra teaspoon of sambal oelek. Cover and refrigerate until set, about 1 hour, before serving.

Fleischsalat

Bologna Salad

PREP TIME: 10 minutes

YIELD: 5 servings

Bologna often gets a bad rap in America, but it's a beloved staple in Germany. Known as fleischwurst or Lyoner, you can find it in many varieties at butcher shops in Germany. Fleischsalat is a creamy, tangy bologna salad made with just three main ingredients: bologna, pickles, and mayonnaise. It's so simple to make and tastes perfect piled high on sliced Körnerbrot (page 85) as part of abendbrot (dinner) or on a Kürbiskernbrötchen (page 18) for frühstück (breakfast). If pork bologna is hard to find, mortadella makes a great substitute.

---

5 ounces (140 g) sliced pork bologna

1 cup (140 g) Gewürzgurken pickles (page 91), juice reserved

⅔ cup (160 ml) mayonnaise

Salt and ground black pepper

Granulated sugar

Chopped fresh parsley, for garnishing (optional)

Chopped fresh chives, for garnishing (optional)

Sliced green onion, for garnishing (optional)

1. On a large cutting board with a sharp knife, cut the bologna into thin strips, about ¼ inch (6 mm) thick. Cut the Gewürzgurken into thin strips roughly the same size as the bologna.

2. In a medium bowl, add the bologna, pickles, and mayonnaise; mix well. Stir in a splash of pickle juice, then season with salt, pepper, and sugar to taste. Garnish with parsley, chives, and/or green onion before serving. The salad can be refrigerated in an airtight container for up to 3 days.

Gewürzgurken

Sweet-and-Sour Pickles

Sweet-and-sour gewürzgurken are perfect for snacking, piled onto fresh baked bread with Leberwurst (page 32); they're great dipped into Käsefondue (page 166); they also make great gifts! Traditionally, you would use small pickling cucumbers; however, unless you grow them yourself, you'll have a hard time finding them unpickled. I like using Persian cucumbers, which are like baby English cucumbers (salatgurke). Make sure to store the cucumbers in the refrigerator before pickling and to let the pickling liquid cool down before adding it to the jar; this will help you get crunchier pickles.

COOK TIME: 5 minutes, plus 1 hour cooling and 1 week fermenting

PREP TIME: 20 minutes

YIELD: About 3 pint-size (480 ml each) glass canning jars

---

1 cup (240 ml) white wine vinegar (about 5% acidity)

¾ cup (90 g) granulated sugar

¼ cup (30 g) salt

18 Persian cucumbers (about 3 pounds), sliced crosswise ½ inch (12mm) thick

3 tablespoons whole mustard seeds

3 bay leaves

6 whole allspice berries

15 whole black peppercorns

3 shallots, thinly sliced

3 sprigs fresh dill

1. In a medium saucepan over high heat, heat the vinegar, sugar, salt, and 2 cups (480 ml) of water; stir occasionally until the sugar has dissolved, about 5 minutes. Set aside to cool completely, about 1 hour.

2. Meanwhile, wash and sterilize the canning jars (see page 11).

3. Divide the cucumbers, mustard seeds, bay leaves, allspice, peppercorns, shallot, and dill among the jars. Pour the cooled pickling liquid into the jars, leaving about ½ inch (12 mm) headspace. Secure the jars with their rubber seals and lids and refrigerate. Let the pickles sit for at least 1 week before eating. They will keep in the refrigerator for up to 3 months.

Abendbrot

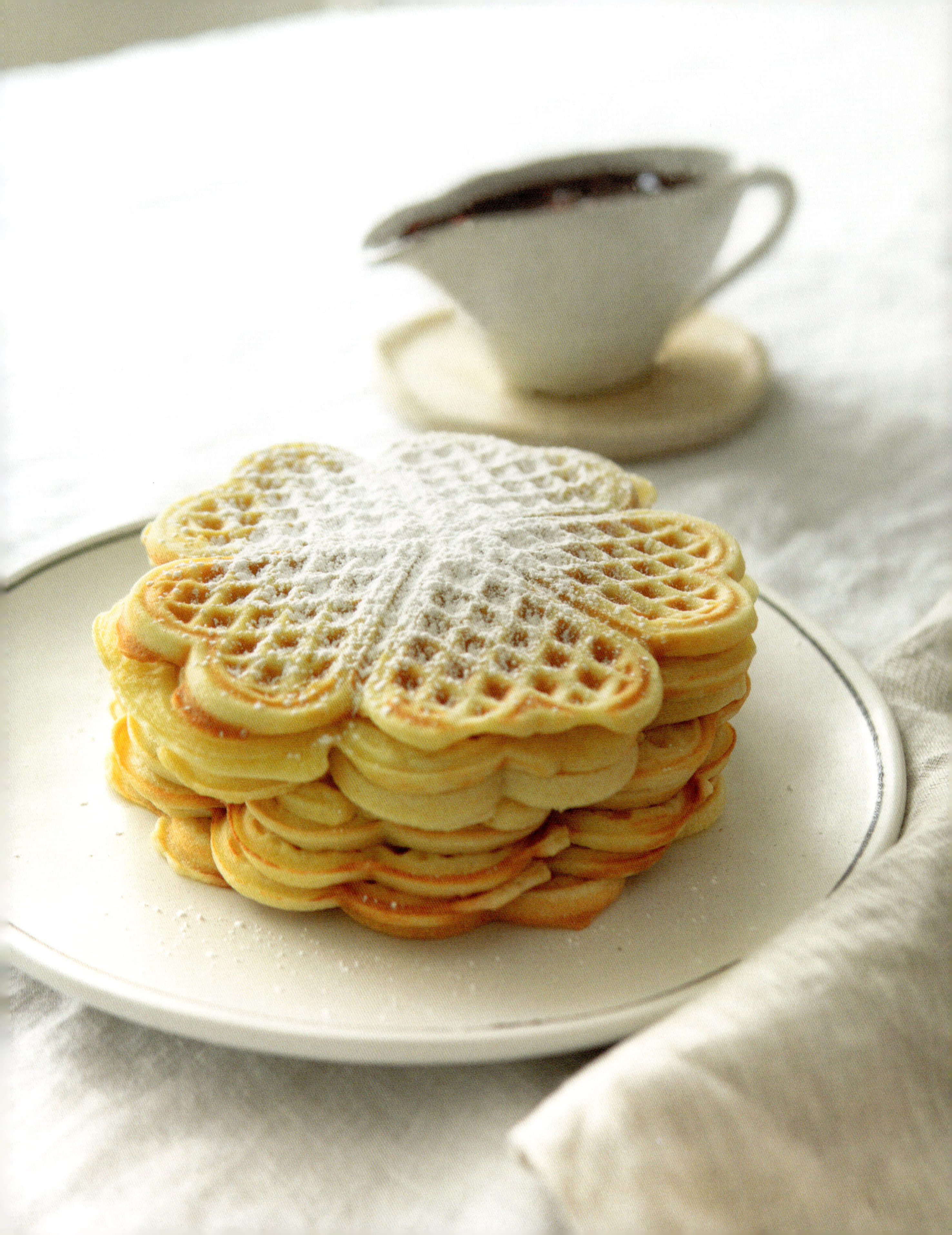

SÜẞE SPEISEN

» *Sweet Meals* «

In Germany, it's perfectly acceptable to have Pfannkuchen (pancakes) for lunch or the fluffiest Dampfnudeln (sweet dumplings with vanilla sauce) for dinner. These sweet—but not-too-sweet—options are also fantastic for a weekend brunch.

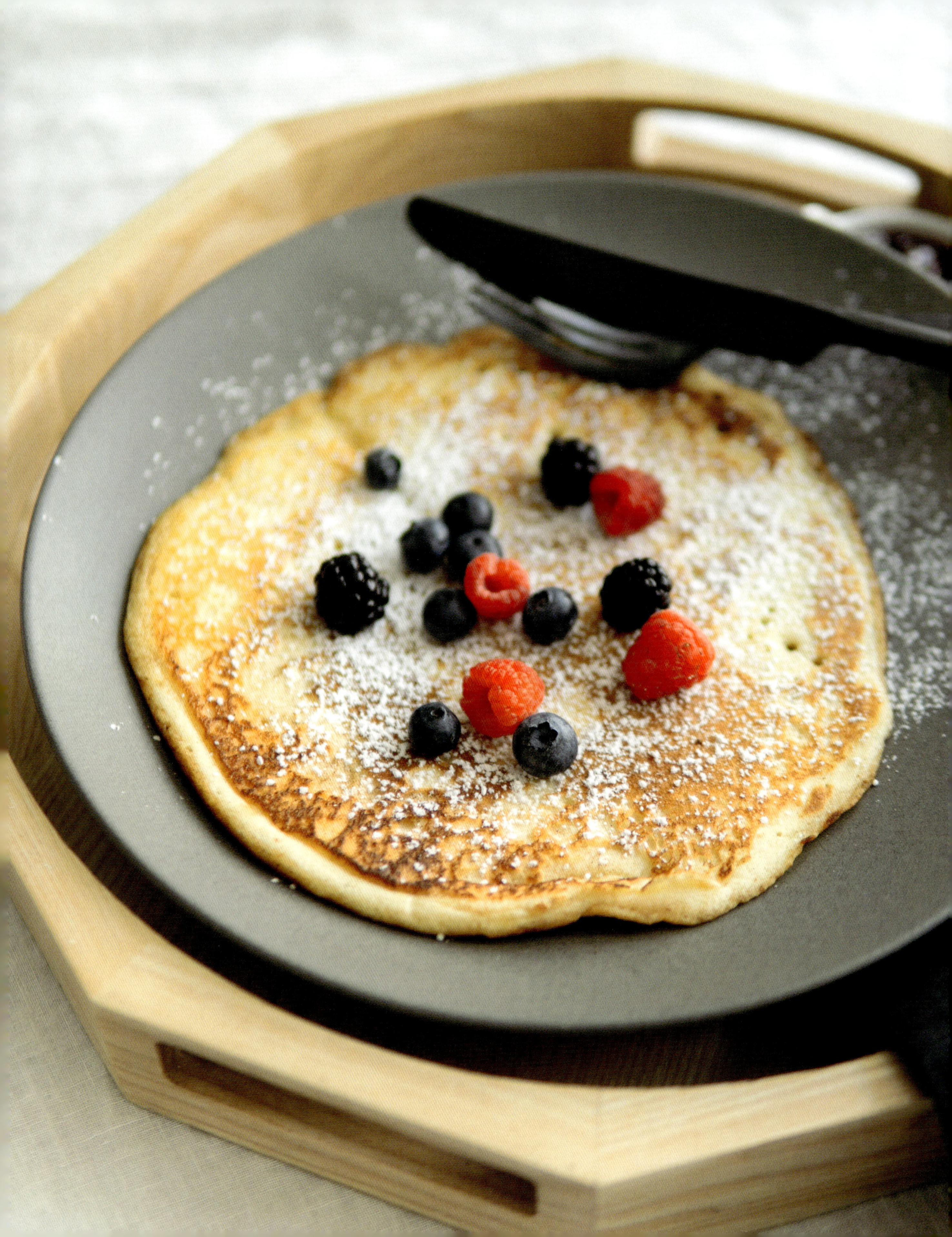

Pfannkuchen

Pancakes

PREP TIME: 10 minutes
COOK TIME: 5 minutes
YIELD: 2 pancakes

I grew up eating pfannkuchen in Germany, and now my kids love them, too. These fall somewhere between American pancakes and French crêpes, with light, fluffy texture from beaten egg whites and a splash of sparkling water. I love them rolled up and filled with Nutella or jam or simply sprinkled with cinnamon sugar.

---

2 large eggs, whites and yolks separated

1 pinch salt

1 teaspoon brown sugar

1 cup (120 g) all-purpose flour

½ teaspoon baking powder

½ cup (120 ml) whole milk

½ cup (120 ml) sparkling water (see Notes)

1 tablespoon unsalted butter, divided

OPTIONAL TOPPINGS AND FILLINGS

Powdered sugar

Cinnamon Sugar (page 7)

Pflaumenmus (page 34) or jam of choice

Chocolate hazelnut spread

1. In the bowl of a stand mixer fitted with the whisk attachment, beat the egg whites and salt at high speed until stiff peaks form.

2. In a large bowl, whisk the egg yolks, sugar, flour, baking powder, milk, and sparkling water until smooth.

3. Gently fold the egg whites into the batter until no white streaks remain. The batter should be thick, fluffy, and barely runny.

4. In a large skillet over medium heat, melt ½ tablespoon of the butter. Pour in half of the batter and cook until the bottom is light golden, 1 to 2 minutes. Flip and cook the other side until light golden, 1 to 2 minutes. Slide the pancake from the skillet directly onto a plate. Repeat with the remaining butter and batter.

5. Top the pancakes as you like, roll them up, slice them into bite-size pieces, and enjoy while still warm.

NOTES

✦ *No sparkling water? While it helps to make the pancakes fluffy and soft, you can replace it with either additional milk or regular water.*

✦ *For apfelpfannkuchen (apple pancakes), add apple slices (I use about ½ medium apple per pancake) to the batter immediately after pouring it into the skillet, before flipping. Top with cinnamon sugar.*

✦ *Pfannkuchen are best enjoyed fresh and don't store well, so make only as many as you plan to eat.*

Süße Speisen

Milchreis

Rice Pudding

Growing up, we made milchreis all the time—always from a prepackaged mix. But when I had to learn to make it from scratch, I realized how surprisingly easy it is. And no, it's not just for kids. I love topping mine with cinnamon sugar, warm cinnamon apple sauce, or warm cherries for a cozy meal or afternoon treat. Get creative and top your milchreis with any of my suggestions or anything you like.

PREP TIME: 10 minutes

COOK TIME: 30 minutes

YIELD: 8 servings (snack) or 4 servings (meal)

---

1 vanilla bean

1 tablespoon unsalted butter

1 cup (250 g) short-grain rice, such as arborio, rinsed

5 cups (1.2 L) whole milk

¼ cup (50 g) granulated sugar

OPTIONAL TOPPINGS

Cinnamon Sugar (page 7)

Warm cinnamon apples or plums (see Notes)

Warm Rote Grütze (page 141)

Applesauce

Warm cherries (see Notes)

Mini chocolate chips

Fresh berries

1. With a sharp knife, cut the vanilla bean lengthwise in half; scrape out the seeds and reserve both the seeds and pod.

2. In a large pot with a lid, melt the butter over medium-high heat. Add the rice and cook, stirring constantly, until fragrant, 1 to 2 minutes. Stir in the milk, sugar, and vanilla seeds and pod. Heat to boiling over high heat, stirring occasionally.

3. Reduce the heat to low, cover, and simmer until most of the milk has been absorbed, about 30 minutes, stirring once halfway through. Remove from the heat.

4. Serve warm or cold—though eating it warm is definitely the best! Remove the vanilla pod, spoon into serving bowls, and top it with whatever you like.

NOTES

✦ *For a dairy-free version, replace the cow's milk with your favorite dairy-free milk. Depending on the type, you may need to add more sugar to replace the natural sugars in milk.*

✦ *To make warm cinnamon apples or plums, in a small saucepan over medium heat, cook apple or plum slices in a bit of avocado oil until soft and starting to brown, about 3 minutes. Sprinkle some cinnamon over the top and serve with your milchreis. To make warm cherries, in a small saucepan over medium heat, warm frozen or canned cherries until soft and heated through.*

✦ *If you have leftovers, warm them up with a bit of milk to bring the milchreis back to life.*

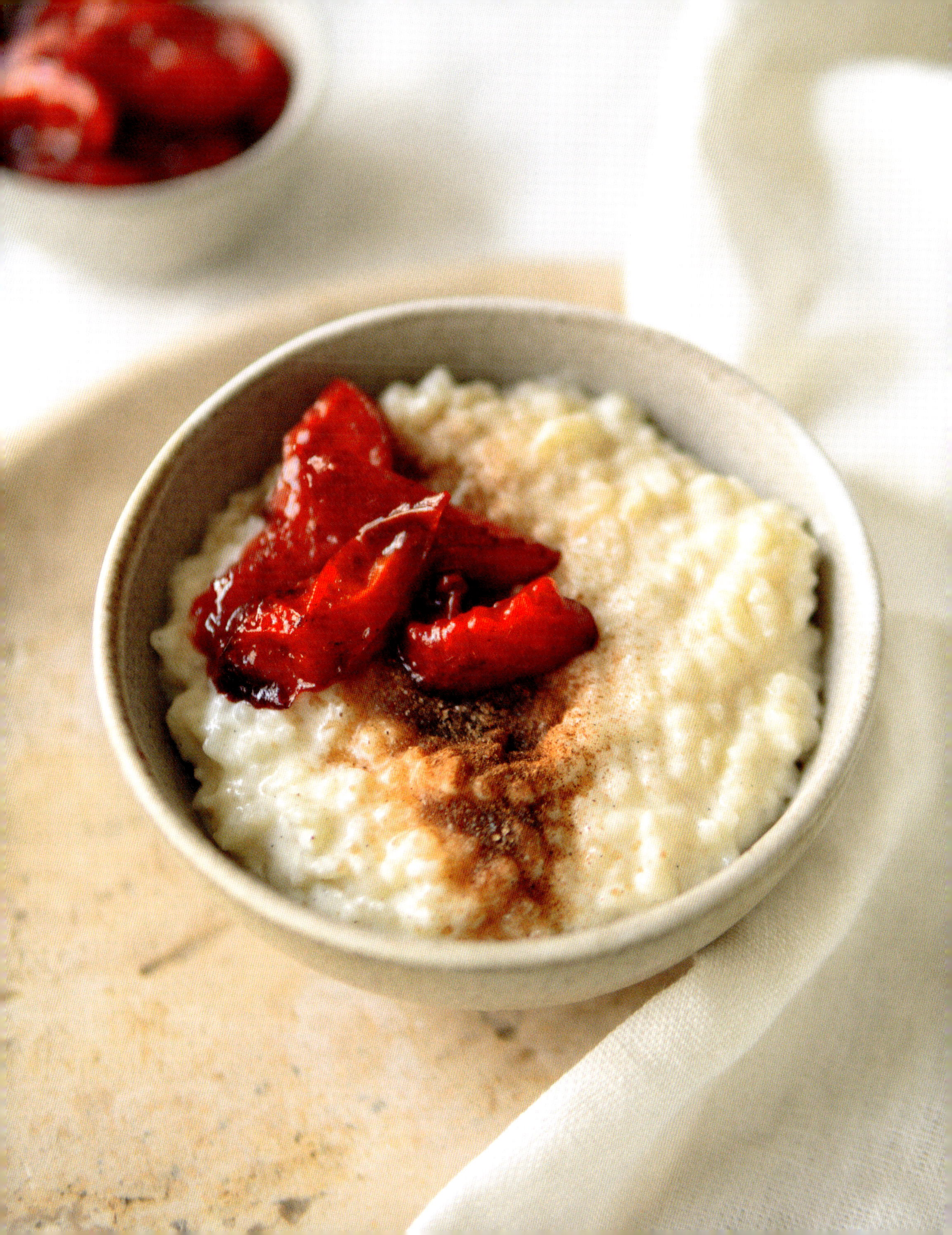

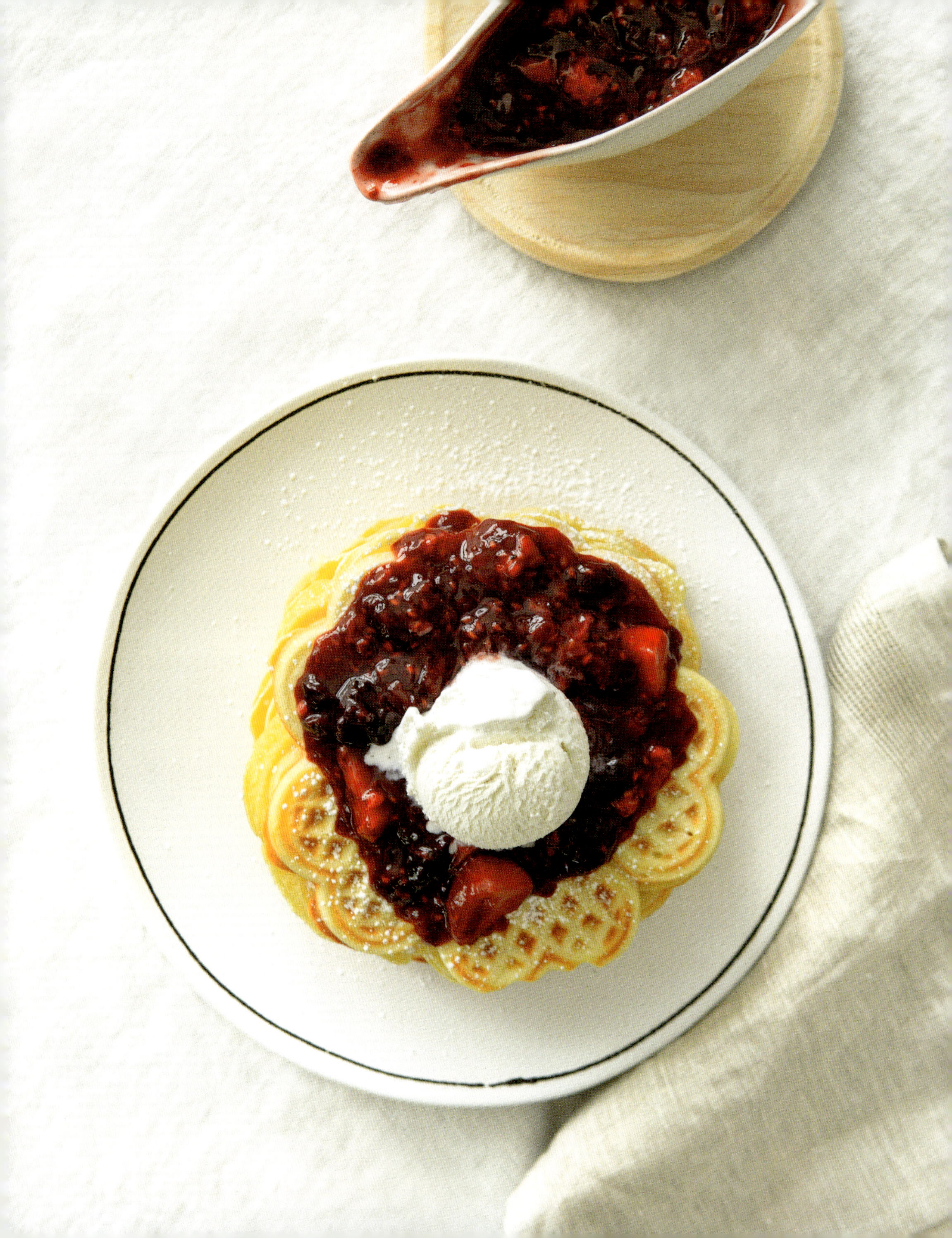

Saure Sahne Waffeln

Sour Cream Waffles

PREP TIME: 10 minutes

COOK TIME: 20 minutes

YIELD: About 10 (7-inch, or 18-cm) waffles

Whenever we visit Germany, we almost always stay with my Uncle Axel and Aunt Heidrun. At some point during those stays, saure sahne waffeln usually make their way to the afternoon kaffee und kuchen table. The recipe is from a super old German cookbook—no pictures, just pages covered in stains from years of use. These waffles are famous in our family, and Uncle Axel makes them at least once a month. I adjusted the recipe to make it my own, using ingredients that are easily available in the United States, while keeping the integrity of the original. For example, I added a pinch of salt, which is not traditionally done in Germany, but enhances the flavors.

---

4 large eggs, whites and yolks separated

3 tablespoons cold water

1 pinch salt

¾ cup plus 2 tablespoons (200 g) unsalted butter, at room temperature, plus 2 tablespoons, melted for brushing

½ cup (100 g) granulated sugar

2 teaspoons vanilla extract

1 cup (240 ml) light sour cream

2 cups (250 g) all-purpose flour, divided

2 teaspoons baking powder

Rote Grütze (page 141), for serving

Whipped cream, homemade (page 9) or store-bought, for serving

Vanilla ice cream, for serving (optional)

1. In a medium bowl, add the egg whites, water, and a pinch of salt; with an electric hand mixer at high speed, beat until stiff peaks form, 4 to 5 minutes. Set aside. No need to clean the whisks for the next step.

2. In a separate large bowl, with the electric hand mixer at high speed, beat the room-temperature butter until creamy, about 2 minutes. Add the sugar, vanilla, egg yolks, sour cream, and 1 cup (125 g) of the flour; mix at medium speed to combine, 1 to 2 minutes. Add the baking powder and the remaining 1 cup (125 g) of flour and mix at medium speed until no lumps remain and a thick batter has formed, about 2 minutes.

3. Preheat the waffle iron. When hot, brush with the melted butter and ladle in some of the batter; cook until golden brown and crispy on the outside. Repeat with the remaining batter, brushing with more butter as needed.

4. Serve them stacked, as Uncle Axel always did, which makes them softer. If you prefer crispier waffles, serve them immediately or keep them warm on a baking sheet in a 150°F (65°C) oven. Either way, top them with the rote grütz, whipped cream, and/or vanilla ice cream (if using).

Süße Speisen

Dampfnudeln

Steamed Dumplings

PREP TIME: 20 minutes, plus 1 hour resting
COOK TIME: 30 minutes
YIELD: 4 dumplings

If you haven't caught on to the trend yet—Germans love dumplings. These fluffy, steamed dampfnudeln are available at all German Christmas markets, and I would not walk, but *run* to get some. I was shocked to find out that they taste even better homemade (yes, even without the Christmas market atmosphere). As they are slowly expanding in your pan, an irresistble caramel crust develops on the bottom of the dampfnudel, which is my favorite feature! Dampfnudeln are typically served with warm vanilla sauce and topped with a nutty poppyseed-sugar mixture. You can also top them with fruit compote, hot cherries (see page 96), or hot berries (skip the poppy seed topping if using fruit). Once you make them yourself, you'll want to make them all year round, not just at Christmas time.

DUMPLINGS

1 teaspoon (3 g) active dry yeast (½ packet)

4½ ounces (125 ml) lukewarm whole milk plus 9 ounces (250 ml) cold, divided

2 cups (250 g) all-purpose flour, plus more for dusting

½ cup (100 g) plus 2 tablespoons granulated sugar, divided

¼ teaspoon salt

2 tablespoons (30 g) melted unsalted butter, plus 7 tablespoons (100 g), cold

1 large egg

VANILLA SAUCE

16 ounces (480 ml) whole milk, divided

2 tablespoons granulated sugar

Seeds from ½ vanilla bean (see page 96)

2 tablespoons cornstarch

1 large egg yolk

1. **Make the dumplings:** In the bowl of a stand mixer fitted with the dough hook attachment, combine the yeast and lukewarm milk and stir. Let activate, about 5 minutes until bubbly. Add the flour, 2 tablespoons of the sugar, the salt, yeast mixture, melted butter, and the egg; mix at low speed until a smooth but slightly sticky dough forms, about 5 minutes. Cover the bowl tightly and let the dough rest in a warm spot until doubled in size, about 1 hour.

2. On a lightly floured work surface, with lightly floured hands, divide the dough into 4 equal pieces and shape each into a ball, tucking the seams underneath.

3. To steam the dumplings, in a large high-rimmed pan (see Notes) with a tight-fitting lid, add the remaining 9 ounces (250 ml) cold milk, ½ cup (100 g) sugar, and 7 tablespoons (100 g) butter; heat to boiling over high heat, stirring until well incorporated, then reduce the heat to medium-low. Carefully place the dumplings, seam sides down, in the pan, leaving plenty of space between them so they can expand. Cover the pan and steam until all the liquid is absorbed, and the dumplings are doubled in size, about 30 minutes—do not lift the lid or they will deflate.

4. **Meanwhile, make the vanilla sauce:** In a small saucepan, add 14 ounces (420 ml) of the milk, the sugar, and vanilla seeds; heat to boiling over medium-high heat, stirring occasionally. In a small bowl, whisk the remaining 2 ounces (60 ml) milk with the cornstarch and the egg yolk until smooth; add to the milk mixture and heat to boiling over high heat, stirring constantly, until thickened, about 1 minute. Keep warm over low heat until ready to serve.

FILLING AND TOPPING

Pflaumenmus (page 34), or compote, or jam of choice, for filling (optional)

Poppy seed sugar (2 parts poppy seeds to 1 part powdered sugar), for topping (optional)

5. If desired, fill your dumplings with any compote or jam you like (pflaumenmus is my favorite). To fill the dumplings, fit a piping bag with a filling tip and add your filling of choice. Insert the entire tip into the side of each cooked dampfnudel and gently squeeze while slowly pulling the tip out.

6. When ready, place the dampfnudeln on individual serving plates, top with the vanilla sauce, and, if desired, sprinkle with the poppy seed sugar. (This is one of the most common ways—and my personal favorite—to enjoy them.)

NOTES

✤ If you're worried about lifting the lid while the dampfnudeln are steaming, use a pan with a glass lid so you can monitor the dumplings without uncovering the pan.

✤ If your pan is too small or too large, you may run into an issue of the steaming liquid either cooking off too fast or not fast enough. A 12-inch (30 cm) pan is a perfect size.

Süße Speisen

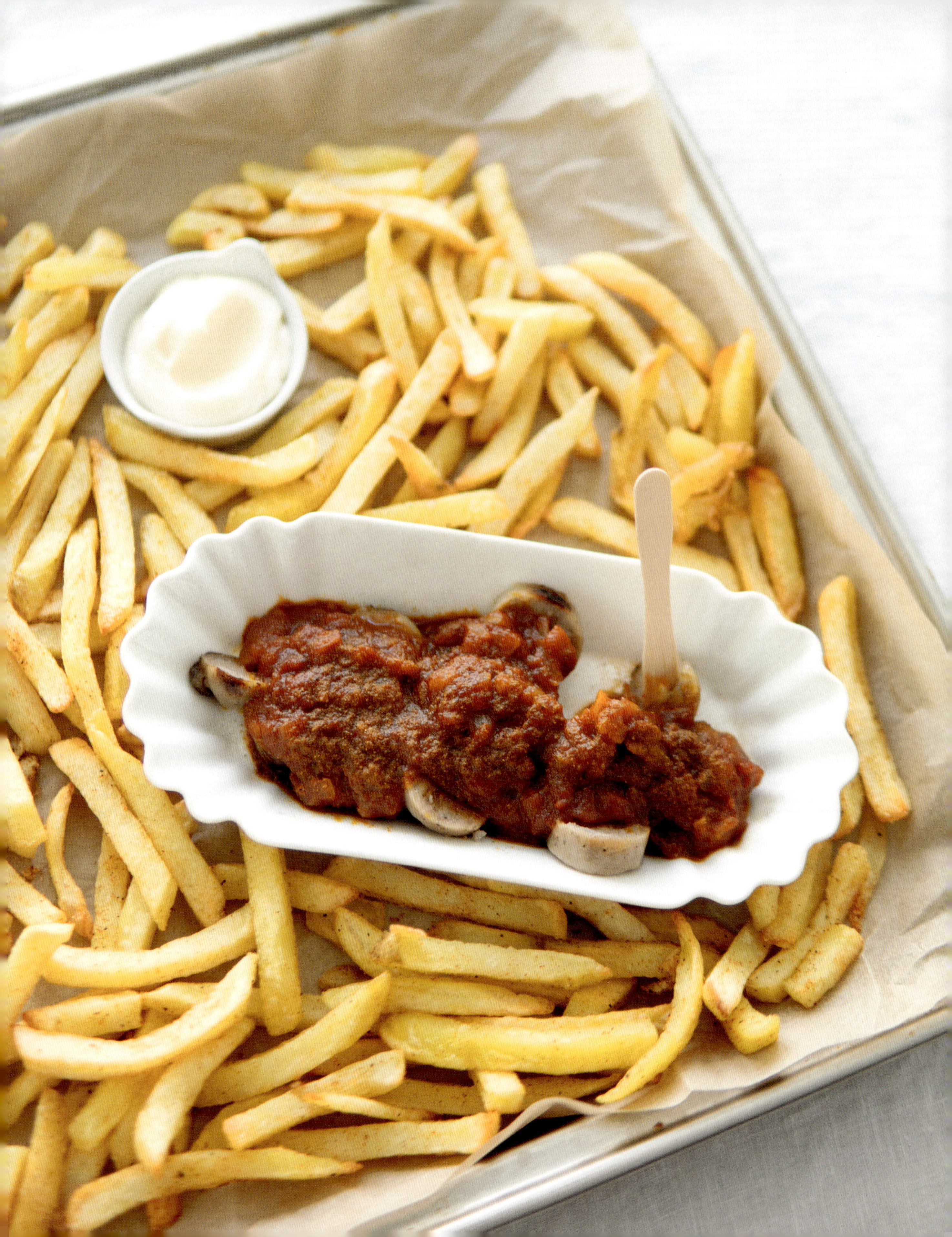

IMBISSBUDE

Street Food

If you've ever visited Germany, you've likely experienced the magic of the OG German "fast food" establishments, Imbissbuden. From the extremely craveable Turkish döner shops to Hamburg-style fish stands, these casual eateries offer quick, affordable bites and a delicious glimpse into the local food culture.

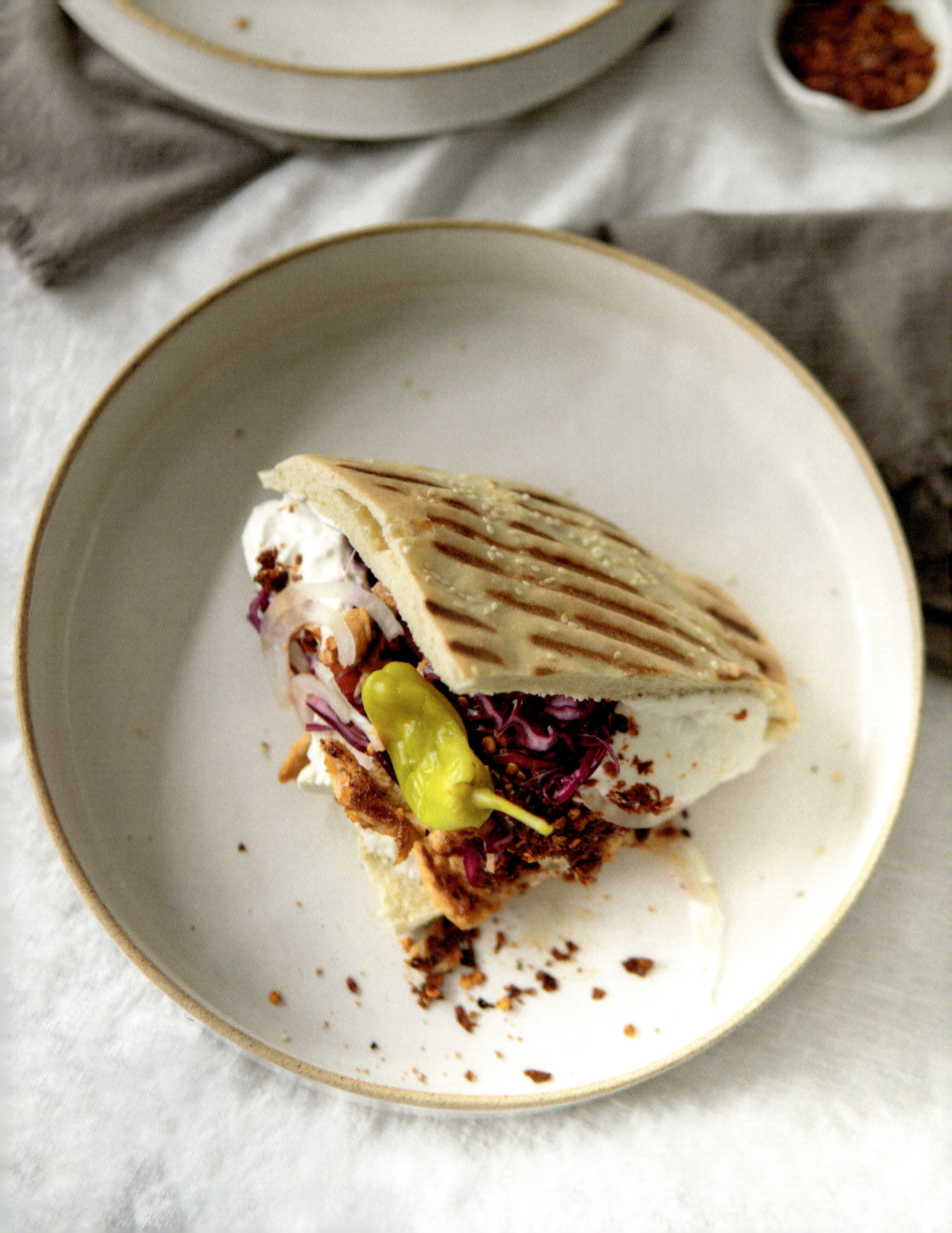

Chicken Döner Kebab

Meat-Stuffed Bread Pockets

PREP TIME: 40 minutes, plus 4 hours resting
COOK TIME: 20 minutes
YIELD: 4 to 6 servings

Döner kebab is Germany's number-one fast food. It's also the best homesickness cure. I developed this recipe to bring the flavors of a German döner shop into my own kitchen. From the homemade pide bread to the perfectly seasoned chicken, creamy garlic sauce, and the pul biber seasoning (for optional scharf—that's German for "spicy"), this is as close as I can get to the real thing. To get the super thin strips of chicken just like from a döner shop, I par-freeze my chicken before slicing, which helps achieve paper-thin pieces. Serve with fries tossed in Pommesgewürz (page 107).

PIDE *(Turkish Bread)*

1 cup (240 ml) lukewarm water

2 teaspoons active dry yeast (1 packet)

1 teaspoon granulated sugar

4 cups (500 g) all-purpose flour, plus more for dusting

3½ tablespoons unsalted butter, at room temperature

2 teaspoons salt

Sesame seeds, for garnishing

DÖNER MEAT

1⅓ pounds (600 g) boneless, skinless chicken breast, par-frozen (see Notes)

1 small yellow onion, finely grated

3 tablespoons Greek yogurt

7 tablespoons extra-virgin olive oil, divided, plus more as needed

1 teaspoon dried oregano

1 teaspoon garlic powder

1 teaspoon sweet paprika

1 teaspoon salt

1 teaspoon ground black pepper

1. **Make the pide:** In the bowl of a stand mixer fitted with the dough hook attachment, combine the water, yeast, and sugar and stir. Let activate, about 5 minutes until bubbly. Add the flour, butter, and salt. Mix at low speed until smooth and elastic, about 5 minutes. Cover tightly and let the dough rest in a warm spot until doubled in size, about 1 hour.

2. Line two baking sheets with parchment paper or silicone baking mats. On a lightly floured work surface, divide the dough in half, then roll each half into a ball. Using a rolling pin, roll out each ball into 10-inch (25 cm) rounds. Transfer to the prepared baking sheet and cover with a clean kitchen towel; let rest until doubled in size, about 1 hour.

3. Meanwhile, preheat the oven to 390°F (200°C). Prepare a shallow bowl with water. Get the sesame seeds handy.

4. Dip the pinky side of your hand into a shallow bowl of water to wet it, then gently press the wet part of your hand into the dough round to create create a diamond pattern with lines that are at a 45-degree angle from each other, about 1 inch (2.5 cm) apart and about ¼ inch (6 mm) deep. Generously sprinkle the top with more water and lightly sprinkle on the sesame seeds. Repeat with the other piece of dough. Bake until the tops are just starting to brown, about 20 minutes. Transfer the pide to the counter, covered with a clean kitchen towel to keep them from drying out until ready to use.

5. **Make the döner meat:** On a large cutting board, using a sharp knife, slice the par-frozen chicken breast against the grain, as thinly as possible. In a large bowl, whisk together the

(CONTINUED)

Imbissbude

MARINATED CABBAGE

½ firm head white or green cabbage, thinly sliced

2 tablespoons white wine vinegar

1 tablespoon extra-virgin olive oil

¼ teaspoon granulated sugar

Salt and ground black pepper

CREAMY GARLIC SAUCE

⅔ cup (165 ml) full-fat Greek yogurt

⅔ cup (165 ml) full-fat sour cream

½ cup (120 ml) mayonnaise

1 tablespoon finely grated (6 g) yellow onion

2 cloves garlic, finely grated

Salt and ground black pepper

PUL BIBER

(*Scharf* Seasoning: optional)

3 tablespoons chili flakes

1 tablespoon sweet paprika

1 tablespoon dried oregano

1 teaspoon onion powder

1 teaspoon garlic powder

1 teaspoon salt

1 teaspoon avocado oil

FOR ASSEMBLY

Iceberg lettuce, thinly sliced

1 tomato, sliced

Thinly sliced sweet or red onion

Feta cheese, sliced or crumbled (optional)

onion, yogurt, 6 tablespoons of the olive oil, the oregano, garlic powder, paprika, salt, and pepper. Add the chicken and toss with your hands until evenly coated. Cover tightly and refrigerate for at least 2 hours and up 1 to day. This helps develop incredible flavor and tender texture.

6. In a large skillet over medium-high heat, heat the remaining 1 tablespoon olive oil until it moves around the skillet like water when tilted, about 1 minute. Working in batches, add just enough chicken to cover the bottom of the skillet and cook, stirring occasionally, until browned and cooked through, 3 to 5 minutes.

7. **Make the marinated cabbage:** In a large bowl, use your hands to knead the sliced cabbage, vinegar, olive oil, and sugar until softened, about 2 minutes. Season with salt and pepper to taste; let marinate at room temperature (no need to cover) for 1 hour.

8. **Make the creamy garlic sauce:** In a medium bowl, whisk together the yogurt, sour cream, mayonnaise, onion, and garlic. Season with salt and pepper to taste. Cover and refrigerate for at least 1 hour. (The sauce can be made up to 1 day in advance.)

9. **Make the pul biber (if using):** In a glass jar or airtight container, combine the chili flakes, paprika, oregano, onion powder, garlic powder, salt, and avocado oil. Store in the pantry for 6 months or in the fridge for up to 1 year.

10. **To assemble:** Quarter a pide bread, then cut the quarters open to create pockets. On a panini grill set to low heat, or in a toaster, warm the pieces (skip this if the pide is fresh out of the oven). Spread some creamy garlic sauce inside each pocket, on one side. Stuff the pockets with the döner meat, marinated cabbage, lettuce, tomatoes, onions, and feta cheese as desired, and drizzle with more garlic sauce. Finish with a sprinkle of pul biber if you like.

NOTES

✣ I freeze my chicken for about 2 hours. The amount of time it takes to par-freeze your chicken will depend on your freezer.

✣ This makes 2 flatbreads, so you will likely have some left over. To store, wrap the bread airtight and store at room temperature for up to 2 days or in the fridge for up to 1 week. The bread can also be frozen for up to 3 months. To use, thaw at room temperature for 2 hours.

✣ The marinated chicken freezes well, as does the pide bread, so consider doubling the recipe and freezing extras, so you're always halfway to a homemade döner.

Pommesgewürz

German Fry Seasoning

PREP TIME: 5 minutes

YIELD: 3¼ ounces (about 100 g)

Next time you make a batch of fries—whether in the oven, air fryer, or deep fryer—toss them in this homemade pommesgewürz! This seasoning takes me straight back to the public pool in Mertesdorf, Germany, where I used to order an an edible wafer cone full of these with lots of mayo (you can have yours with ketchup if you prefer). This is also a great all-purpose seasoning for meat, veggies, and more. And it makes a great gift! Fill small glass jars, add homemade labels (totally optional but fun), and share with all your fry-loving friends and family.

¼ **cup (60 g) fine sea salt**

1 **teaspoon garlic powder**

2 **teaspoons sweet paprika**

2 **teaspoons garam masala**

½ **teaspoon mild curry powder**

½ **teaspoon cayenne pepper**

½ **teaspoon ground black pepper**

In a glass jar or airtight container, add the salt, garlic powder, paprika, garam masala, curry powder, cayenne pepper, and black pepper. Seal the container and shake to combine. Store away from light or heat, and it will stay fresh for 1 to 3 years.

NOTES

✤ *Making a large batch? Mix the ingredients in a bowl, then use a funnel to transfer the seasoning into jars.*

Imbissbude

Frikadellen

German Hamburgers

While Germans think hamburgers are from Hamburg, there is evidence that the hamburger was, in fact, invented in the United States. They do look very similar, both being meat patties, but frikadellen are always perfectly seasoned with a mixture of spices, herbs, onion, and garlic. They are a staple at German imbissbuden (the OG German food truck), where they are served on the go with mustard on a crusty Weizenbrötchen (page 16). But they are just as popular to eat at home with mashed potatoes or Kartoffelsalat (page 125), Bratkartoffeln (page 55), or roasted veggies or Gemischter Salat (page 48).

PREP TIME: 30 minutes
COOK TIME: 15 minutes
YIELD: 4 servings

---

1 crusty white roll, such as Weizenbrötchen (page 16)

1 tablespoon unsalted butter

1 medium yellow onion, finely diced

½ pound (225 g) ground pork

½ pound (225 g) ground beef

1 teaspoon salt

1 teaspoon mustard of choice, preferably German

1 teaspoon dried marjoram

1 teaspoon sweet or hot paprika, or a mixture of both

1 teaspoon chili powder

3 tablespoons finely chopped fresh parsley

3 cloves garlic, minced

1 large egg

1 tablespoon avocado oil

1. Place the roll in a small bowl and cover with water; soak until softened, 10 to 15 minutes. Discard the water, squeeze the roll dry, tear it into small pieces, and return them to the bowl.

2. In a small skillet over medium heat, melt the butter until foamy. Add the onion and cook, stirring occasionally, until translucent and lightly browned, about 5 minutes. Transfer to a large bowl.

3. To the softened onions, add the pork, beef, salt, mustard, marjoram, paprika, chili powder, parsley, garlic, and egg. Using your hands, knead until combined. Add the bread and continue to knead until well incorporated (it's okay if small pieces of bread are still visible).

4. Line a large plate with paper towels. Pinch off a walnut-size piece of the meat mixture and shape it into a small patty.

5. In a large skillet over medium heat, heat the oil until it moves like water and easily coats the pan when swirled, about 1 minute. Add the test patty and sear on both sides. Taste and adjust the seasoning of the meat mixture as desired. Divide the mixture into quarters and shape into patties.

6. Sear until thoroughly browned on the first side, 3 to 5 minutes. Flip the patties, reduce the heat to medium-low, and continue cooking until fully cooked through, about 10 minutes. Transfer the frikadellen to the prepared plate and let rest for 3 to 5 minutes before serving.

NOTES

✦ *Frikadellen make great leftovers! You can reheat them or enjoy them cold (and no, eating them cold is not weird, although I personally prefer them hot).*

✦ *I love making mini frikadellen for parties and serving them on toothpicks with some mustard and a slice or two of Gewürzgurken (page 91). Serve with Brezeln (page 39).*

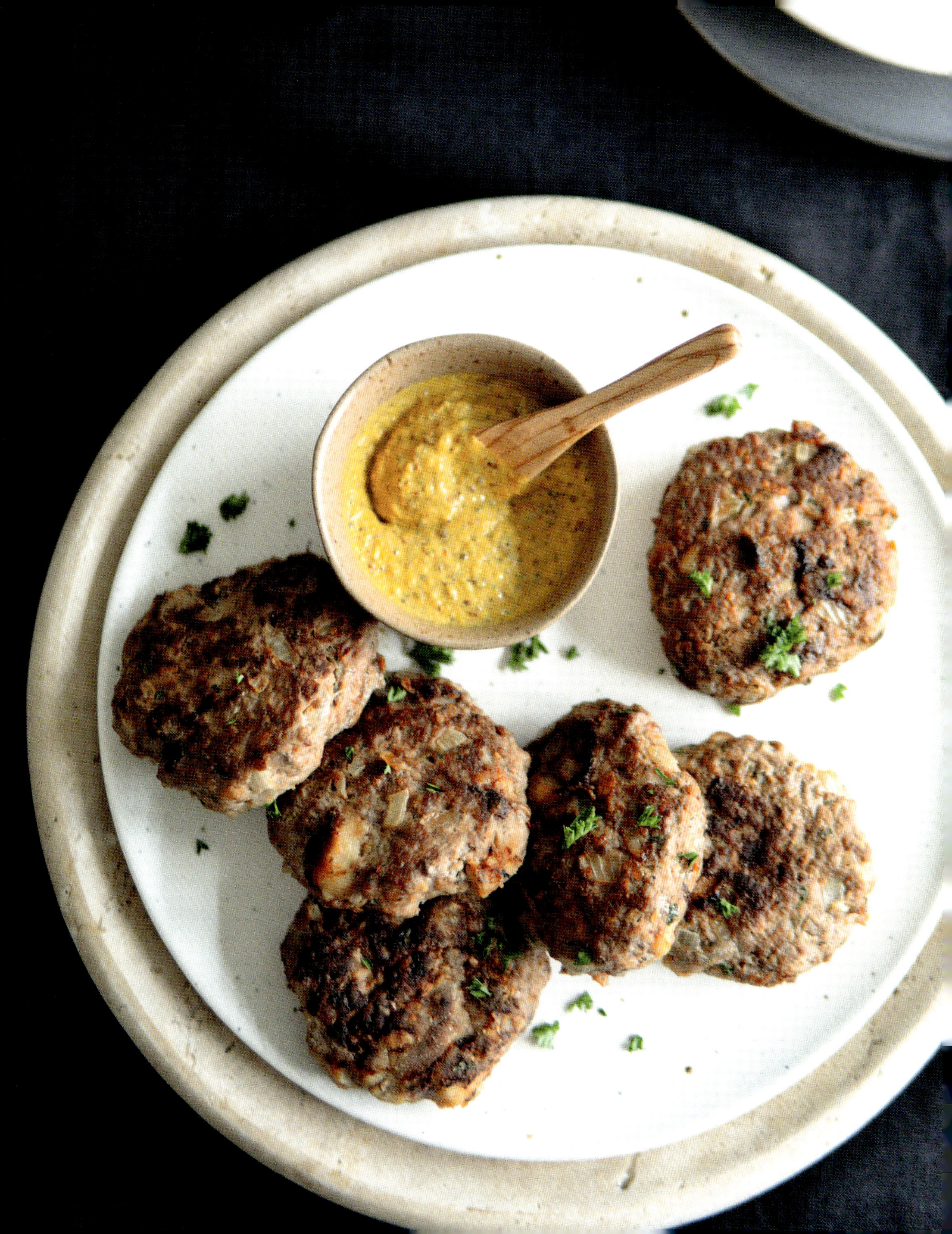

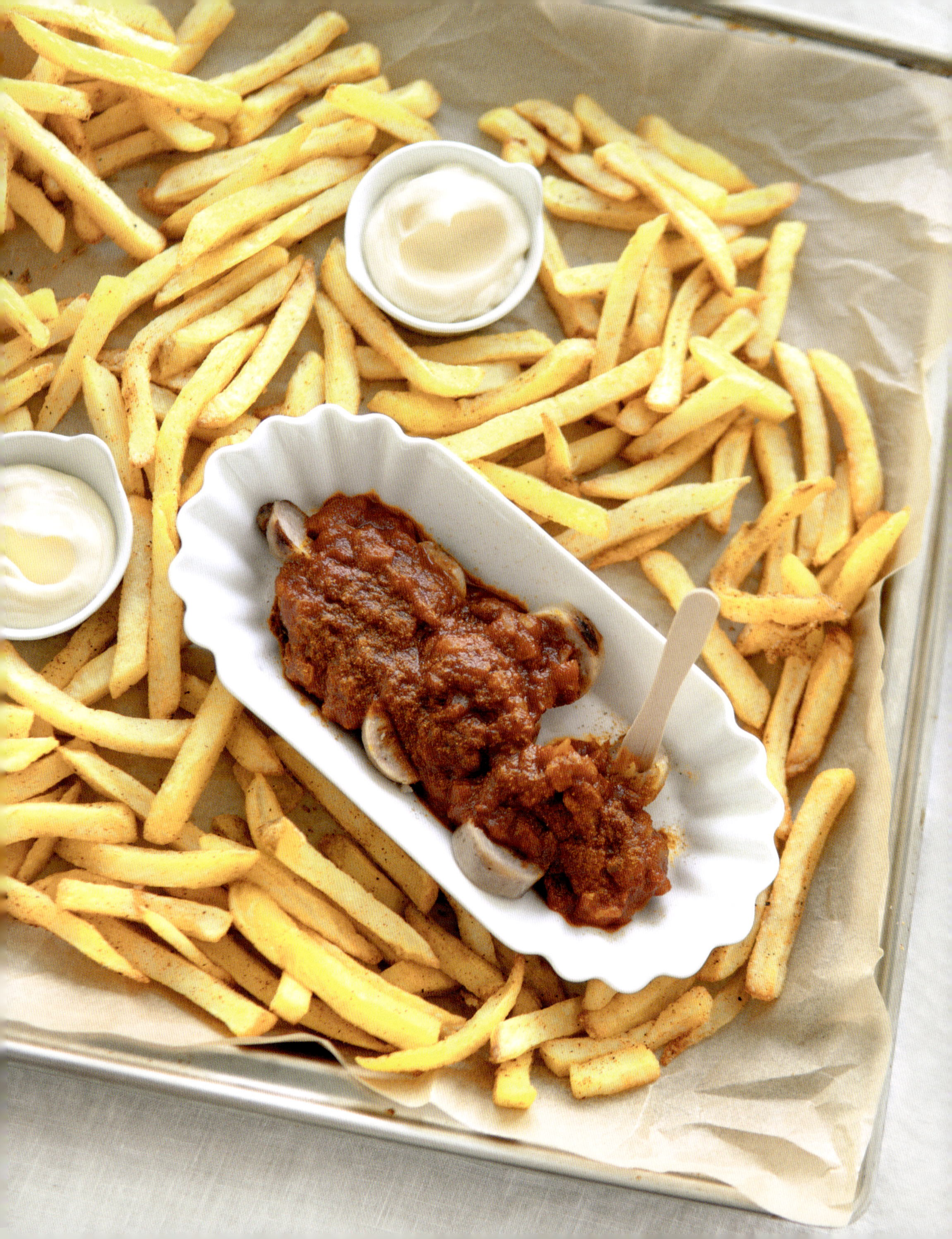

Currywurst

Bratwurst with Curry Ketchup

PREP TIME: 10 minutes
COOK TIME: 10 minutes
YIELD: 12 servings

Currywurst is one of the most common street foods at the OG food trucks of Germany, die imbissbuden (literally "snack shacks," which I love the sound of!). Germans fight about whether currywurst was invented in Berlin or Hamburg, but one thing is sure: those snack shacks usually can't compete with homemade currywurst. For a true German experience, serve with tiny wooden forks. I know it sounds silly, but this is how currywurst is traditionally eaten at imbissbuden across Germany—a nostalgic touch for those who grew up eating it and an authentic experience for those trying it for the first time. Serve with french fries seasoned with Pommesgewürz (page 107), along with extra curry sauce and mayonnaise for dipping.

---

12 bratwurst links

1 tablespoon avocado oil

1 large yellow onion, finely diced

1 tablespoon tomato paste

17 ounces (500 ml) ketchup

3 tablespoons balsamic vinegar

2 tablespoons honey

1 dash soy sauce

2 tablespoons mild curry powder, plus more for topping

Cayenne pepper

Mayonnaise, for serving

1. On a grill or griddle over medium heat, cook the bratwurst, turning every 3 to 5 minutes until slightly charred on all sides and they reach an internal temperature of at least 160°F (71°C), 15 to 20 minutes.

2. In a medium skillet over medium heat, heat the oil until it easily moves around the pan when swirled, about 1 minute. Add the onion and cook, stirring occasionally, until translucent (do not brown), about 2 minutes. Add the tomato paste and stir until fragrant, about 1 minute. Add 2 tablespoons of water and stir until the paste dissolves, about 30 seconds. Add the ketchup, vinegar, and honey; stir to combine. Add the soy sauce, curry powder, and cayenne pepper to taste. Heat to boiling over high heat, then reduce the heat to low.

3. Slice the bratwurst into bite-size pieces and arrange them on individual plates. Remove the sauce from the heat and spoon it over the bratwurst and sprinkle a bit of curry powder on top.

NOTE

✣ *I love switching things up by topping my currywurst with crumbled goat cheese, honey, and fresh thyme—an idea inspired by my favorite currywurst restaurant in Saarbrücken, Kalinski's Wurstwirtschaft.*

Flieten

Fried Chicken Wings

PREP TIME: 10 minutes

COOK TIME: 30 minutes

YIELD: 2 servings

Summer always has me craving flieten—the crispy, spice-rubbed chicken wings I grew up eating in my German hometown of Trier. If you haven't been to Trier, you may not have heard of flieten, but if you have (by chance or by plan), you might already be hooked. These non-breaded wings are a local specialty, seasoned with a bold blend of sweet paprika, oregano, cayenne pepper, and a hint of curry. And it's SO LECKER (yummy)! Traditionally, flieten are served with slices of Roggenmischbrot (page 82) or fries seasoned with Pommesgewürz (page 107). You can also add a Gemischter Salat (page 48) as a side. Guten Appetit!

---

1 teaspoon sea salt

1 teaspoon ground black pepper

1 teaspoon sweet paprika

¼ teaspoon cayenne pepper

¼ teaspoon mild curry powder

¼ teaspoon dried oregano

Avocado oil, for deep frying

10 large whole chicken wings, patted dry

1. In a small bowl, add the salt, pepper, paprika, cayenne, curry powder, and dried oregano; stir to combine.

2. Preheat the oven to 150°F (65°C).

3. Set up your frying station: Place a cooling rack on top of a baking sheet. Pour enough oil into a large pot to reach a depth of 3 inches (7.5 cm) of oil and clip a frying thermometer to it. Heat the oil over high heat until it reaches 350°F (175°C).

4. Working in batches, use tongs to carefully lower the wings into the hot oil, adding only as many as you can fit in a single layer. Fry until golden brown and the internal temperature in the thickest part of the wing reads 165°F (74°C) or higher, 10 to 15 minutes. (As you lower the raw chicken in the hot oil, it may splatter. To protect yourself, use a splatter guard if needed.)

5. Using clean tongs, transfer the fried wings to the prepared rack and let the excess oil drain for about 1 minute. Gently toss with the spice mixture until evenly coated (they should only be lightly coated, otherwise they get too spicy). Transfer the wings to a baking sheet and keep warm in the oven while you fry the remaining wings. Serve warm.

NOTE

❖ *The oil temperature will drop slightly when you add the chicken— that is normal. Adjust the heat as needed to keep it between 325° to 350°F (163° to 175°C) for consistent frying. A deep fryer makes this process easier, but if you don't have one (I don't either!), a saucepan and a reliable thermometer work just fine.*

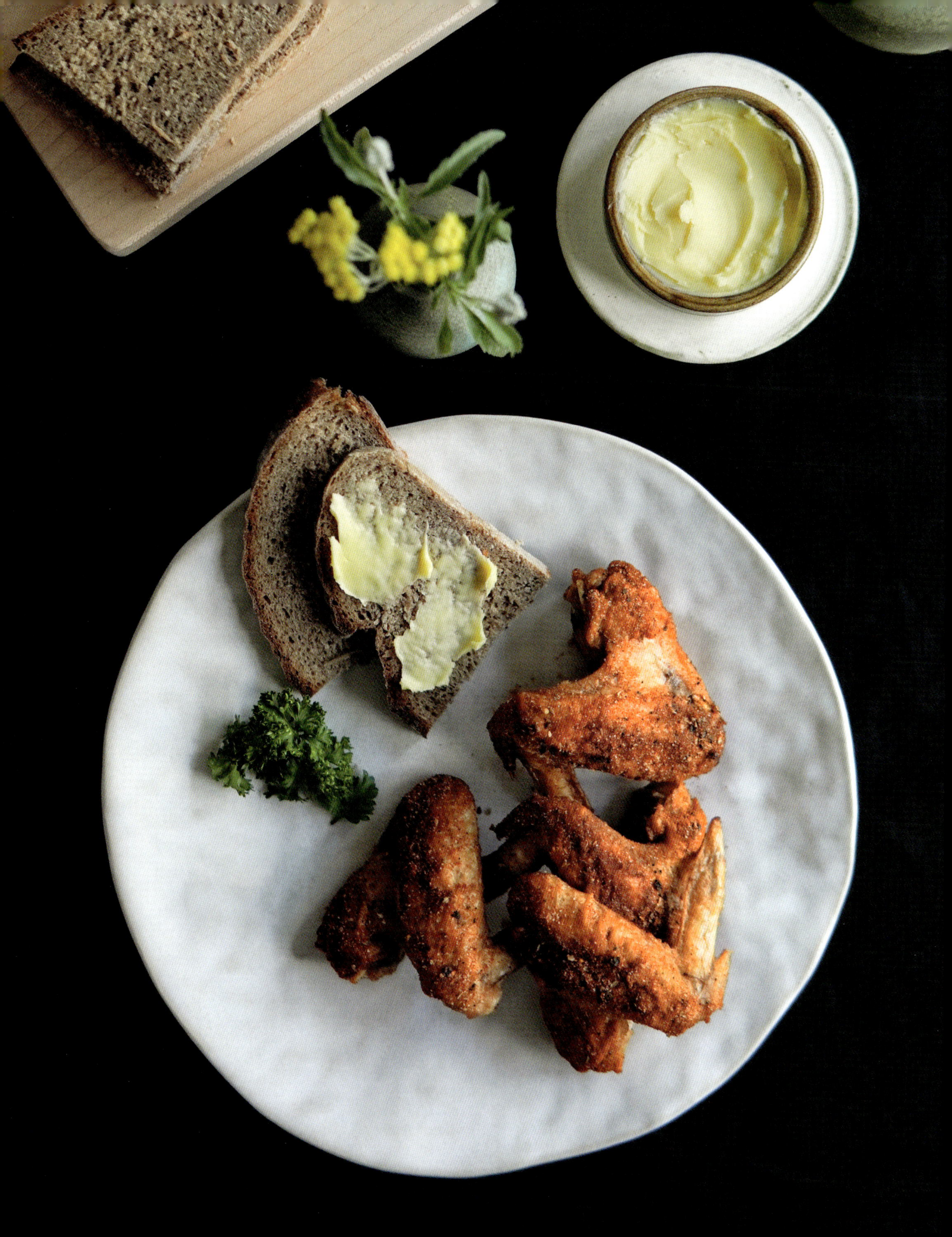

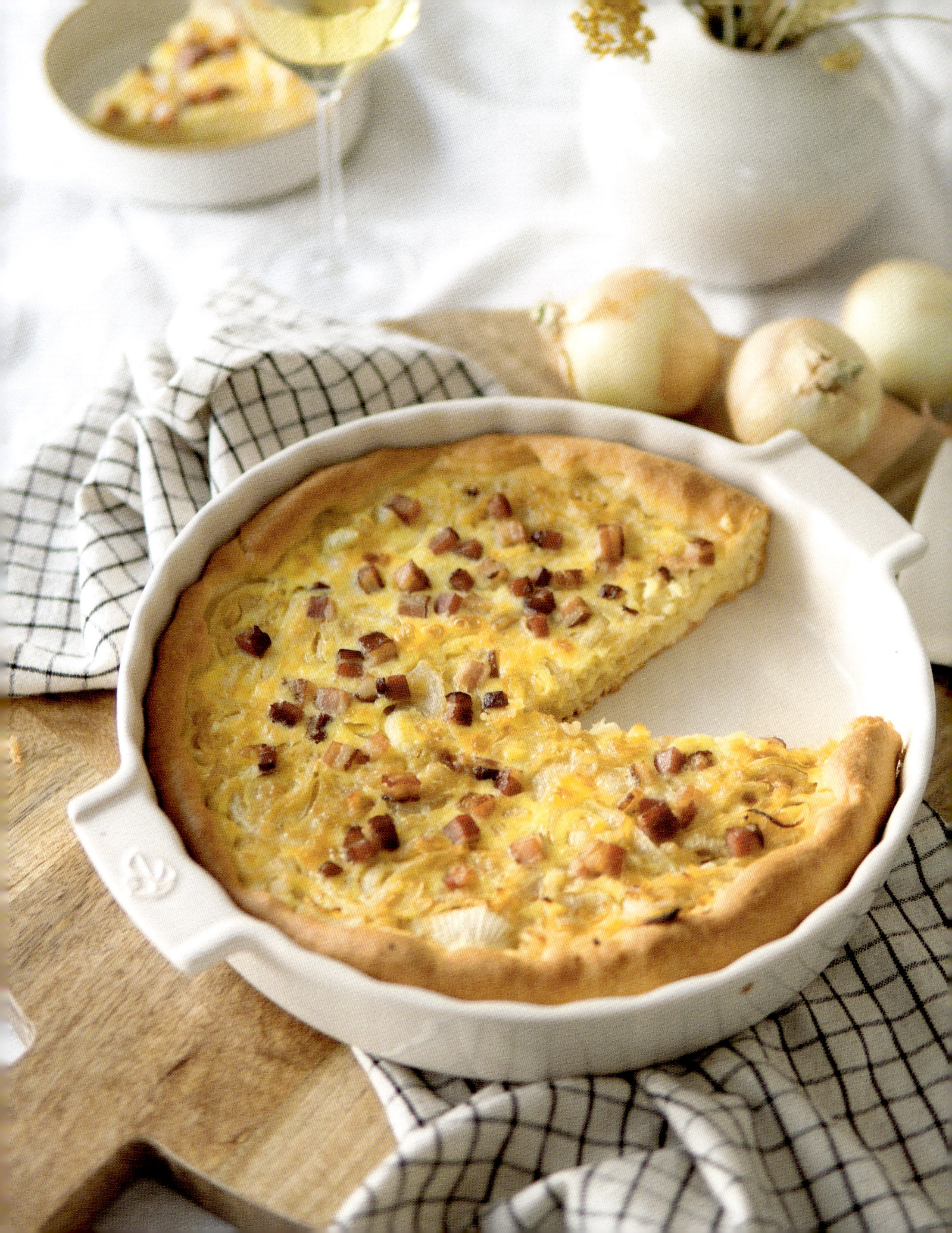

AUS OMA SIEGHILDES KÜCHE

From Oma Sieghilde's Kitchen

Oma Sieghilde had a gift for transforming the simplest ingredients into some of the tastiest meals—often with tons of elbow grease and a little help from my sister and me. From Klösschen to Zwiebelkuchen, each dish is filled with unique memories that I hope to never forget. The biggest challenge in recreating her meals was that she didn't really use recipes. Meaning I got to spend lots of time on the phone with her when she was still around. And then even more time in my kitchen testing. Oma never traveled by air in her lifetime, but I hope her spirit will shine in your kitchen wherever you are, as you cook and bake her beloved recipes.

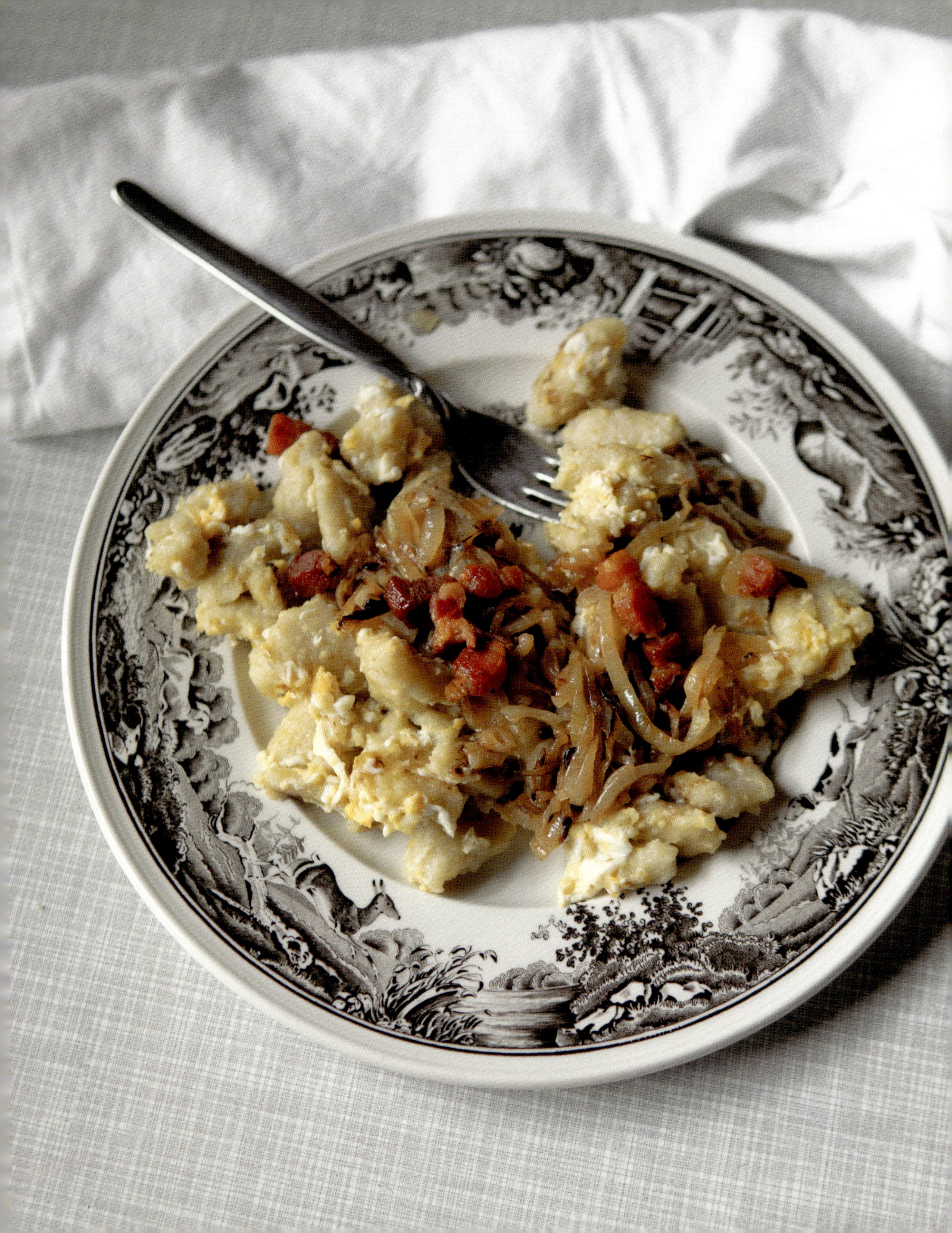

Klößchen

Mini Potato Dumplings

PREP TIME: 1 hour
COOK TIME: 30 minutes
YIELD: 4 servings

Making potato dumplings is hard work, but I didn't realize this until I started making klößchen on my own. That's when I finally understood why my Oma would sigh rather heavily whenever we begged her to make them. Oma's bite-size potato dumplings, made from finely shredded potatoes, are cooked with eggs in a skillet and topped with caramelized onions and crisped bacon. This was my Oma's signature dish, and it feels like a hug from her whenever I make them for my family (danke, Oma). Invite a friend to help—just like my sister and I used to help our Oma; it makes the work lighter and the experience twice as fun.

---

4 pounds (2 kg) starchy potatoes, peeled and finely grated

¼ cup (35 g) potato starch or cornstarch, plus more as needed

4 teaspoons salt, plus more for boiling

4 tablespoons unsalted butter, divided

2 large yellow onions, sliced into half-moons

1 pound slab bacon, cut into ½-inch (12 mm) strips (this is also known as lardons)

4 large eggs

1. Working in batches, place orange-size portions of the grated potatoes in a thin linen towel or cheesecloth and wring out as much liquid as possible.

2. To a large bowl, add the strained potatoes, potato starch, and salt. Knead with your hands until a just-barely sticky dough forms, about 2 minutes. If the dough feels too wet, wring out more moisture or add in more starch.

3. Heat a large pot of salted water to boiling over high heat. Place a colander in a large bowl.

4. On a small cutting board, spread out a layer of dough, about ½ inch (12 mm) thick. Dip a soup spoon into the boiling water, then, working in batches, scrape bite-size dumplings directly from the cutting board into the pot, wetting your spoon with the boiling water as the dough gets stuck (about every 5 scrapes). Boil until the dumplings float to the top, about 3 minutes. Using a skimmer, transfer the dumplings to the prepared colander.

5. In a large skillet over medium-low heat, add 2 tablespoons of the butter and the onions and cook, stirring occasionally, until caramelized, about 30 minutes. Remove from the heat.

6. Line a large plate with paper towels. Place the bacon in a small skillet and cook, stirring often, over medium heat until crispy, about 10 minutes. Transfer to the prepared plate.

7. In a large nonstick skillet over medium-high heat, melt the remaining 2 tablespoons butter, then add the drained potato dumplings. Cook, stirring occasionally, until just starting to adopt a golden color, about 3 minutes. Crack the eggs directly into the skillet and scramble until cooked through, 1 to 2 minutes. Season with salt to taste.

8. Serve immediately, topped with the caramelized onions and crisped bacon.

Aus Oma Sieghildes Küche

Erbsbrei

Mashed Peas

Erbsbrei was always one of the most requested dishes at Oma Sieghilde's house. Made primarily from mashed peas and potatoes, the dish may look like baby food to some, but don't be fooled—it's actually quite delicious. A bonus is that it's super budget-friendly. Serve erbsbrei, like Oma did, with a generous scoop of crisped hand-cut lardons (grieben) and loads of sauerkraut and a glass of buttermilk. And to make the meal complete, don't forget the Wiener sausages!

PREP TIME: 20 minutes
COOK TIME: 1 hour
YIELD: 4 servings

---

16 ounces (455 g) green split peas, rinsed and picked through

28 ounces (800 g) waxy potatoes, peeled

2 bay leaves

16 ounces (455 g) slab bacon, cut into ½-inch (12 mm) strips (this is also known as lardons)

1 medium yellow onion, chopped

35 ounces (1 kg) sauerkraut, homemade (page 60) or store-bought, drained

4 to 8 Wiener sausages

Salt

Chopped fresh parsley, for garnishing (optional)

1. In a large pot, add the split peas, potatoes, bay leaves, and just enough water to cover them. Heat to boiling over high heat. Reduce the heat to low, cover the pot, and simmer, stirring occasionally, until the potatoes are cooked through and the split peas start falling apart, about 45 minutes.

2. Meanwhile, if there are any uneven pieces of bacon, chop them into little bits and reserve for later.

3. Line a large plate with paper towels. Place the bacon in a small skillet and cook over medium heat, stirring often, until crisp, about 10 minutes. Using a slotted spoon, transfer the bacon to the prepared plate. Keeping 2 tablespoons of the bacon grease in the skillet, pour the excess into a small bowl and reserve for later.

4. In the same skillet over medium heat, cook the onion in the remaining bacon grease, stirring occasionally, until it starts to brown, about 15 minutes. Stir in the sauerkraut, and any little bits of odd-size bacon. Reduce the heat to low and nestle in the sausages.

5. Using a fine mesh sieve, drain the peas and potatoes, then return them to the pot. Remove and discard the bay leaves. Using an immersion blender or a potato masher, puree or mash the peas and potatoes until smooth (see Notes). Stir in some of the reserved bacon grease for extra flavor, then season with salt to taste.

6. To assemble, place the mashed peas on a plate, top with the sauerkraut, followed by the sausages and crisped bacon. Garnish with parsley, if you like.

NOTES

✤ Erbsbrei should be the consistency of mashed potatoes. If yours are too thin, you can sprinkle in some potato starch or cornstarch and stir until it thickens; if too thick, stir in a little water or milk until it's just right.

✤ Erbsbrei freezes and reheats beautifully. Store in an airtight container in the fridge for up to 4 days or in the freezer for up to 3 months. Thaw in the the refrigerator one day before. Reheat, place it in a saucepan with some water, then stir over medium-low heat until heated through, adding a bit of water as needed.

✤ Leave the bacon and bacon grease out and you have a delicious vegetarian version that is packed with protein and fiber, thanks to the lovely peas and potatoes.

Aus Oma Sieghildes Küche

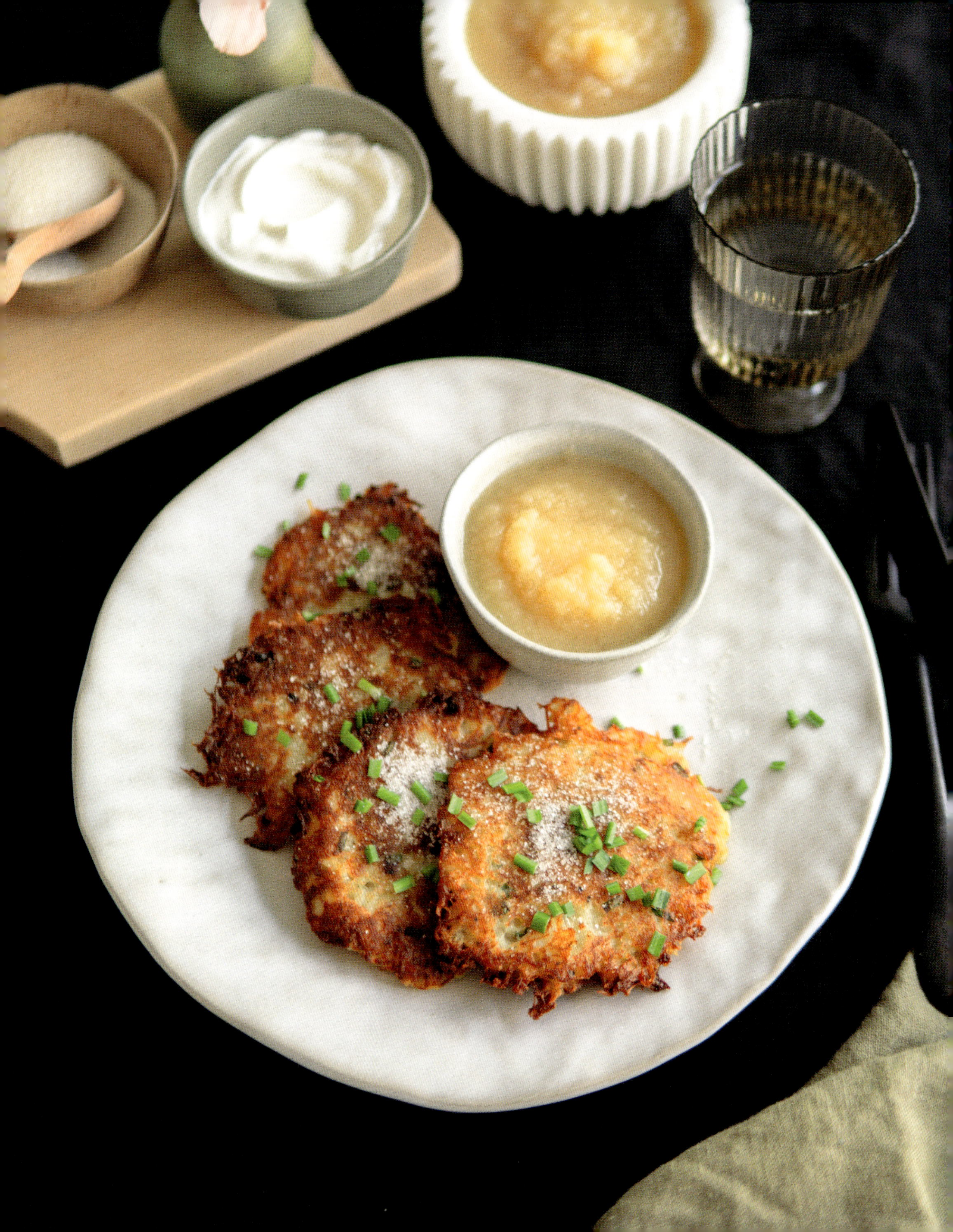

Kartoffelpuffer

Potato Pancakes

PREP TIME: 1 hour
COOK TIME: 30 minutes
YIELD: 6 servings

My Oma loved us so much that she made us homemade kartoffelpuffer whenever we wanted them! While they are quite a bit of work—shredding all of those potatoes and onions is no small task—the result is a super delicious comfort meal. Eating them hot out of the pan at her kitchen table brings back the best memories. I like to top them with a sprinkle of sugar, chives, applesauce, and a dollop of sour cream—just the way we ate them at Oma Sieghilde's house when we were kids. Other popular ways to eat kartoffelpuffer are with herbed salt, strawberry jam, smoked salmon, shredded parsnip salad, Pflaumenmus (page 34), or grafschafter goldsaft (sugar beet syrup). For a complete vegetarian meal, try serving the pancakes with Quark Dips (page 87) and Gemischter Salat (page 48).

5½ pounds (2½ kg) starchy potatoes, peeled and finely grated

3 large yellow onions, peeled and finely grated

½ cup (60 g) all-purpose flour

2 large eggs

¼ cup (12 g) finely chopped chives, plus more for garnish (optional)

2 teaspoons salt

½ teaspoon ground black pepper

1 cup (240 ml) avocado oil, for frying

Granulated sugar, for sprinkling (optional)

Applesauce, for serving (optional)

Sour cream, for serving (optional)

1. Working in batches, place orange-size portions of the grated potatoes and onions in a thin linen towel or cheesecloth and wring out as much liquid as possible. Place in a large bowl.

2. Add the flour, eggs, chives, salt, and pepper to the bowl. Using your hands, knead the mixture until a just-barely sticky dough forms, about 2 minutes. If the dough feels too wet, wring out more moisture or add in more starch.

3. Place a wire rack on top of a baking sheet. In a large skillet over medium-high heat, heat the oil until it bubbles around a wooden toothpick or utensil, about 2 minutes. Working in batches, scoop 2 heaping tablespoons per potato pancake into the skillet and flatten into 3-inch (7.5 cm) rounds. Cook until golden brown and crispy on both sides, about 2 minutes per side. Transfer the pancakes to the prepared rack to drain excess oil.

4. Serve immediately, with sugar and chives for sprinkling and sides of applesauce and sour cream.

Zwiebelkuchen

Onion Pie

It's not really fall until I have made zwiebelkuchen! This German specialty is a seasonal must-bake that takes me right back to the vineyards where I grew up—literally surrounded by vines in every direction. My Oma Sieghilde made her onion pie on a baking sheet (see Note), but I love the way it looks in a round pie dish. In Germany, a warm slice of zwiebelkuchen is not complete without a glass of chilled Federweißer—a young, sweet wine that has just started to ferment. It's hard to find outside of Germany, but a semidry Riesling will be a delicious alternative. Serve warm with a Gemischter Salat (page 48) or a simple green salad on the side.

PREP TIME: 30 minutes, plus 1 hour and 30 minutes resting

COOK TIME: 35 to 45 minutes

YIELD: 8 servings

DOUGH

1½ teaspoons (5 g) active dry yeast

1 teaspoon granulated sugar

⅔ cup (165 ml) lukewarm milk

2 cups (250 g) all-purpose flour

¼ cup (55 g) unsalted butter, softened, plus more for greasing

1 teaspoon salt

FILLING

¼ cup (55 g) unsalted butter

1 pound (455 g) yellow onions (about 4 medium), sliced into rings or half-moons

1 tablespoon all-purpose flour

1 teaspoon salt

2 large eggs

½ cup (120 ml) heavy cream

2 slices slab bacon, cut into ½-inch (12 mm) cubes or strips

1 teaspoon caraway seeds (optional)

1. **Make the dough:** In a small bowl, add the yeast, sugar, and lukewarm milk; mix well. Set aside to activate, about 5 minutes. It should look bubbly and happy.

2. In the bowl of a stand mixer fitted with the dough hook attachment, add the yeast mixture, flour, butter, and salt. Mix at low speed until a smooth, elastic dough forms, about 5 minutes. Cover the bowl and set aside in a warm spot until doubled in size, 1 to 1½ hours.

3. Preheat the oven to 380° F (200° C). Grease a 9½-inch (24 cm) pie dish (see Note) with butter.

4. **Make the filling:** In a large skillet over medium heat, melt the butter until foamy, about 1 minute. Add the onions and cook, stirring every 30 seconds or so, until soft and translucent (avoid browning them), 5 to 10 minutes. Sprinkle the flour and salt evenly over the onions and briefly stir to combine. Remove from the heat.

5. In a small bowl, whisk together the eggs and cream.

6. Using your hands, press the dough into an even layer in the baking dish, going up about 1 inch (2.5 cm) on the sides. Spread the onions over the dough, pour the egg-cream mixture on top, and evenly distribute the bacon. Sprinkle with the caraway seeds (if using).

7. Bake on the middle rack until the crust is nice and golden and the middle does not wiggle, 35 to 45 minutes. Transfer to a wire rack to cool for at least 10 minutes before slicing.

NOTES

✤ *If your pie dish is larger, your zwiebelkuchen won't be quite as tall. You could also make it on a rimmed baking sheet like my Oma always did, then cut it into squares after baking (you will want to double the recipe if doing so).*

✤ *Make it vegetarian by skipping the bacon.*

Aus Oma Sieghildes Küche

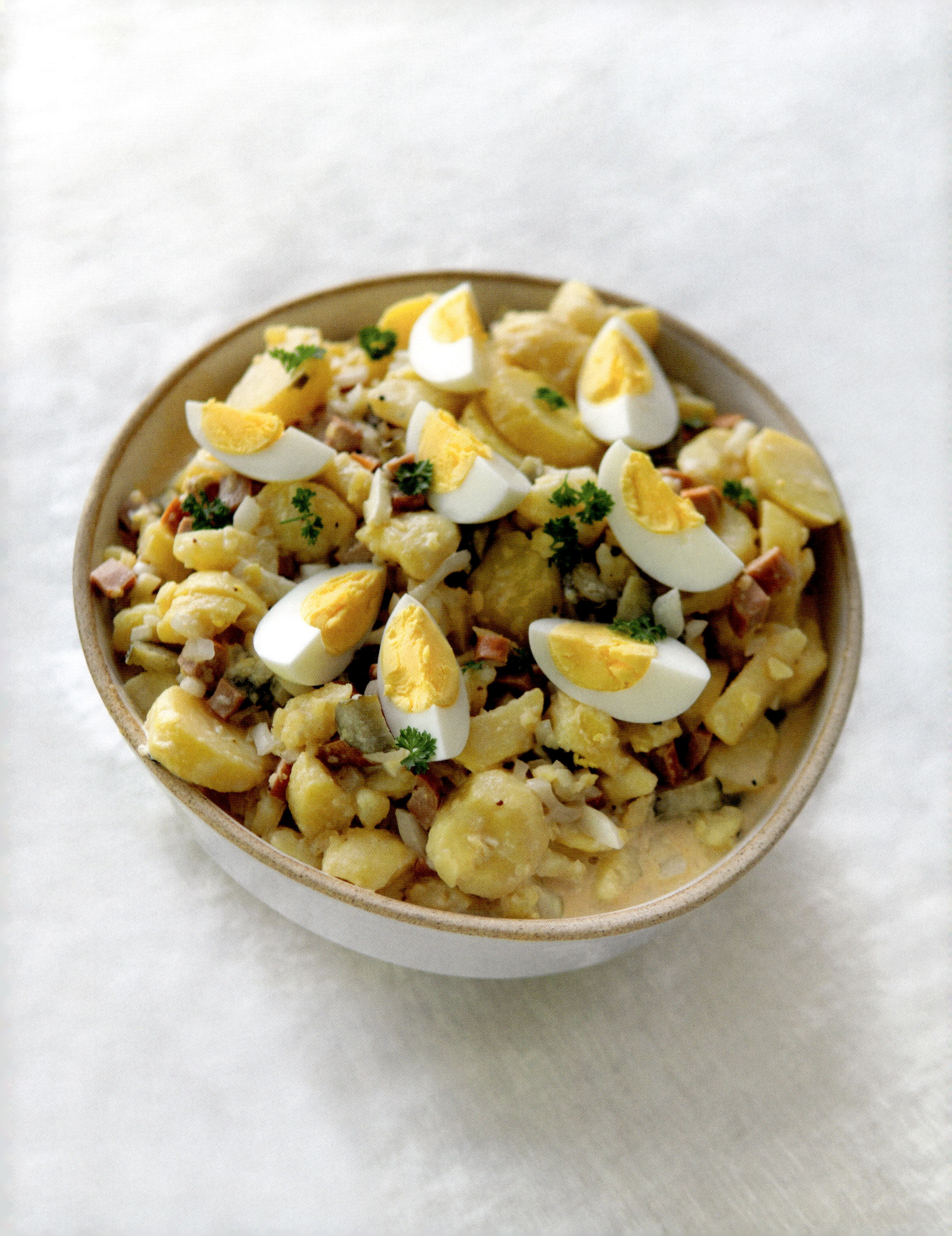

Kartoffelsalat

Potato Salad

PREP TIME: 1 hour
COOK TIME: 30 minutes
YIELD: 10 servings

Each German family has their own version of potato salad, and this is ours. My Oma Sieghilde's creamy, mayo-based kartoffelsalat is packed with dill pickles, eggs, Wiener sausages, and—you guessed it—plenty of potatoes. It makes a great contribution to an outdoor or indoor gathering with family and friends. When I'm in Germany in the summer, it's a must-have for grilling outside, served alongside a variety of grilled meats, bratwurst, and good bread.

4½ pounds (2 kg) waxy or all-purpose potatoes, boiled (see Note)

1 medium yellow onion, finely chopped

7 ounces (200 g) Gewürzgurken (page 91) or dill pickles, medium diced, plus more for garnishing (optional)

4 Wiener sausages, medium diced

1⅔ cups (400 ml) vegetable broth

½ cup (120 ml) pickle juice

3 tablespoons apple cider vinegar

1 teaspoon Dijon or medium-spicy mustard of choice

Salt and ground black pepper

Granulated sugar

1 cup (240 ml) mayonnaise

7 hard-cooked eggs, 5 diced and 2 quartered, divided

Fresh parsley leaves, for garnishing (optional)

1. Using a paring knife, peel the skin off the boiled potatoes and cut them into slices about ¼ inch (6 mm) thick.

2. In a serving bowl, add the potatoes and onion; toss gently to mix, trying to keep the potato slices intact (some will break, and that's totally fine).

3. In a small bowl, add the pickles and sausages; toss to combine.

4. In a medium saucepan, add the broth, pickle juice, vinegar, and mustard and heat to boiling over high heat. Season with salt, pepper, and sugar to taste (it should not be too sour or else Oma gets mad!). Remove from the heat and let cool slightly, about 10 minutes. Pour over the potato-onion mixture and let marinate for 10 minutes.

5. Stir in the mayonnaise, then gently fold in the diced eggs, pickles, and sausages. The dressing will be quite runny at first, but it will thicken as the salad sits. Garnish with the egg quarters, parsley, and pickles. Serve either right away (it will still be somewhat loose) or refrigerate for at least 2 hours to let it firm up.

NOTES

✣ In a time crunch? You can boil the potatoes on the same day you make the salad. They may be a bit softer and break apart more easily, but this salad is not entering a beauty contest. It will taste amazing regardless.

✣ The salad tastes even better the next day when the flavors have had time to soak more deeply into the potatoes. Make sure to scoop from the bottom of the bowl when serving to get the juiciest bites.

✣ For a vegetarian version, simply leave out the sausages.

Baumkuchen

Tree Cake

I almost gave up on this recipe after burning seven cakes trying to get the baking method to work with an American oven (see Note). My Oma Sieghilde helped me figure it out when I first moved to the United States. Traditionally, baumkuchen is baked on rotating wooden rods next to an open fire, with layers of batter brushed on one layer at a time, creating a tree-ring effect. We can't quite recreate that at home, but we can get close by layering the batter in a springform pan. Danke, Oma.

PREP TIME: 30 minutes, plus 2 hours resting
COOK TIME: 35 minutes
YIELD: 12 servings

CAKE

1 cup plus 1½ tablespoons (250 g) unsalted butter, at room temperature, plus more for greasing

2½ cups (250 g) granulated sugar

6 large eggs, whites and yolks separated

1 teaspoon vanilla extract

3½ ounces (100 g) marzipan

3 tablespoons amaretto

1¼ cups (150 g) all-purpose flour

¾ cup (100 g) cornstarch

1 tablespoon baking powder

1 pinch salt

LEMON GLAZE

¾ cup (100 g) powdered sugar

1 tablespoon fresh lemon juice

CHOCOLATE GANACHE
(optional)

2 ounces (55 g) bittersweet chocolate

2 ounces (55 ml) heavy cream

1. Preheat the broiler or oven (see Notes). Line the bottom of a 9-inch (23 cm) dark metal springform pan with parchment paper and secure the ring around it. Trim the paper edges. Grease the sides of the pan with butter and dust with flour. (Alternatively, grease a 9-inch, or 23 cm, cake pan, line the bottom with a parchment paper circle, then dust the sides with flour.)

2. **Make the cake:** In a large bowl, whisk the butter, granulated sugar, egg yolks, and vanilla until smooth.

3. In a small, microwave-safe bowl, heat the marzipan and amaretto in 10-second increments until warmed. (Alternatively, heat in a small saucepan over medium heat.) Whisk until smooth; stir into the butter mixture.

4. In a medium bowl, sift together the flour, cornstarch, and baking powder; whisk into the butter mixture, 1 tablespoon at a time, until a thick, lump-free batter forms.

5. In a large bowl, whisk the egg whites and a pinch of salt until stiff peaks form. Fold into the batter until just combined.

6. Spread about ½ cup (130 g) of batter evenly over the bottom of the prepared pan. Bake until the top starts to turn golden brown, 3 to 4 minutes. Repeat, carefully adding and spreading each new layer, with the remaining batter for 9 layers. Keep a close eye on the cake, as it can burn easily. Insert a cake tester or a toothpick into the center of the cake. If it doesn't come out clean, adjust the oven to 350°F (180°C) and bake until the cake is cooked through, 5 to 7 minutes. Let cool on a wire rack for about 5 minutes. Run a thin knife around the cake to loosen it from the pan, then carefully remove the springform ring. Cover the cake with a clean kitchen towel and let cool completely, about 1 hour.

German Home Kitchen

7. **Make the lemon glaze:** In a small bowl, whisk the powdered sugar and lemon juice until thick and smooth, like honey. Spread the glaze over the top of the cooled cake.

8. **Make the ganache (if using):** Place the chocolate in a small bowl. In a small saucepan over medium heat, warm the heavy cream, whisking periodically, until just about to boil. Pour it over the chocolate and let sit for 1 minute. Stir until smooth. Let the ganache cool until thick enough to pipe, stirring periodically (refrigeration will speed this up). Fit a piping bag with a small round tip, add the ganache, and draw pretty tree-like rings on the cake.

NOTE

✦ *Here's how to adjust your oven: If you have three broil settings, use Broil 2 (450°F, or 230°C) and bake the cake on the bottom rack. If you have two broil settings (high and low), use the low option (400°F, or 200°C) and bake on the middle rack. If you're in Germany, use oberhitze (top heat only) and select 200°C. Bake your cake on the middle rack.*

Aus Oma Sieghildes Küche

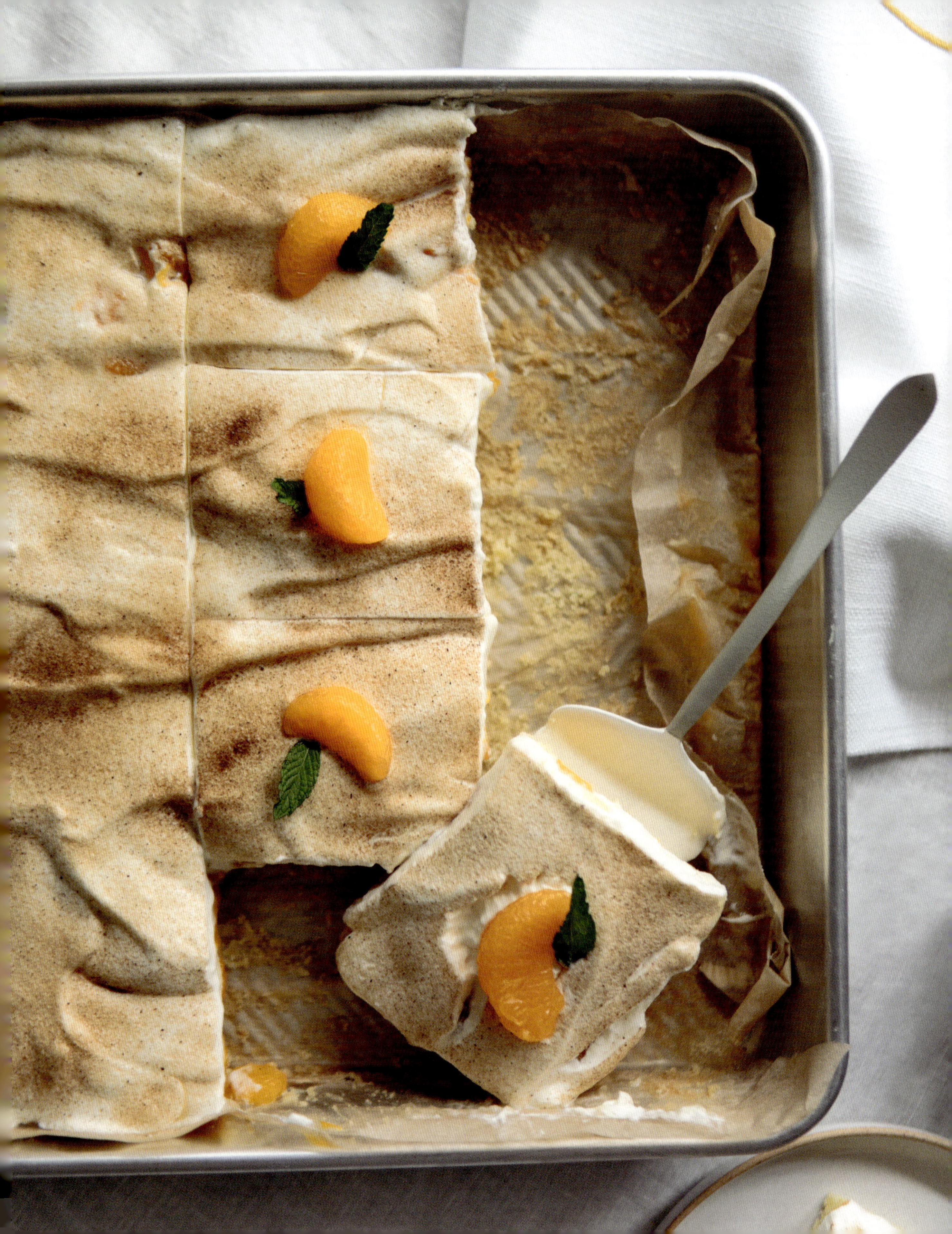

KAFFEE & KUCHEN

» *Afternoon Coffee & Cake* «

Germany's beloved "fourth meal," Kaffee und Kuchen, is an afternoon coffee break centered around cake but often accompanied by other sweet treats like pastries, fluffy braids, strudel, and ice cream. While I usually skip the sweets during the week and just go for an afternoon coffee, I love baking something special for a weekend afternoon to create a moment to slow down and savor the day. Inviting friends to share this tradition makes it even more special, and I hope you will do the same. The kuchen and torte (coffee cakes and layered cakes) in this chapter—some simple, some more elevated—are perfect for celebrating the Kaffee und Kuchen tradition. Versatile and indulgent, they can be a birthday cake, a "just because" treat, or a fun addition to brunch.

Hefezopf

Yeast Braid

Hefezopf is a big bang for your effort kind of recipe and one of the fluffiest braided breads! The pearl sugar sprinkled over the top before baking is mainly decorative (and optional), but iconic. While it's not typical to add flavoring to a hefezopf, I love the addition of vanilla or lemon zest for a subtle aromatic note. My Oma Sieghilde often purchased braids from a bakery to enjoy with her afternoon cup of coffee. Hefezopf is great on its own, but it's easily taken to the next level with a spread of butter and jam or Pflaumenmus (page 34). Store any leftovers in an airtight container or freeze for later.

PREP TIME: 30 minutes, plus 2 hours resting
COOK TIME: 30 minutes
YIELD: 18 slices

---

5 teaspoons active dry yeast (2 packets)

7 ounces (210 ml) lukewarm whole milk plus 3 tablespoons cold, divided

4 cups (500 g) all-purpose flour, plus more for dusting

⅓ cup (75 g) granulated sugar

1 pinch salt

5½ tablespoons unsalted butter, at room temperature

3 large eggs, divided

1 teaspoon vanilla extract or ½ teaspoon freshly grated lemon zest (optional)

Pearl sugar, for sprinkling (optional)

1. In a small bowl, combine the yeast and the lukewarm milk. Set aside to activate, about 5 minutes, or until bubbly.

2. In the bowl of a stand mixer fitted with the dough hook attachment, stir together the flour, granulated sugar, and salt. Add the bubbly yeast mixture, butter, 2 of the eggs, and vanilla or lemon zest (if using). Mix at low speed until a smooth dough forms, about 8 minutes. Cover the bowl tightly and let the dough rest in a warm spot until doubled in size, about 1 hour.

3. Preheat the oven to 320°F (160°C) on the convection (umluft) setting or to 345°F (175°C) for a non-convection oven. Line a baking sheet with parchment paper or a silicone baking mat.

4. On a clean work surface, using a bench scraper or a sharp knife, divide the dough into 3 equal pieces. Briefly knead each piece to remove major air bubbles. Using your hands, roll each piece into a log, about 20 inches (51 cm) long. Line up the logs vertically and pinch the ends together at the top, facing away from you. Braid the dough, then tuck the ends under to create an even braid with a neat finish. Transfer to the prepared baking sheet, cover loosely with a clean kitchen towel, and let rest in a warm spot until doubled in size, about 30 minutes.

5. In a small bowl, whisk together the remaining egg and the 3 tablespoons cold milk. Brush the egg wash over the braid, sprinkle with pearl sugar (if using), and bake on the middle rack until golden brown, 30 to 35 minutes. At the 20-minute mark, tent the braid with foil so it does not get too dark. Transfer to a wire rack and let cool for about 30 minutes before slicing and serving.

NOTES

✣ *For a wreath version (often made for Easter), roll the logs into 30-inch (75 cm) ropes, braid them, and pinch both ends together to form a circle. Nestle dyed boiled eggs in the center after baking for a festive touch.*

✣ *While hefezopf is best fresh, you could freeze a freshly baked braid after it cools down to preserve the fluffiness. To thaw, leave at room temperature for 3 hours.*

Kaffee & Kuchen

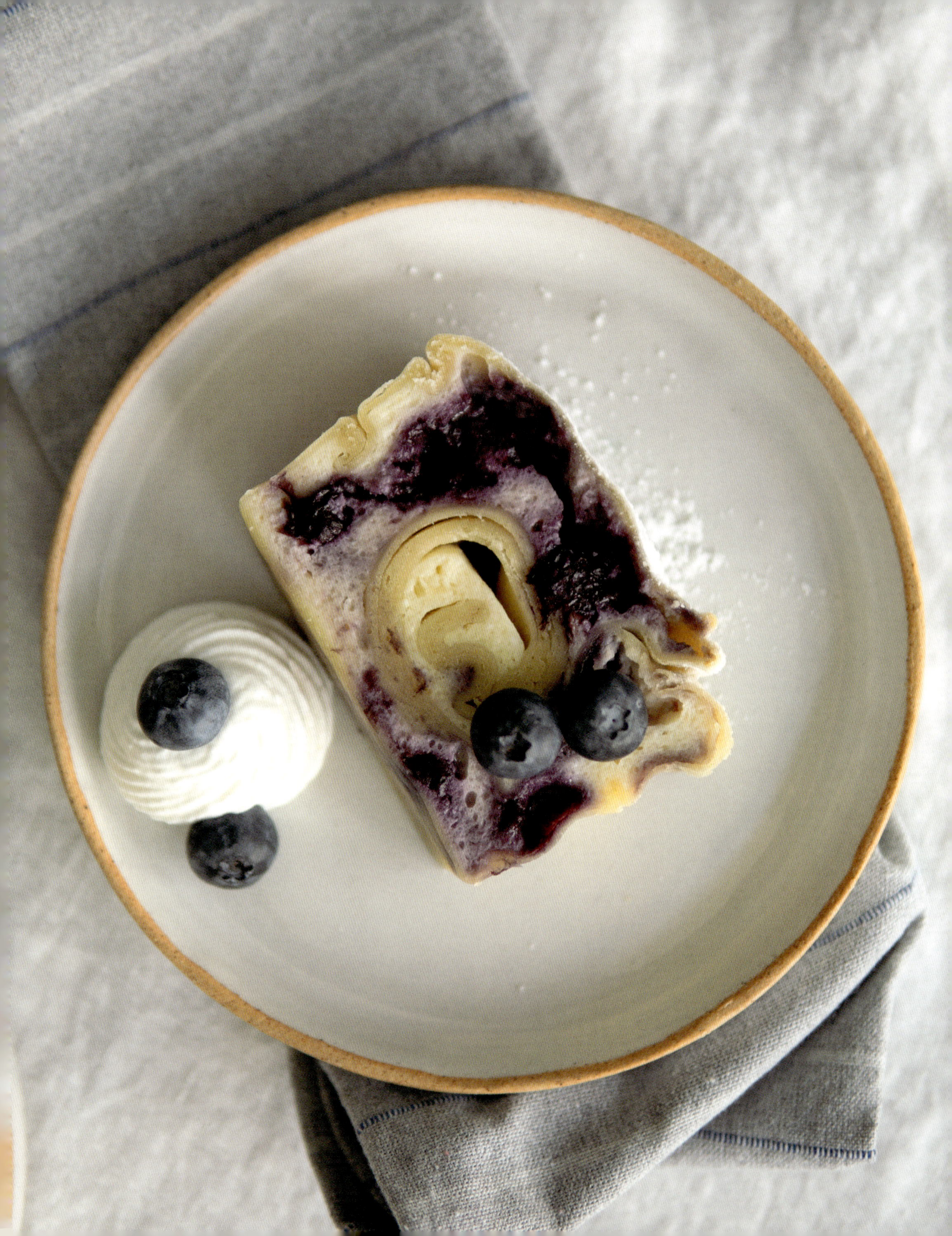

Blaubeer Quarkstrudel

Quark and Blueberry Strudel

PREP TIME: 20 minutes, plus 1 hour resting
COOK TIME: 50 minutes
YIELD: 12 slices

This treat combines a rich, cheesecake-like quark filling with juicy blueberries between thin, delicate layers of strudel dough. It's a fresh take on the wintry classic Austrian apple strudel. To keep the quarkstudel from losing its shape, I started baking it in a loaf pan, creating uniform slices that not only hold their structure but also look gorgeous.

STRUDEL DOUGH

2 cups (250 g) all-purpose flour, plus more for rolling

¼ teaspoon salt

1 large egg

½ cup (120 ml) lukewarm water

4 teaspoons plus 2 tablespoons avocado oil, divided

2 tablespoons melted unsalted butter, divided

BLUEBERRIES

2 cups (300 g) fresh or frozen blueberries

2 tablespoons granulated sugar

1 teaspoon cornstarch

1 tablespoon cold water

QUARK FILLING

2 large eggs, whites and yolks separated

1 pinch salt

2 cups (480 ml) Quark (page 12) or full-fat Greek yogurt

1½ tablespoons spiced rum

1. Preheat the oven to 375° F (190° C) and line the bottom and sides of a 4 by 10-inch (10 by 25 cm) loaf pan with parchment paper, leaving some overhang on the two long sides for easy removal.

2. **Make the strudel dough:** In the bowl of a stand mixer fitted with the dough hook attachment, add the flour, salt, egg, water, and 4 teaspoons of the oil and mix at low speed until a smooth, elastic dough forms, about 5 minutes. Shape the dough into a ball, place it in a bowl just big enough to fit it, and then pour the remaining 2 tablespoons oil over it. Cover the bowl with plastic wrap or a tight-fitting lid and let rest at room temperature for 30 minutes—this helps the gluten to relax, making the dough easier to stretch without tearing.

3. **Meanwhile, make the blueberries:** In a small saucepan, add the blueberries and granulated sugar; cook, stirring occasionally, over medium heat until bubbly, about 5 minutes. In a small bowl, whisk the cornstarch and cold water until smooth, then stir into the blueberry mixture. Cook, stirring constantly, until the sauce is thick and syrupy, 1 to 2 minutes. Remove from the heat.

4. **Make the quark filling:** In a large bowl, with a wire whisk, beat the egg whites and a pinch of salt until stiff peaks form. In a medium bowl, add the egg yolks, quark, rum, butter, vanilla, powdered sugar, and cornstarch; whisk to combine. Stir in the lemon zest, then the bread crumbs. Gently fold in the beaten egg whites until no white streaks remain.

(CONTINUED)

Kaffee & Kuchen

3½ tablespoons unsalted butter, at room temperature

1 teaspoon vanilla extract

1 cup (130 g) powdered sugar, plus more for dusting

3 tablespoons cornstarch

Grated zest of ½ lemon

3 tablespoons bread crumbs

Whipped cream, homemade (page 9) or store-bought, for serving

5. Place a small handful of flour on a clean work surface. Remove the dough from the oil bath, letting excess drip off, then roll it in the flour to coat evenly. On a clean work surface, lay out a thin, cotton kitchen towel, about 26 by 27 inches (66 by 69 cm) and lightly dust it with flour. Place the dough in the middle and, using a rolling pin, roll it out to a rectangular shape close to the size of the kitchen towel. Carefully stretch the dough, using your hands with your knuckles facing up, until it is almost see-through. Roll it out some more if needed and alternate between the two methods to get your dough to be the approximate size of the kitchen towel. (This dough is super flexible, and I don't usually have any issues with tearing, but any holes can be pinched back together.) Brush with 1 tablespoon of the melted butter.

6. Spread the quark filling evenly over the dough, leaving a 2-inch (5 cm) border on each side. Distribute the blueberries over the filling. Using the kitchen towel for support, fold in the shorter edges first, then fold in the longer edges, making sure it matches up with the long side of the loaf pan. Roll the entire strudel into a 10-inch-long (25 cm) log and transfer it to the prepared pan with the help of the kitchen towel.

7. Bake on the middle rack until the top is light brown, about 40 minutes. Check at the 30-minute mark; if the top is browning too quickly, cover it with foil for the remaining bake time. Transfer to a wire rack and immediately brush the top with the remaining 1 tablespoon melted butter; this helps crisp up the top layer. Let it cool in the pan for about 30 minutes, or until the filling is set. Dust the top with powdered sugar before slicing. Serve warm with whipped cream.

NOTES

✤ *Quarkstrudel is best served warm, as that's when the strudel crust is the flakiest. It becomes hard when it's cold, but you could easily reheat your strudel in the oven or microwave to bring it back to life.*

✤ *For storage, let the strudel cool completely, then wrap it tightly with plastic wrap and refrigerate for up to 5 days. For longer storage, cut into individual slices, wrap tightly with plastic wrap, and freeze for up to 3 months.*

Schwarzwälder Kirschtorte

Black Forest Cherry Cake

PREP TIME: 30 minutes, plus 1 hour cooling
COOK TIME: 45 minutes
YIELD: 12 slices

Black forest cake is the most iconic, internationally famous German chocolate cake. I call it the *real* German chocolate cake because it's not the "German chocolate cake" that's popular in the United States. (Fun fact: That cake was actually invented by an American man named Samuel German.) Schwarzwälder kirschtorte is a staple for special occasions like birthdays. With three delicious layers of chocolate sponge cake, Kirschwasser-infused cherries, and vanilla whipped cream frosting, it's nothing like the American cake with pecans and coconut. Plus, you can use frozen, jarred, or fresh cherries, making it easy to enjoy year-round.

CHOCOLATE SPONGE CAKE

- 1¼ cups (140 g) semisweet chocolate chips
- 5 tablespoons cold unsalted butter, cubed
- 6 large eggs, whites and yolks separated
- 1 pinch salt
- 1 cup (180 g) granulated sugar
- ¾ cup (100 g) all-purpose flour, plus more for dusting
- ⅓ cup (50 g) cornstarch
- 2 teaspoons baking powder
- 2 ounces (60 ml) Kirschwasser

CHERRY FILLING

- 28 ounces (800 g) frozen, jarred, or fresh pitted cherries (see Notes)
- 2 cups (480 ml) cherry juice
- ⅓ cup (40 g) cornstarch
- 2 tablespoons granulated sugar, or more to taste
- 2 ounces (60 ml) Kirschwasser

1. **Make the chocolate sponge cake:** Preheat the oven to 350°F (180°C). Place a piece of parchment paper on the bottom of a 9-inch (23 cm) springform pan and secure the ring around it. Trim the edges. Grease the sides of the pan and dust with flour. (Alternatively, grease a 9-inch, or 23 cm, cake pan and line the bottom with a parchment paper circle, then dust the sides with flour.)

2. In a double boiler or a bowl placed over a saucepan of boiling water, melt the chocolate chips and butter; stir until completely melted and smooth. (Alternatively, microwave for 30-second increments, stirring in between, until melted.) Set aside to cool.

3. In the bowl of a stand mixer fitted with the whisk attachment (or in a large bowl using an electric hand mixer), whisk the egg whites and a pinch of salt at high speed until stiff peaks form.

4. In a large bowl, whisk the egg yolks and granulated sugar until foamy. Whisk in the melted chocolate until combined. Sift together the flour, cornstarch, and baking powder through a fine-mesh sieve right into the chocolate mixture. Whisk until smooth with no lumps remaining, about 1 minute. Carefully fold in the beaten egg whites until just combined. Transfer the batter to the prepared pan.

(CONTINUED)

Kaffee & Kuchen

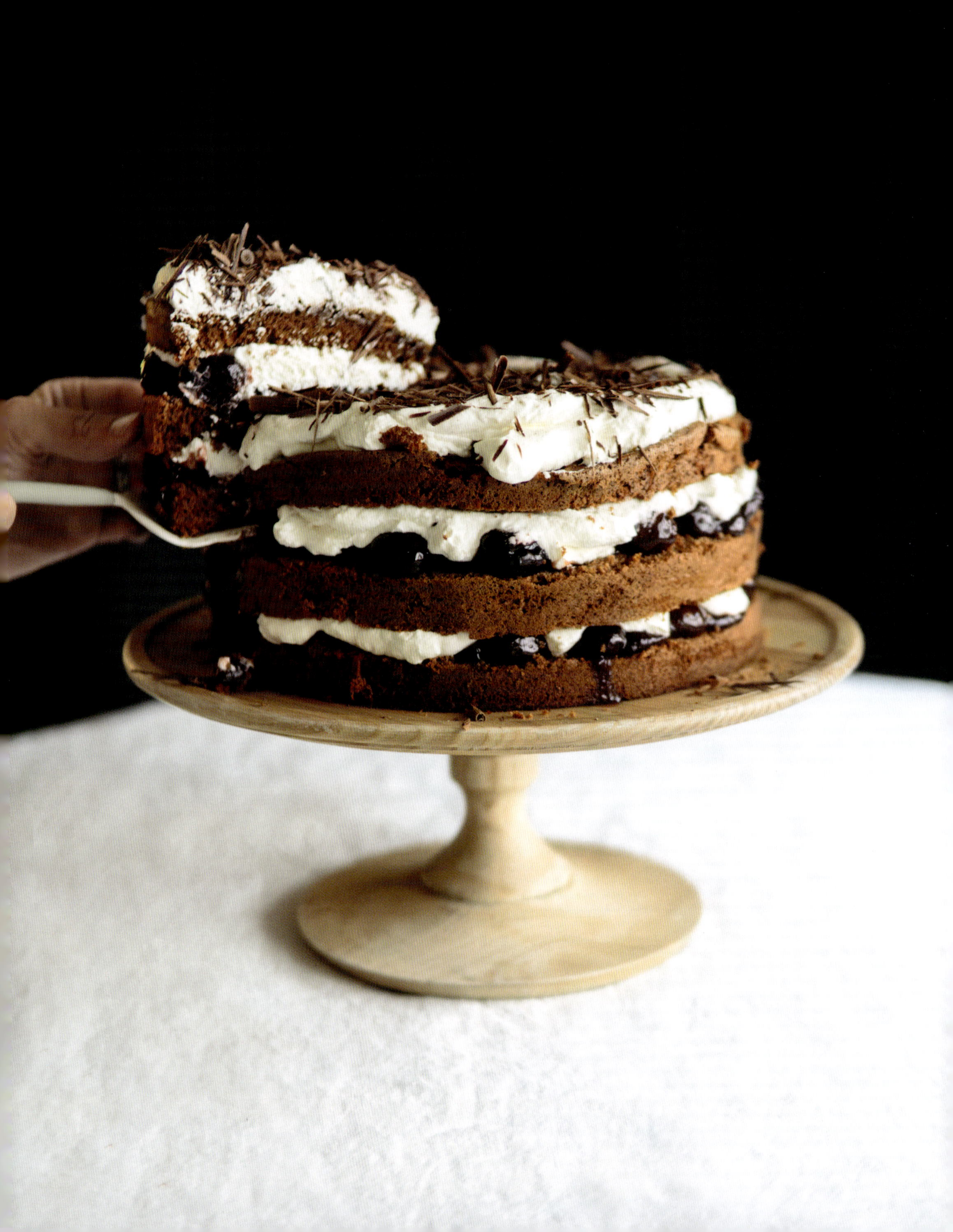

WHIPPED CREAM FROSTING

3½ cups (840 ml) heavy cream

¼ cup (25 g) powdered sugar

2 teaspoons vanilla extract

TOPPING

Shaved chocolate or chocolate sprinkles

NOTES

✦ *If using jarred or canned cherries, the drained weight should be 28 ounces (800 g). Make sure the cherries are in juice, not in syrup, and reserve the liquid to use for making the cherry sauce.*

✦ *Kirschwasser is a clear cherry brandy that enhances this cake's aroma, reinforcing its deep cherry flavor. If you prefer, you can leave it out or substitute it with another clear fruit brandy, like German fruit Schnaps (around 40 percent alcohol).*

✦ *Store leftovers covered (with a cake dome or in a sealed container) and refrigerated for up to 3 days, or frozen for up to 3 months. To thaw, transfer to the fridge a day before serving.*

5. Bake until a cake tester or toothpick inserted into the center of the cake comes out clean, 40 to 45 minutes. Transfer to a wire rack, cover with a clean kitchen towel (to prevent it from drying out), and let cool for 5 minutes. Run a thin knife around the edges to loosen the cake, remove the springform ring, then carefully lift up the cake, keeping the parchment on the bottom, onto the rack. Cover with a clean kitchen towel and let cool completely, about 2 hours.

6. On a cutting board, remove the parchment and, using a large, serrated knife, cut the cake horizontally into 3 even layers. Brush each layer with the Kirschwasser.

7. **Make the cherry filling:** Place the cherries in a large bowl. In a small bowl, whisk together ¼ cup (60 ml) of the cherry juice, the cornstarch, and granulated sugar. In a small saucepan, heat the remaining 1¾ cups (440 ml) cherry juice to boiling over high heat and whisk in the cornstarch mixture. Continue boiling, stirring constantly, until thickened to a pudding-like consistency, about 1 minute. Remove from the heat and transfer to the bowl with the cherries. Let cool for 15 minutes, then stir in the Kirschwasser.

8. If desired, reserve some of the cherries for decorating the top of the cake. Divide the remaining filling between two of the cake layers, spreading it evenly. Let the cherry filling cool and set, about 1 hour.

9. **Make the whipped cream frosting:** In the bowl of a stand mixer fitted with the whisk attachment (or a large bowl using an electric hand mixer), add the heavy cream, powdered sugar, and vanilla; beat at high speed until soft peaks form, 2 to 3 minutes. Refrigerate until ready to assemble.

10. **To assemble:** Place one of the cherry-covered cake layers on a cake platter, then spread a quarter of the whipped cream frosting evenly over it. Place the other cherry-covered layer on top and spread another quarter of the frosting over it. Top with the final cake layer, then frost the top of the cake with the remaining frosting. Decorate with shaved chocolate or chocolate sprinkles. For a traditional look, pipe whipped cream rosettes around the outer edge, then top each with a cherry—either fresh, maraschino, or from the filling—and press chocolate shavings against the sides of the cake.

Kaffee & Kuchen

Spaghettieis

Spaghetti Ice Cream

PREP TIME: 15 minutes, plus 30 minutes freezing

YIELD: 4 servings

Spaghettieis (pronounced "spaghetti ice") may look like a plate of pasta with tomato sauce from a distance, but don't be fooled. This playful dessert, said to be invented by a seventeen-year-old named Dario Fontanella at his father's ice cream shop in Mannheim, Germany, skillfully combines vanilla ice cream pressed through a spätzle press, arranged over whipped cream, and topped with strawberry sauce (wannabe tomato sauce), grated white chocolate (wannabe Parmesan cheese), and fresh mint leaves (wannabe basil). The best part for me is when the ice cream meets the whipped cream and freezes it just a little. When visiting Germany, I eat one almost every other day. But now that I've perfected this recipe to make it taste just like from the best ice cream shops in Germany, I can control myself a bit better at home.

---

1 pound (500 g) fresh strawberries, hulled

¼ cup (30 g) powdered sugar

1 teaspoon vanilla extract

3 pints (1.4 L) vanilla ice cream or gelato

1 cup (240 ml) whipped cream, homemade (page 9) or store-bought

2 ounces (50 g) white chocolate bar

Fresh mint leaves, for garnishing (optional)

1. In a food processor fitted with the knife blade, add the strawberries, powdered sugar, and vanilla; puree until smooth. Strain through a fine-mesh sieve into a small bowl and keep refrigerated until ready to serve.

2. At least 30 minutes before serving, put a spätzle press or potato ricer and serving bowls in the freezer; this helps prevent the ice cream from melting right away and keeps it looking like spaghetti longer.

3. About 10 minutes before serving, set the ice cream out at room temperature to soften slightly, making it easier to press.

4. To assemble, divide the whipped cream evenly among the serving bowls. For each bowl, place about 1½ cups (375 ml) of ice cream into the spätzle press and press, creating spaghetti-like strands, over the whipped cream. Spoon about 2 to 3 tablespoons of the strawberry sauce over the ice cream noodles. Using a rasp-style grater or the finest setting on a box grater, shave the white chocolate on top. Garnish with a mint leaf (if using). Eat before it melts!

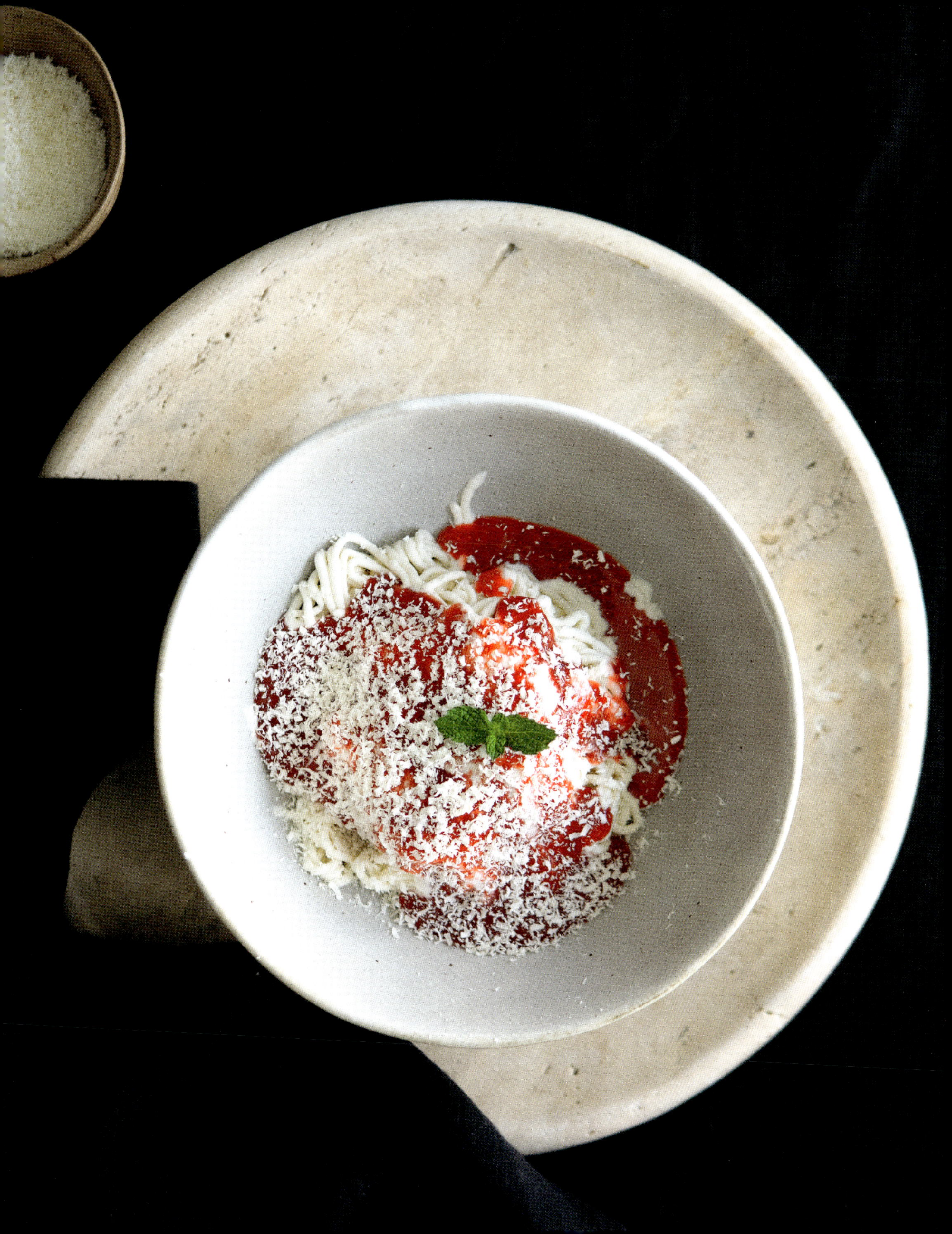

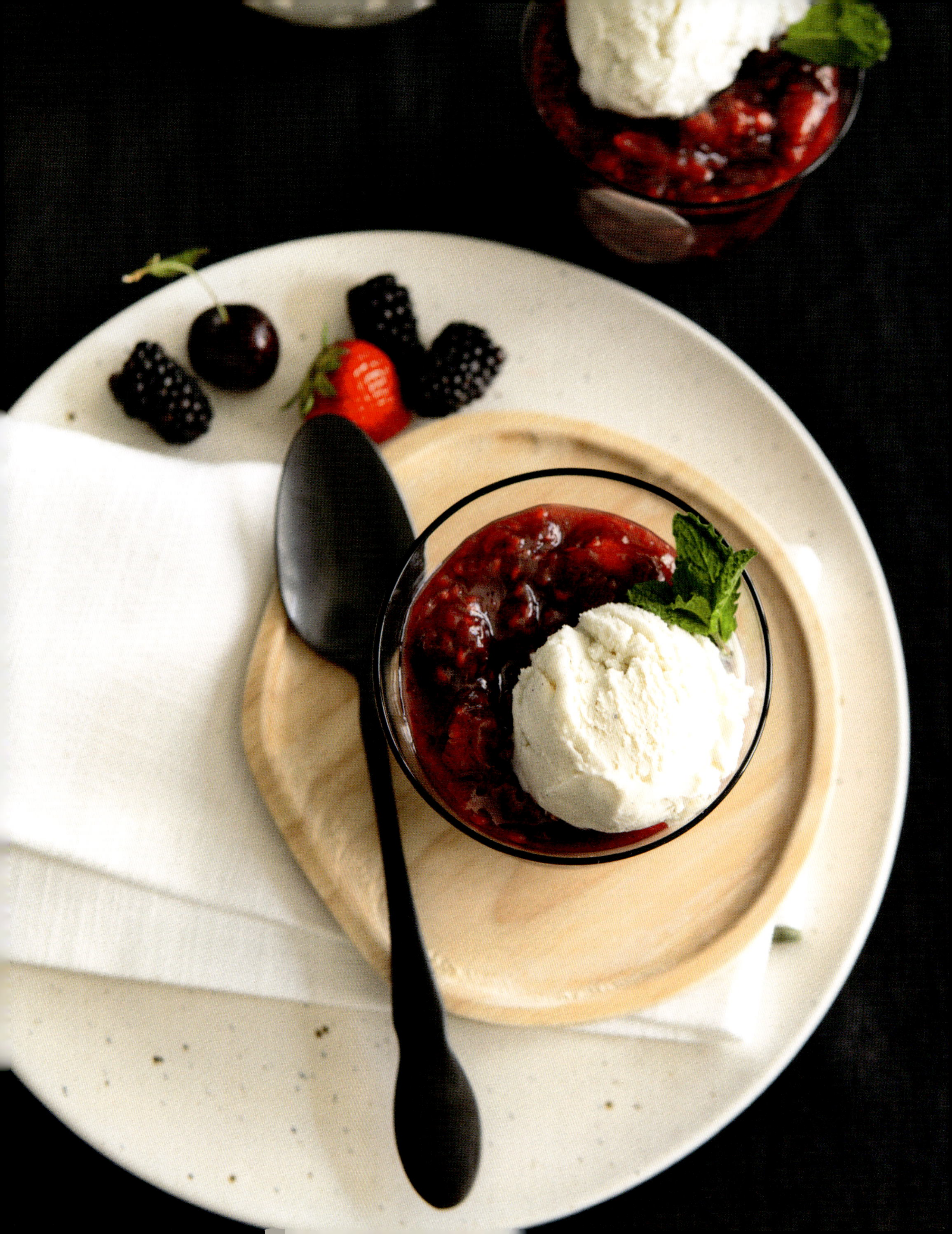

Rote Grütze

Berry Grits

PREP TIME: 15 minutes
COOK TIME: 15 minutes
YIELD: 4 servings

Don't be confused by the translation, this has nothing to do with grits as they're known in English. Rote grütze is the perfect light summer dessert—ripe, juicy berries simmered with fruit juice and warm spices. The gentle hint of cinnamon and vanilla bring out the rich red-fruit flavors. Serve with vanilla ice cream or vanilla sauce (page 100) because, in my opinion, nothing is more satisfying when you're craving something refreshing and sweet at the same time. Rote grütze tastes the best with fresh, ripe berries in season, though frozen berries are an option during the colder months. It is also amazing served with my Uncle Axel's Saure Sahne Waffeln (page 99) or on top of Dampfnudeln (page 100).

½ **vanilla bean**

6 ounces (180 ml) **unsweetened cherry or cranberry juice**

¾ cup (150 g) **granulated sugar**

1-inch (2.5 cm) piece **cinnamon stick**

1 cup (250 g) **pitted cherries divided**

1 cup (125 g) **strawberries, divided**

1 cup (125 g) **blackberries, divided**

1 cup (200 g) **raspberries, divided**

¼ cup (30 g) **cornstarch**

2 tablespoons **cold water**

Vanilla ice cream or vanilla sauce (page 100), for serving (optional)

Saure Sahne Waffeln (page 99), for serving (optional)

1. With a sharp knife, cut the vanilla bean lengthwise in half, scrape the seeds, and reserve for later.

2. In a medium pot, add the scraped vanilla bean pod, juice, sugar, cinnamon stick, and 4 ounces (125 ml) of water and heat to boiling over high heat. Add half of the fruit, reduce the heat to medium, and cook, stirring occasionally, until softened, about 10 minutes.

3. In a small bowl, whisk the cornstarch and cold water until smooth and stir into the fruit mixture. Heat to boiling over medium-high heat, stirring constantly until thickened, about 1 minute. Stir in the remaining half of fruit and the reserved vanilla seeds. Remove from the heat and let cool for about 5 minutes. Remove and discard the vanilla pod.

4. Serve warm or cold with vanilla ice cream or vanilla sauce and/or saure sahne waffeln.

NOTES

❖ *You can customize your own fruit blend, swapping out any berries or fruit depending on what's available. I like a good mix of sweet fruit (like raspberries) and tart fruit (like tart cherries) to keep the flavor balanced.*

❖ *Make extra rote grütze and freeze it for a taste of summer during the colder months—it's like a cheerful summer greeting that will totally lift your mood.*

Kaffee & Kuchen

Käsekuchen im Glas

Raspberry Cheesecake in a Jar

This is my go-to käsekuchen recipe for a few reasons: it's easy, it's fast and there is no significant waiting time after baking and before they can be eaten. I love serving these little cheesecakes warm from the oven, but they're just as good reheated later. This is the perfect way to use up extra quark while transporting yourself to Germany in under an hour. No jars? Use mugs! You can also bake them in even smaller jars for a fun party treat.

PREP TIME: 15 minutes

COOK TIME: 25 minutes

YIELD: About 39 ounces (1.2 ml) or enough to fill 6 (10-ounce, or 290-ml) jars

---

KÄSEKUCHEN BATTER

8½ tablespoons butter, at room temperature, plus more melted butter for greasing

⅔ cup (125 g) granulated sugar

Grated zest of ½ lemon

1 pinch salt

3 large eggs, at room temperature

2 tablespoons plus 1 teaspoon all-purpose flour

2 tablespoons plus 2 teaspoons cornstarch

1⅔ cups (400 ml) Quark (page 12; or substitute with strained Greek yogurt), at room temperature

RASPBERRY FILLING

2 cups (280 g) frozen raspberries

3 tablespoons granulated sugar

1 teaspoon cornstarch

1 tablespoon cold water

1. Wash and sterilize your jars (see page 11).

2. **Make the batter:** In a large bowl, whisk the butter, granulated sugar, lemon zest, and salt until smooth. Add one egg at a time, mixing until incorporated after each addition. Sift the flour and cornstarch over the mixture; whisk until smooth. Whisk in the quark until just combined.

3. **Make the filling:** In a medium saucepan, heat the raspberries and granulated sugar to boiling over medium-high heat. In a small bowl, whisk the cornstarch and cold water until smooth; add to the raspberry mixture, stirring constantly, until thickened, about 1 minute. Remove from the heat.

4. Preheat the oven to 320°F (160°C) on the convection (umluft) setting or 345°F (175°C) for a non-convection oven. Brush the insides of the jars with melted butter.

5. Spoon 1 tablespoon of the raspberry sauce into the bottom of each jar (see Notes). With a spoon or a large piping bag (without a decorating tip), fill the jars about two-thirds full with the batter. Spoon some of the remaining raspberry filling on top, if desired. Wipe the rims of the jars clean with a paper towel.

6. Bake the jars directly on the middle rack until the käsekuchen have puffed up, the centers are no longer wobbly, and the tops are golden, 20 to 25 minutes. Transfer to a cooling rack. If serving warm (my preferred way), let sit until cool enough to handle, about 15 minutes; otherwise, let cool to room temperature, 2 to 3 hours, then refrigerate until ready to serve. If desired, garnish with a dusting of powdered sugar, fresh raspberries, and mint leaves.

OPTIONAL GARNISHES

Powdered sugar

Fresh raspberries

Fresh mint leaves

NOTES

✤ *For a fun marbled effect, layer the raspberry filling between spoonfuls of the batter, then swirl it with a fork or knife.*

✤ *You can use any fruit you like in this recipe. I love fresh or canned apricots, plums, blueberries, cherries, strawberries, blackberries, and more. Cooked cinnamon apples are another amazing option.*

✤ *Canning jars are freezer-safe. Freeze for up to 3 months. Thaw at room temperature for about 2 hours, then reheat in the oven at 350°F (175°C) for 8 minutes.*

Kaffee & Kuchen

Apfelkuchen

Apple Cake

Apfelkuchen was my Oma Sieghilde's specialty, and I know you will love this simple recipe that I have been making for years. The buttery, cinnamon-almond streusel topping adds the most fantastic finishing touch.

PREP TIME: 30 minutes

COOK TIME: 30 to 35 Minutes

YIELD: 16 servings

CAKE BATTER

1 cup plus 2 tablespoons (250 g) unsalted butter, at room temperature, plus more for greasing

1¼ cups (250 g) granulated sugar

½ teaspoon salt

4 large eggs

¼ cup (60 g) whole milk

3¼ cups (400 g) all-purpose flour

4 teaspoons baking powder

APPLES

5 large tart apples (see Note), cut into ½-inch-thick (12 mm) slices

Juice of 1 lemon

STREUSEL TOPPING

½ cup (60 g) all-purpose flour

2 tablespoons (30 g) sliced almonds

2½ tablespoons (30 g) granulated sugar

2½ tablespoons (40 g) unsalted butter, cold and cut into pieces

1 teaspoon (3 g) ground cinnamon

FOR SERVING

Whipped cream, homemade (page 9) or store-bought,

1. Preheat the oven to 340°F (170°C). Line the bottom of an 11 by 17-inch (28 by 43 cm) baking pan with parchment paper and grease the sides with butter.

2. **Make the cake batter:** In the bowl of a stand mixer fitted with the whisk attachment, beat the butter, sugar, and salt at medium-high speed until light and fluffy, about 2 minutes. With the mixer at medium speed, add the eggs, one at a time, until incorporated. Add the milk and mix until worked in, about 30 seconds. Sift the flour and baking powder into the egg mixture and mix until a thick, lump-free batter forms, about 2 minutes. Use a rubber spatula to transfer the batter to the prepared baking pan and spread it into an even layer.

3. **Prepare the apples:** In a large bowl, toss the apple slices with the lemon juice to prevent browning. Arrange them, cut side down, in neat rows, pressing them halfway into the batter.

4. **Make the streusel topping:** In a large bowl, add the flour, almonds, sugar, butter, and cinnamon. Using an electric hand mixer, mix at medium speed to combine. Using your hands, crumble the mixture, forming the streusel. Evenly distribute the streusel over the cake. If you would like the apple rows to remain visible, sprinkle the streusel between the rows instead of covering the entire surface.

5. Bake on the middle rack until a cake tester or a toothpick inserted into the center of the cake comes out clean, 30 to 35 minutes. To add an extra tan to the streusel topping, adjust the oven control to the broiler setting and broil for 1 to 2 minutes, watching carefully to prevent burning. Transfer to a wire rack and let cool for 5 minutes. Slice and serve warm with whipped cream.

NOTES

✤ *You can use any type of apple, but tart varieties help balance the sweetness of the streusel. I don't peel my apples because I love the color contrast, but feel free to peel yours if you prefer. Try swapping out apples for plums or pitted cherries (frozen cherries work especially well for convenience).*

✤ *Store in an airtight container or wrapped in plastic wrap at room temperature for 2 to 3 days, in the fridge for up to 6 days, or in the freezer for up to 3 months. Reheat at 350°F (180°C) until warm, about 5 minutes. If frozen, thaw at room temperature for 2 to 3 hours, before reheating.*

Kaffee & Kuchen

Rhabarberstreusel

Rhubarb Streusel Cake

PREP TIME: 25 minutes, plus 1 hour resting

COOK TIME: 30 minutes

YIELD: 16 slices

My Mama Ute is the ultimate rhubarb fanatic in my life. She's the one who taught me to love rhubarb, so I always think of her when I make this cake. While my mom doesn't cook many traditional German dishes, her fun and experimental approach to baking and cooking very much inspires me. I know you will love the sweet and tart flavors in this cake, with the fluffy yeast-raised base and the crunchy-sweet streusel topping. While rhubarb is my favorite for this cake, you can swap in fresh, frozen, or canned apples, apricots, plums, cherries, blueberries, raspberries, currants . . . the possibilities are endless!

RHUBARB CAKE

2 teaspoons active dry yeast (1 packet)

1 cup (240 ml) lukewarm milk

4 cups (500 g) all-purpose flour

⅓ cup (75 g) granulated sugar, plus more for sprinkling (optional)

1 teaspoon salt

Grated zest of ½ lemon

1 large egg

7 tablespoons unsalted butter, at room temperature

4 large or 8 to 10 small stalks rhubarb, cut into 1-inch (2.5 cm) pieces (see Notes)

STREUSEL TOPPING

2 cups (250 g) all-purpose flour

¾ cup (150 g) granulated sugar

⅔ cup (150 g) unsalted butter

1 pinch salt

1 teaspoon vanilla extract

Whipped cream, homemade (page 9) or store-bought, for serving

1. **Make the rhubarb cake:** In a small bowl, combine the yeast and milk. Let it activate for about 5 minutes until bubbly.

2. In the bowl of a stand mixer fitted with the dough hook attachment, sift together the flour, sugar, and salt. Add the yeast mixture, lemon zest, egg, and butter and mix at low speed until a smooth, elastic dough forms, 5 to 10 minutes; it shouldn't stick to the sides of the bowl. Cover the bowl tightly and let the dough rest in a warm spot until doubled in size, about 1 hour.

3. Preheat the oven to 390°F (200°C) and line a 13 by 18-inch (33 by 46 cm) rimmed baking sheet with parchment paper.

4. **Meanwhile, make the streusel topping:** In a large bowl, combine the flour, sugar, butter, salt, and vanilla. Using an electric hand mixer, mix at medium speed to combine. Using your hands, crumble the mixture, forming the streusel.

5. Turn the dough out onto the prepared baking sheet. Using your hands, spread it in an even layer to cover the entire surface of the prepared baking sheet. Evenly distribute the rhubarb on top. If desired, sprinkle a little sugar on top like my Oma did (though I think the streusel adds enough sweetness), then the streusel topping.

6. Bake on the middle rack until the edges and streusel start to brown and a cake tester or a toothpick inserted into the center of the cake comes out clean, about 30 minutes. Let cool for 10 minutes before cutting into 16 squares. Serve warm or at room temperature with whipped cream.

NOTES

✤ *There's no need to peel rhubarb, especially if it's early in the season.*

✤ *The cake freezes very well—perfect for satisfying rhubarb cravings (and sugar lows) long after the season ends. Store it in freezer-safe containers or bags. Thaw at room temperature for 2 to 3 hours, then reheat it in a 350ºF (180ºC) oven for 5 minutes to restore its fluffy texture.*

Marmorkuchen

German Marble Cake

This fluffy vanilla-and-chocolate marble cake, enhanced with hints of rum and lemon, and finished with a luxurious chocolate glaze, was my twin sister and my most favorite birthday cake when we were growing up. We'd go wild decorating it with sprinkles, chocolate candies, and gummy bears. But it's just as perfect without all the extras. Enjoy it fresh out of the oven, simply dusted with some powdered sugar, or covered in a rich dark chocolate glaze, which helps lock in moisture. The quality of the cocoa powder and chocolate chips really makes all the difference, so I would not cut corners here!

PREP TIME: 20 minutes

COOK TIME: 40 to 55 minutes (see Note)

YIELD: 12 slices

CAKE BATTER

7 tablespoons unsalted butter

1½ cups (300 g) granulated sugar, divided

1 teaspoon vanilla extract

1 teaspoon freshly grated lemon zest

1 ounce (30 ml) spiced rum

6 large eggs, whites and yolks separated

1 pinch salt

2¼ cups (280 g) all-purpose flour

2 teaspoons baking powder

3½ ounces (100 ml) plus 1½ tablespoons whole milk, divided

¼ cup (20 g) good-quality cocoa powder

CHOCOLATE GLAZE (OPTIONAL)

¾ cup (140 g) good-quality semisweet chocolate chips

3 tablespoons unsalted butter, cubed

1. Preheat the oven to 310°F (155°C) on the convection (umluft) setting or 335°F (170°C) for a non-convection oven. Line the bottom and sides of a 4 by 10-inch (10 by 25 cm) loaf pan with parchment paper, leaving some overhang on the long sides.

2. **Make the vanilla cake batter:** In the bowl of a stand mixer fitted with the paddle attachment, mix the butter, ¾ cup (150 g) of the sugar, the vanilla, lemon zest, and spiced rum at medium-high speed until creamy, scraping down the sides of the bowl as needed, about 3 minutes. With the mixer at medium speed, add 1 egg yolk at a time until incorporated.

3. In a separate bowl of a stand mixer, switching to the whisk attachment (or in a large bowl using an electric hand mixer), beat the egg whites and a pinch of salt at high speed until soft peaks form, about 4 minutes. Gradually add the remaining ¾ cup (150 g) sugar and beat until glossy, stiff peaks form, about 4 minutes.

4. In a medium bowl, sift together the flour and baking powder. Switch back to the paddle attachment on the stand mixer with the butter mixture. Add half of the flour mixture and mix at low speed until combined, scraping down the sides of the bowl as needed, about 1 minute. Add 3½ ounces (100 ml) of the milk; mix at low speed until combined, about 1 minute. Add the beaten egg whites and the remaining flour mixture; mix at low speed until no lumps of flour or streaks of egg white remain, about 1 minute. Transfer half of the batter to the prepared pan.

5. **Make the chocolate cake batter:** Sift the cocoa powder into the remaining batter, fold in the remaining 1½ tablespoons milk until thoroughly combined; spoon over the vanilla cake batter. Using a fork, swirl the batters together, creating a marbled effect.

German Home Kitchen

6. Bake on the middle rack until a cake tester inserted into the center comes out clean, 40 to 55 minutes. (Rotate the cake halfway through if using a non-convection oven.) Cool on a wire rack for 5 minutes. Then invert the pan and gently jiggle the cake onto the rack.

7. **Make the chocolate glaze (if using):** In a double boiler over low heat or a metal bowl over a saucepan of boiling water, whisk the chocolate until just melted. Add the butter and whisk until smooth; the glaze should be thick but spreadable. Spread the glaze over the cake (the cake does not need to be cool before glazing). Gently tap the cooling rack on the countertop to encourage the glaze to run down the sides of the cake. Decorate (or don't) as desired.

NOTE

✣ *Store leftover cake at room temperature in an airtight container, under a cake dome, or sealed with plastic wrap for 3 days or refrigerate for up to 1 week. This cake also freezes well. Store slices in freezer-safe containers or bags for up to 3 months. Thaw at room temperature for 2 to 3 hours before serving.*

Kaffee & Kuchen

Rotweinbirnenkuchen

Red Wine Pear Cake

PREP TIME: 20 minutes
COOK TIME: 40 minutes
YIELD: 12 slices

When I left Germany to become an exchange student, a friend gave me a homemade red wine cake as a farewell present. I know—such a sweet German thing to do. I love red wine cake on its own, but my absolute favorite version includes pears. This mildly spiced cake is freckled with chocolate bits and baked with whole, cored pears nestled inside. The result is a beautifully rustic, moist cake that's best served with spoonfuls of whipped cream (a must!). Let me do some girl math for you: Juicy Pears + Rich Chocolate + Red Wine + Fluffy Whipped Cream = Heaven.

¾ cup plus 2 tablespoons (200 g) unsalted butter, plus more for greasing

1 cup (200 g) granulated sugar

2 teaspoons vanilla extract

1 tablespoon spiced rum

4 large eggs

2 cups (250 g) all-purpose flour, plus more for dusting

2 tablespoons cocoa powder

2 teaspoons baking powder

½ teaspoon ground cinnamon

½ teaspoon salt

3½ ounces (100 g) semisweet chocolate chips or chocolate bar (35 to 65% cocoa), chopped into small chunks

½ cup (120 ml) red wine (any kind you like)

4 small, very ripe pears, such as Bosc or Anjou, at room temperature (see Notes)

Powdered sugar, for dusting

Whipped cream, homemade (page 9) or store-bought, for serving

1. Preheat the oven to 350°F (180°C). Place a piece of parchment paper on the bottom of a 9-inch (23 cm) springform pan, secure the ring around it, and trim any excess paper. Grease the sides of the pan with butter and dust with flour. (Alternatively, grease a 9-inch (23 cm) cake pan, line the bottom with a parchment paper circle, then dust the sides with flour.)

2. In the bowl of a stand mixer fitted with the paddle attachment (or in a large bowl using an electric hand mixer), beat the butter and granulated sugar at medium-high speed, scraping down the sides of the bowl as needed, until light and fluffy, about 5 minutes. Add the vanilla and rum, and with the mixer at medium speed, add one egg at a time, until incorporated.

3. In a medium bowl, sift together the flour, cocoa powder, baking powder, cinnamon, and salt. Stir in the chocolate chips, making sure they are evenly coated; add to the butter mixture and whisk until a thick batter forms. Add the wine and continue whisking until no dry bits remain. Transfer to the prepared springform pan and smooth out the top.

4. Using a small cookie scoop or spoon, core each pear from the bottom end while keeping the stem intact. With the stems facing up, push the pears into the batter until they touch the bottom of the pan.

5. Bake on the middle rack until a cake tester inserted into the center comes out clean, 40 to 50 minutes. Cool on a wire rack for about 5 minutes. To remove, run a thin knife around the edges, loosen the springform ring, and carefully lift out the cake with the parchment still attached. Let cool on the wire rack for at least 15 minutes before slicing. Remove the parchment paper.

6. Dust with powdered sugar, slice, and serve with whipped cream.

NOTES

✤ *If your pears aren't soft yet and you don't want to wait, you can poach them first before using them in the recipe. But, trust me, the result of making this cake with fresh, ripe pears is definitely worth the wait!*

✤ *To store, let the cake cool completely, about 2 hours, before wrapping it in plastic wrap or storing it under a cake dome to keep it moist.*

Kaffee & Kuchen

Tante Heidruns Mandarinen-Schmand-Kuchen

Mandarin Orange Sour Cream Cake

PREP TIME: 30 minutes, plus 4 hours cooling

COOK TIME: 20 minutes

YIELD: About 20 slices

I loved spending summer afternoons at my aunt Heidrun's house for two main reasons: sunbathing with my cousin Anna by their private pool (a rare luxury in Germany) and eating a few slices of this mandarin orange sour cream cake; it always lit me up when my aunt made it. Years later, these are still two of my favorite things to do—only now, my cousin and I have our own kids splashing in the pool and we have to share this cake with them. The cake has a soft, moist base, a bright mandarin orange filling, and a creamy, just-sweet-enough frosting. A final sprinkle of cinnamon sugar ties it all together. One of the best things about this cake is that you can make it year-round thanks to canned mandarin oranges, which bring a refreshing citrus flavor.

CAKE

3 large eggs, yolks and whites separated

1 pinch salt

1½ cups (300 g) granulated sugar

¾ cup (180 ml) avocado oil

2¼ cups (270 g) all-purpose flour

2 teaspoons baking powder

¾ cup (180 ml) juice from canned mandarin oranges

MANDARIN ORANGE FILLING

5 cans (10½ ounces, or 300 g, each) mandarin oranges in juice, fruit and juice separated and 2 cups (480 ml) juice reserved, divided

¼ cup (25 g) cornstarch

1 teaspoon vanilla extract

1. Preheat the oven to 350°F (180°C) and grease a 13 by 18-inch (33 by 46 cm) cake pan (see Notes) and line the bottom with parchment paper.

2. **Make the cake:** In the bowl of a stand mixer fitted with the whisk attachment, beat the egg whites and a pinch of salt at medium-high speed until stiff peaks form.

3. In a large bowl, whisk the granulated sugar, oil, flour, baking powder, and juice until smooth. Fold in the egg whites until just combined and no white streaks remain. Transfer the batter to the prepared pan.

4. Bake until the top starts to turn golden and a cake tester or toothpick inserted into the center of the cake comes out clean, 18 to 20 minutes. Remove from the pan and transfer on the parchment to a wire rack to cool completely, about 2 hours.

5. **Meanwhile, make the mandarin orange filling:** Place the oranges in a large bowl. In a small bowl, whisk together ½ cup (120 ml) of the reserved mandarin juice with the cornstarch. In a small saucepan, heat the remaining 1½ cups (360 ml) reserved mandarin juice to boiling over high heat, then whisk in the cornstarch mixture. Continue boiling, stirring constantly, until thickened to a pudding-like consistency, about 1 minute. Transfer to the bowl with the mandarin oranges. Stir in the vanilla and mix gently until everything is evenly incorporated. Let cool completely, about 2 hours.

German Home Kitchen

FROSTING

⅓ cup (40 g) powdered sugar

2 teaspoons vanilla extract

2 cups (480 ml) heavy cream

3 cups (720 ml) sour cream (see Note)

TOPPING

⅓ cup (75 g) granulated sugar

1 teaspoon ground cinnamon

6. **Meanwhile, make the frosting:** In the bowl of a stand mixer fitted with the whisk attachment (or in a large bowl and using an electric hand mixer), beat the powdered sugar, vanilla, and heavy cream at high speed until stiff peaks form, 2 to 3 minutes. Gently fold in the sour cream until just combined. Refrigerate until ready to assemble.

7. **To make the topping:** In a small bowl, stir together the granulated sugar and cinnamon.

8. **Assemble the cake:** Remove the parchment and either return the cake to the pan or place it on a platter with a rectangular cake ring. Evenly spread the mandarin orange mixture over the cooled cake. Top with the frosting, then sprinkle with the cinnamon-sugar mixture. Refrigerate for 2 hours before slicing and serving. (This cake tastes great the next day but doesn't keep well beyond that, and it is not freezer-friendly.)

NOTE

❖ *The cake is traditionally made with Schmand, German sour cream, which has a fat content of 20 to 29% as opposed to American sour cream which has 16% fat content. Light sour cream (8% fat) works as well, but regular sour cream makes the frosting creamier.*

Erdbeerrolle

Sponge Cake with Strawberries and Cream Filling

This fluffy, rolled German sponge cake filled with whipped strawberry cream is surprisingly quick and easy to make. It's a go-to in our family for birthdays and as an afternoon treat, especially in late spring and summer when strawberries are in season. In fact, it was our littlest one's first birthday cake—much less sweet than typical American birthday cakes—and Maximilian loved it! The recipe is flexible and can be adjusted to suit the season or your preferences (see Notes for ideas), but the strawberry filling is always a winner!

PREP TIME: 30 minutes, plus 30 minutes resting
COOK TIME: 10 minutes
YIELD: 12 slices

SPONGE CAKE

5 large eggs, whites and yolks separated

1 pinch salt

½ cup (100 g) granulated sugar, divided, plus more for sprinkling

Grated zest of 1 lemon

⅔ cup (80 g) all-purpose flour

¼ cup (30 g) cornstarch

½ teaspoon baking powder

STRAWBERRIES AND CREAM FILLING

1⅔ cups (400 ml) heavy cream

½ cup (50 g) powdered sugar, plus extra for dusting

1 teaspoon vanilla extract

8 ounces (230 g) fresh strawberries, trimmed and chopped, plus 4 ounces (120 g) pureed

½ cup (120 ml) strawberry jam

1. **Make the sponge cake:** Preheat the oven to 390°F (200°C) and line a baking sheet with parchment paper.

2. In the bowl of a stand mixer fitted with the whisk attachment, beat the egg whites and a pinch of salt at high speed until soft peaks form, about 2 minutes. With the mixer at low speed, gradually add 6 tablespoons (75 g) of the sugar. Continue whisking at high speed until glossy, stiff peaks form, about 4 minutes.

3. In a large bowl, whisk the egg yolks, remaining 2 tablespoons granulated sugar, and lemon zest until creamy, about 2 minutes. Sift together the flour, cornstarch, and baking powder right into the yolk mixture and stir until no lumps remain. Gently fold in the egg whites until just combined and no white streaks remain. (Avoid overmixing, as it can deflate the egg whites.) Spread the batter in an even layer on the prepared baking sheet.

4. Bake until the top is lightly golden and the cake springs back when lightly pressed in the center, about 10 minutes. Meanwhile, lay out a clean kitchen towel, about 15 by 20 inches (38 by 50 cm), on a work surface and sprinkle with granulated sugar. Once the cake is done, immediately flip it onto the prepared towel. Leave the parchment paper on and let cool completely, about 30 minutes.

5. **Make the strawberries and cream filling:** In a large bowl, add the cream, powdered sugar, and vanilla and, using an electric hand mixer with the whisk attachments, beat at high speed until stiff peaks form, 2 to 3 minutes. Fold in the strawberry purée and chopped strawberries.

6. In a small saucepan over medium-low heat, warm the jam until loosened up and easy to stir. Remove the parchment paper from the cake. Spread the jam evenly onto the cake and let cool for about 5 minutes. Spread the filling over the jam.

7. With the long side of the cake facing you, use the towel to help roll the cake into a tight log. Carefully transfer to a serving platter, seam side down. Wipe the platter clean. Dust the cake with powdered sugar. Slice and serve tableside. Optional: For a more polished look, trim the ends.

NOTE

❖ *Substitute mixed berries for strawberries, or swap rhubarb compote for pureed strawberries.*

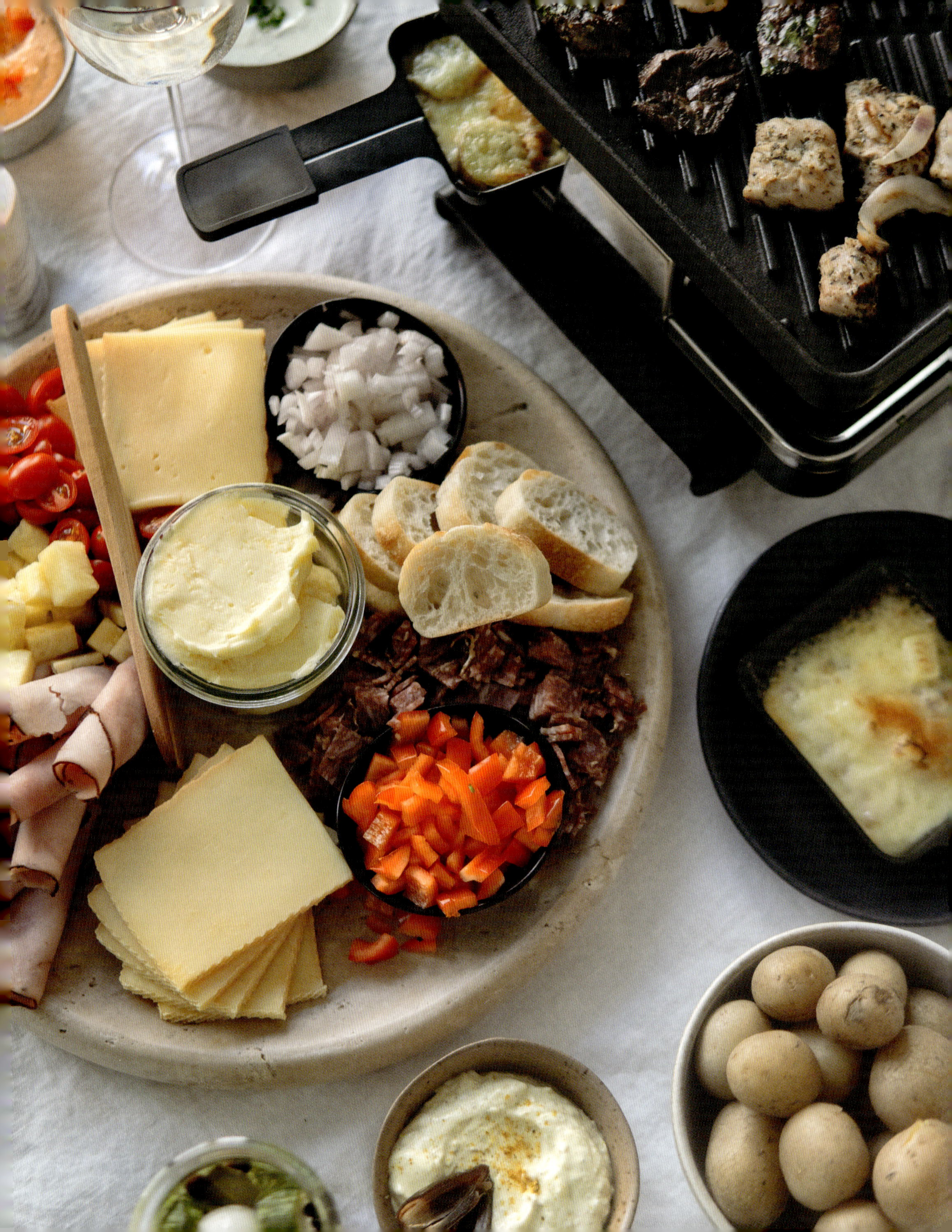

WEIHNACHTEN

>> *Christmas* <<

There is nothing quite like Christmas in Germany—twinkle lights strung across the streets, the warm scent of sweet spices in the air, and cherished celebrations like St. Nicholas Day morning and the most magical Christmas Eve. It can also be a bittersweet time of year for those spending the season far from family. If that's you, consider the recipes in this love-filled chapter a warm hug.

Vanillekipferl

Vanilla Bean Cookies

Vanillekipferl are my favorite German Christmas cookies, and my Oma Sieghilde made at least one batch every Christmas season. I think it's because they're quick and easy to make, buttery, and perfectly sweet. Using real vanilla bean adds the coziest flavor.

PREP TIME: 15 minutes, plus 1 hour resting
COOK TIME: 12 minutes
YIELD: 40 cookies

---

1 vanilla bean (see Notes)

15 tablespoons (210 g) unsalted butter, at room temperature

¾ cup plus 2 tablespoons (100 g) almond flour (see Notes)

⅓ cup (70 g) granulated sugar

½ teaspoon (3 g) salt (not traditional, but I love it)

2 cups (250 g) all-purpose flour, plus more for dusting

Powdered sugar, sifted, for topping

1. With a sharp knife, cut the vanilla bean lengthwise in half, then scrape out the seeds.

2. In a medium bowl, add the vanilla seeds, butter, almond flour, granulated sugar, salt, and all-purpose flour. Using your hands, knead until a smooth dough forms. Divide the dough into 2 equal pieces.

3. On a lightly floured surface, roll out each piece into a log 10 inches (25 cm) long. Wrap the logs separately in parchment paper or plastic wrap and refrigerate for 1 hour.

4. Preheat the oven to 390° F (200° C). Line two baking sheets with parchment paper.

5. On a clean work surface, cut each log crosswise ½-inch-thick (12 mm) slices; you should have 20 slices per log. Roll each slice into pencil-thick rope, about 2-inches (5 cm) long, with tapered ends, then curve the ends in to make crescent moons. Don't make the ends too thin, as they can burn easily. Arrange the cookies on the prepared baking sheets, 20 cookies per sheet.

6. Bake on the two racks closest to the middle of the oven until just starting to brown on the ends, 9 to 11 minutes. Transfer to a wire rack to cool completely. Once cool, either roll (Oma's way) or dust (my preferred way) them in powdered sugar.

NOTES

❖ Don't have a vanilla bean? Use 1 tablespoon of vanilla paste instead. Never waste a scraped vanilla bean! Use it to make Vanilla Sugar (see page 7).

❖ For the traditional pale-yellow appearance, use blanched almond flour (with skins removed). You can use ground almonds or almond meal (with skins), but it will make the cookies darker. Both taste great!

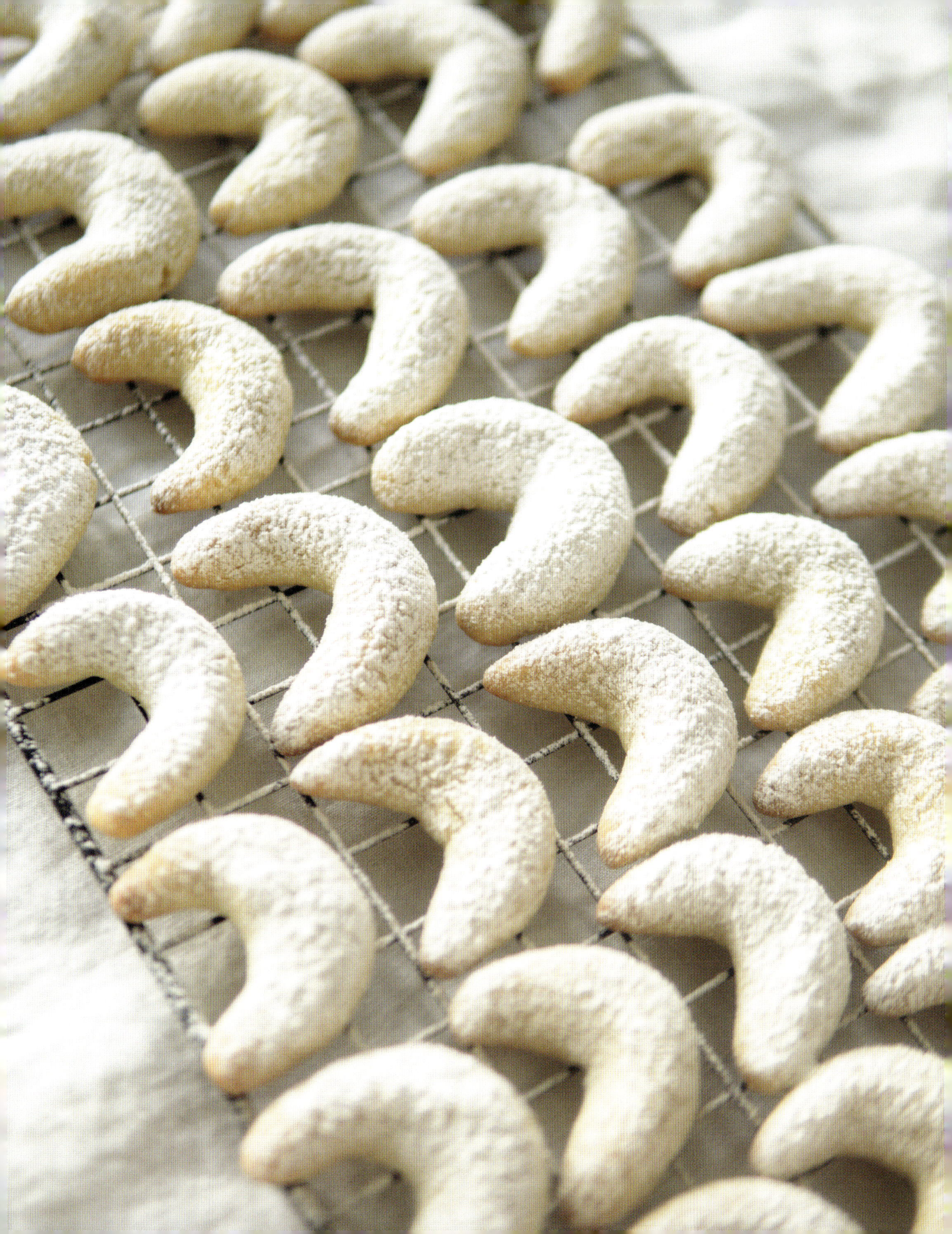

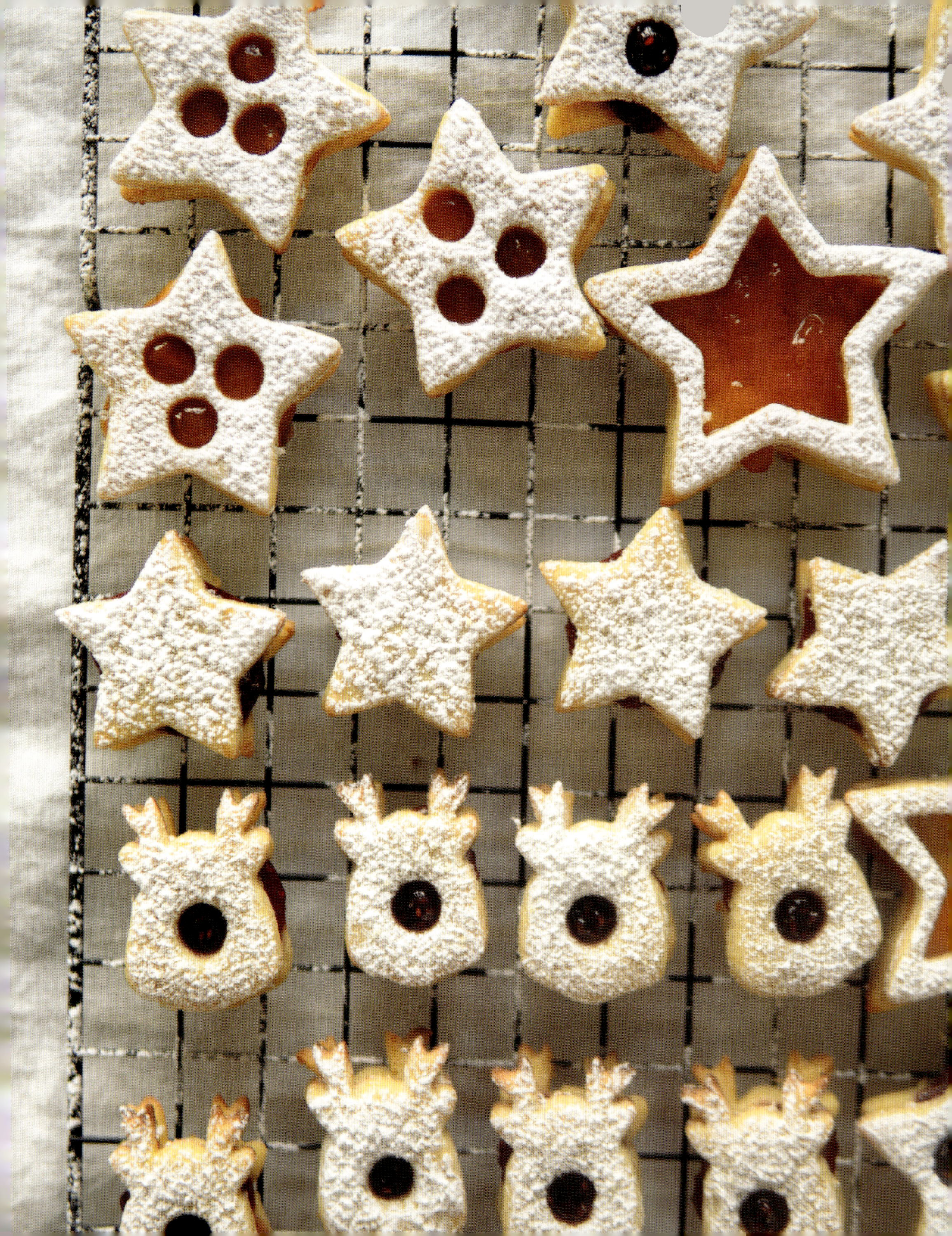

Spitzbuben

Jam-Filled Cookies

I used to make spitzbuben with my Oma Sieghilde every year. These buttery, flaky, jam-filled cookies dusted with powdered sugar have long been a family favorite, and you will be so happy that you put spitzbuben on your baking list this year! As for the jam filling, just use your favorite flavor. I love raspberry, apricot, or cherry.

PREP TIME: 20 minutes, plus 1 hour resting

COOK TIME: 8 minutes

YIELD: 40 (3-inch, or 7.5 cm) cookies

---

3 hard-cooked eggs, yolks only

2 large egg yolks

¾ cup plus 2 tablespoons (200 g) unsalted butter, at room temperature

½ teaspoon salt (not traditional, but I love it)

⅔ cup (140 g) granulated sugar

Freshly grated zest of ½ lemon

2½ cups (300 g) all-purpose flour, plus more for dusting

1 tablespoon whole milk

Powdered sugar, for dusting

3½ ounces (105 ml) jam of choice

NOTES

❖ If your jam is thick, warm it slightly to make it easier to spread.

❖ For storage, layer the cookies between sheets of parchment or wax paper to prevent sticking. Store in a cookie jar for up to 3 weeks (but there's no way they'll last that long!).

1. Using the back of a spoon, press the yolks of the hard-cooked eggs through a fine-mesh sieve (the finer, the better) set over a medium bowl. Add the egg yolks. Using a fork, stir until a smooth paste forms. Add the butter, salt, granulated sugar, and lemon zest; whisk until incorporated. Add the flour and milk and, using your hands, knead until a smooth dough forms. Wrap the dough in plastic wrap and refrigerate for 1 hour.

2. Preheat the oven to 390°F (200°C). Line two baking sheets with parchment paper or silicone baking mats.

3. On a lightly floured work surface, roll out the dough to ⅛-inch (3 mm) thickness. Cut out 40 of your favorite shapes (this number could change, depending on the size of your cookie cutters; just remember that each cookie needs a top and a bottom). Cut a small hole in the centers of the tops. (You can use a special cookie cutter or create your own peek-a-boo holes.) Arrange the cookie tops on one of the prepared baking sheets and the bottoms on the other.

4. Bake on two racks closest to the middle of the oven, until just golden around the edges, 8 to 10 minutes (the tops will brown about 1 minute faster). If baking one sheet at a time, reduce the bake time by about 1 minute. Let cool on the baking sheets until firm and cool enough to handle, about 5 minutes, then lift the parchment paper with the cookies still on it and transfer to a wire rack to finish cooling.

5. Dust the cookie tops with powdered sugar. Spread about ½ teaspoon of jam on each bottom cookie and place a sugar-dusted cookie on top.

Glühwein

Mulled Wine

PREP TIME: 5 minutes, plus 10 minutes steeping

YIELD: 4 servings

This is the coziest, most delicious drink to help you warm up. Served at every German Christmas market, Glühwein fills the air with the most wonderful scent. We love making a batch while decorating our home for Christmas. In just 10 minutes of steeping, the sweet scent of citrus and spices in wine fills your home and transports you to Germany. Best of all, it's as easy as making tea!

---

1 bottle (750 ml) wine (see Note)

1 medium organic lemon, cut into thin slices

2 strips (3 by ½ inches each) orange peel (see Notes)

3 tablespoons granulated sugar

1 cinnamon stick

3 whole cloves

1 cardamom pod or 1 pinch ground cardamom

Rum, cognac, or schnapps (optional)

1. In a medium saucepan over medium heat, warm the wine until it just begins to boil. Remove from the heat. Add the lemon slices, orange peel, sugar, cinnamon stick, cloves, and cardamom; stir. Cover the pan and let steep for 10 minutes.

2. Using a skimmer, remove and discard the fruit and spices. Serve warm, adding a shot of rum, cognac or schnapps (if using). In case there is any left, keep it warm over low heat.

NOTE

✦ *Red and white glühwein are both common in Germany. For red, use a low-tannin wine like Pinot Noir or Merlot. For white, use a dry Riesling or other dry, unoaked whites. For both versions, don't use the best wine, but don't use bad wine either.*

Raclette

Tableside Cheese Meal

PREP TIME: 1 hour, plus 4 hours marinating

COOK TIME: 1 hour

YIELD: 1 raclette dinner

I can't remember a Christmas Eve or New Year's Eve without raclette on the table. The ultra-cheesy tableside dinner experience is popular in Germany because everyone gets to eat whatever they want—the only rule being that everything gets smothered in melted cheese. Raclette is the Swiss cheese that gives this traditional Swiss meal its name. While the Swiss keep it simple—melting the cheese on a grill and scraping it over boiled potatoes and vegetables—we use a raclette grill, which has a stone or cast-iron cooktop for grilling vegetables and marinated meats, plus individual pans for layering toppings and melting cheese over everything. There really isn't a better way to enjoy German-style raclette than with a tableside grill, so just get one (I promise you won't regret it!). I stock up on raclette cheese as soon as it hits store shelves. It keeps well, and leftovers are great in omelets, on pizza, in pasta sauce, or in anything that loves a good cheese. Don't judge raclette by the way it smells before cooking—it can be intense, but it's really the perfect, most delicious cheese for melting.

TOPPINGS *(Everything except the Raclette and potatoes is up to you!)*

Raclette cheese (see Notes)

Boiled mini potatoes

Sliced ham (typically cooked, smoked ham)

Garlic butter (I always start by putting some in the bottom of my raclette pan—it makes all the difference.)

Salami (Not traditional, but THE KIDS LOVE IT.)

Mixed Pickles (page 46) or Gewürzgurken (page 91)

Fresh pineapple, cut into bite-size pieces (Raclette Hawaii!)

Bell pepper, cut into bite-size pieces

Tomatoes, cut into small pieces, or cherry or grape tomatoes, halved

Onions, small diced (Just have extra handy. We like to use them a lot.)

Store-bought marinated mushrooms (Good for grilling, as they don't always heat through in the raclette pan.)

Canned corn (It's my sister's favorite.)

Crusty, white bread, like Weizenbrötchen (page 16) (I love sliding the hot, melty contents of my raclette pan onto a slice of bread.)

Salad greens and herb vinaigrette from Gemischter Salat (page 48)

Quark Dips (page 87) (They make the best sauces for meat and potatoes—the curry-date quark pairs well with pork and shrimp, while the spicy pepper quark and the chive quark go with any meat.)

Weihnachten

SCHWENKBRATEN-STYLE PORK

2 boneless thin-cut pork loin chops, trimmed and cut into bite-size pieces

1 shallot, finely chopped

1 clove garlic, minced

¼ teaspoon dried thyme

1 teaspoon dried oregano

¼ teaspoon ground cloves

¼ teaspoon ground allspice

1 tablespoon extra-virgin olive oil

½ teaspoon salt

¼ teaspoon ground black pepper

In a small bowl, add the pork, shallot, garlic, thyme, oregano, cloves, allspice, oil, salt, and pepper; using your hands, toss to coat evenly. Cover and refrigerate for at least 4 hours and up to 1 day.

CHIMICHURRI-INSPIRED STEAK

¾ pound (340 g) steak (your choice, we use rib eye or New York strip), cut into bite-size pieces

1 tablespoon extra-virgin olive oil

½ tablespoon red wine vinegar

1 clove garlic, minced

2 tablespoons chopped fresh parsley

¼ teaspoon crushed red pepper

¼ teaspoon dried oregano

½ teaspoon salt

¼ teaspoon ground black pepper

In a small bowl, add the steak, oil, vinegar, garlic, parsley, crushed red pepper, oregano, salt, and black pepper; using your hands, toss to coat evenly. Cover and refrigerate for at least 4 hours and up to 1 day.

LEMON-GARLIC SHRIMP

1 pound (455 g) shrimp, peeled and deveined

1 tablespoon extra-virgin olive oil

1 tablespoon fresh lemon juice

2 cloves garlic, minced

1 tablespoon chopped fresh parsley

½ teaspoon salt

¼ teaspoon ground black pepper

In a small bowl, add the shrimp, oil, lemon juice, garlic, parsley, salt, and pepper; using your hands, toss to coat evenly. Cover and refrigerate for 30 minutes before cooking.

TO SERVE

1. Arrange all of the toppings on platters with serving utensils.

2. Grill the marinated meats in batches and distribute when cooked. (To avoid cross-contamination, raw meat should never touch anything but the grill.)

3. Mix and match your favorite toppings, melt raclette over everything, and enjoy!

NOTES

✤ *Plan 1 package of raclette cheese for every 2 people, or about 6 slices per person. Kids will likely eat less depending on their age.*

✤ *Plan on ½ pound (227 g) of meat or seafood per person. Make sure everything is cut into even, bite-size pieces.*

✤ *Prep the raw meat first, as it needs time to marinate (except for shrimp). For a vegetarian raclette, marinate vegetables, tofu, or mushrooms.*

✤ *Small toppings work best so they get a chance to soften in the raclette pans while the cheese melts on top, so aim for bite-size pieces when you're cutting things up.*

✤ *To avoid cross-contamination, we simply grill meat in batches, then distribute it when cooked. This way, only one person needs to handle raw meat.*

✤ *If you can't find raclette cheese, good substitutes include mild or aged Swiss cheeses (such as Emmentaler and Gruyère), Gouda, Cheddar, or mozzarella.*

Weihnachten

Käsefondue

Cheese Fondue

PREP TIME: 30 minutes
COOK TIME: 10 minutes
YIELD: 4 servings

I have so many memories of my mom running around frantically on Christmas Eve because her cheese fondue had split—leaving us with a glob of cheese swimming in wine. Fast-forward to today, and this was one of the first recipes I set out to perfect just for her. With this recipe, you will get consistent, stress-free results and fondue parties filled with happy dancing (and happy stomachs). Every. Single. Time. If you don't have a fondue set, place a small saucepan on either a teapot warmer (with a tealight) or an electric warming plate (easier to control the heat) and use regular forks for dipping.

1½ pounds (700 g) imported Swiss cheese, shredded (see Notes)

3 tablespoons cornstarch

3 cloves garlic, 1 halved and 2 minced, divided

1½ cups (360 ml) dry white wine (see Notes)

1½ tablespoons fresh lemon juice

2 tablespoons Kirschwasser

¾ teaspoon dry mustard or 1½ teaspoons Dijon mustard

1 teaspoon freshly grated nutmeg

Salt

DIPPERS

1 loaf Roggenmischbrot (page 82), cut into 1-inch (2.5 cm) cubes and covered with a clean linen napkin to keep from drying out

8 ounces (125 g) dry-aged ham, such as Prosciutto di Parma, thinly sliced

8 ounces (125 g) sliced salami

1. In a large bowl, toss the shredded cheese with the cornstarch until evenly coated.

2. If using a fondue pot that's stovetop-safe, place it directly on the burner; otherwise, use a medium saucepan. Rub the inside of the pot with the halved garlic clove, then discard the garlic. Add the wine and lemon juice and heat to a gentle simmer over medium heat. Gradually add the cheese, using a wooden spoon to stir in a figure-eight motion (a trick I ironically learned from my mom!) until smooth, about 5 minutes. (Adding the cheese gradually and melting it slowly ensures a smooth fondue.)

3. Once smooth, stir in the minced garlic, Kirschwasser, mustard, and nutmeg. Season with salt to taste. Place the fondue pot on the warmer and keep on a low flame (or on low heat if using an electric warmer).

4. **To serve:** Pick up dippers with the fondue forks, dip into the fondue, swirl, and enjoy. Dropped a dipper in the cheese? Take a shot of Kirschwasser! At least that was a rule in my family!

1 cup (150 g) Gewürzgurken (page 91) or Mixed Pickles (page 46)

2 pears (we like Bartlett) or apples (we like Granny Smith), cubed and tossed with a squeeze of lemon juice

2 large red or orange bell peppers, cores and seeds removed and cut into bite-size pieces

2 cups (290 g) cherry tomatoes

1½ pounds (680 g) boiled mini potatoes (serve these hot!)

NOTES

❖ *Traditional cheeses to use are Emmentaler, Gruyère, Appenzeller, Comté, Bergkäse. It's important to keep a mix of mostly harder, aged cheeses (like aged Gruyère or aged Emmentaler) and some younger cheeses like young Emmentaler.*

❖ *Typical Swiss wines for cheese fondue include Chasselas, Fendant, Riesling-Sylvaner, Müller-Thurgau. Riesling, the grape I grew up with in Trier, is also a great pairing.*

❖ *Refrigerate any leftover cheese in an airtight container for up to 3 days or in the freezer for up to 3 months. Thaw in the fridge 1 to 2 days before reheating. Reheat in a fondue pot or double boiler over medium heat, stirring occasionally.*

Weihnachten

Recipe Index by Keyword

Here's a quick way to reference the recipes in this book, whether you want to make something in advance, quick for a weeknight meal, as a gift, for a dinner party, and more!

FREEZER-FRIENDLY

Weizenbrötchen (White Rolls), 16
Kürbiskernbrötchen (Pumpkin Seed Rolls), 18
Müslibrötchen (Granola Rolls), 20
Plunderteig (German Croissant Dough), 25
Franzbrötchen (Croissant-Style Cinnamon Rolls), 28
Laugenecken (Lye Pastries), 30
Leberwurst (Liver Paté), 32
Pflaumenmus (Plum Butter), 34
Brezeln (Pretzels), 39
Rotkohl (Braised Red Cabbage), 59
Sauerbraten (Sweet-and-Sour Beef Roast), 64
Linsensuppe (Lentil Soup), 68
Rinderrouladen (Beef Roulade), 70
Kohlrouladen (Stuffed Cabbage Rolls), 72
Jägerschnitzel (Pork Schnitzel with Creamy Mushroom Sauce), 78
Roggenmischbrot (Rye and Wheat Bread), 82
Körnerbrot (Seeded Bread), 85
Milchreis (Rice Pudding), 96
Saure Sahne Waffeln (Sour Cream Waffles), 99
Chicken Döner Kebab (Meat-Stuffed Bread Pockets), 105
Frikadellen (German Hamburgers), 108
Klößchen (Mini Potato Dumplings), 117
Erbsbrei (Mashed Peas), 118
Baumkuchen (Tree Cake), 126
Hefezopf (Yeast Braid), 130
Blaubeer Quarkstrudel (Quark and Blueberry Strudel), 133
Schwarzwälder Kirschtorte (Black Forest Cherry Cake), 135
Rote Grütze (Berry Grits), 141
Käsekuchen im Glas (Raspberry Cheesecake in a Jar), 142
Apfelkuchen (Apple Cake), 144
Rhabarberstreusel (Rhubarb Streusel Cake), 146
Marmorkuchen (German Marble Cake), 148

Erdbeerrolle (Sponge Cake with Strawberries and Cream Filling), 154
Vanillekipferl (Vanilla Bean Cookies), 158
Spitzbuben (Jam-Filled Cookies), 161
Käsefondue (Cheese Fondue), 166

GIFTABLE

Franzbrötchen (Croissant-Style Cinnamon Rolls), 28
Laugenecken (Lye Pastries), 30
Leberwurst (Liver Paté), 32
Pflaumenmus (Plum Butter), 34
Mixed Pickles (Pickled Vegetables), 47
Sauerkraut (Fermented Cabbage), 60
Roggenmischbrot (Rye and Wheat Bread), 82
Körnerbrot (Seeded Bread), 85
Fleischsalat (Bologna Salad), 90
Gewürzgurken (Sweet-and-Sour Pickles), 91
Chicken Döner Kebab (Meat-Stuffed Bread Pockets), 105
Pommesgewürz (German Fry Seasoning), 107
Zwiebelkuchen (Onion Pie), 122
Baumkuchen (Tree Cake), 126
Hefezopf (Yeast Braid), 130
Schwarzwälder Kirschtorte (Black Forest Cherry Cake), 135
Rote Grütze (Berry Grits), 141
Käsekuchen im Glas (Raspberry Cheesecake in a Jar), 142
Marmorkuchen (German Marble Cake), 148
Rotweinbirnenkuchen (Red Wine Pear Cake), 150
Erdbeerrolle (Sponge Cake with Strawberries and Cream Filling), 154
Spitzbuben (Jam-Filled Cookies), 161

HOSTING

Leberwurst (Liver Paté), 32
Brezeln (Pretzels), 39
Obatzda (Bavarian Beer Cheese Spread), 41
Gebackener Camembert (Baked Camembert), 42
Gemischter Salat (German Mixed Salad), 48
Kartoffelklöße (Potato Dumplings), 51
Semmelknödel (Bread Dumplings), 52
Spätzle (German Egg Noodles), 57
Rotkohl (Braised Red Cabbage), 59
Sauerbraten (Sweet-and-Sour Beef Roast), 64
Käsespätzle (Cheese Spätzle Noodles), 67
Rinderrouladen (Beef Roulade), 70
Kohlrouladen (Stuffed Cabbage Rolls), 72
Königsberger Klopse (German Meatballs), 76
Körnerbrot (Seeded Bread), 85
Quark Dips, 87
Frikadellen (German Hamburgers), 108
Currywurst (Bratwurst with Curry Ketchup), 111
Zwiebelkuchen (Onion Pie), 122
Kartoffelsalat (Potato Salad), 125
Baumkuchen (Tree Cake), 126
Hefezopf (Yeast Braid), 130
Blaubeer Quarkstrudel (Quark and Blueberry Strudel), 133
Schwarzwälder Kirschtorte (Black Forest Cherry Cake), 135
Rote Grütze (Berry Grits), 141
Käsekuchen im Glas (Raspberry Cheesecake in a Jar), 142
Marmorkuchen (German Marble Cake), 148
Rotweinbirnenkuchen (Red Wine Pear Cake), 150
Tante Heidruns Mandarinen-Schmand-Kuchen (Mandarin Orange Sour Cream Cake), 152
Erdbeerrolle (Sponge Cake with Strawberries and Cream Filling), 154
Vanillekipferl (Vanilla Bean Cookies), 158
Glühwein (Mulled Wine), 162
Raclette (Tableside Cheese Meal), 163
Käsefondue (Cheese Fondue), 166

MAKE AHEAD

Plunderteig (German Croissant Dough), 25
Leberwurst (Liver Paté), 32
Pflaumenmus (Plum Butter), 34
Brezeln (Pretzels), 39
Obatzda (Bavarian Beer Cheese Spread), 41
Mixed Pickles (Pickled Veggies), 47

Kartoffelklöße (Potato Dumplings), 51
Semmelknödel (Bread Dumplings), 52
Rotkohl (Braised Red Cabbage), 59
Sauerkraut (Fermented Cabbage), 60
Gemischter Salat (German Mixed Salad), 48
Sauerbraten (Sweet-and-Sour Beef Roast), 64
Linsensuppe (Lentil Soup), 68
Rinderrouladen (Beef Roulade), 70
Kohlrouladen (Stuffed Cabbage Rolls), 72
Königsberger Klopse (German Meatballs), 76
Jägerschnitzel (Pork Schnitzel with Creamy Mushroom Sauce), 78
Quark Dips, 87
Fleischsalat (Bologna Salad), 90
Gewürzgurken (Sweet-and-Sour Pickles), 91
Milchreis (Rice Pudding), 96
Saure Sahne Waffeln (Sour Cream Waffles), 99
Chicken Döner Kebab (Meat-Stuffed Bread Pockets), 105
Pommesgewürz (German Fry Seasoning), 107
Frikadellen (German Hamburgers), 108
Currywurst (Bratwurst with Curry Ketchup), 111
Klößchen (Mini Potato Dumplings), 117
Zwiebelkuchen (Onion Pie), 122
Kartoffelsalat (Potato Salad), 125
Baumkuchen (Tree Cake), 126
Hefezopf (Yeast Braid), 130
Blaubeer Quarkstrudel (Quark and Blueberry Strudel), 133
Schwarzwälder Kirschtorte (Black Forest Cherry Cake), 135
Rote Grütze (Berry Grits), 141
Käsekuchen im Glas (Raspberry Cheesecake in a Jar), 142
Apfelkuchen (Apple Cake), 144
Rhabarberstreusel (Rhubarb Streusel Cake), 146
Marmorkuchen (German Marble Cake), 148
Rotweinbirnenkuchen (Red Wine Pear Cake), 150
Tante Heidruns Mandarinen-Schmand-Kuchen (Mandarin Orange Sour Cream Cake), 152
Erdbeerrolle (Sponge Cake with Strawberries and Cream Filling), 154
Vanillekipferl (Vanilla Bean Cookies), 158
Spitzbuben (Jam-Filled Cookies), 161
Glühwein (Mulled Wine), 162
Raclette (Tableside Cheese Meal), 163

Recipe Index by Keyword

MAKE WITH A FRIEND

Plunderteig (German Croissant Dough), 25

Franzbrötchen (Croissant-Style Cinnamon Rolls), 28

Laugenecken (Lye Pastries), 30

Spargelsuppe (White Asparagus Cream Soup), 45

Brezeln (Pretzels), 39

Rinderrouladen (Beef Roulade), 70

Königsberger Klopse (German Meatballs), 76

Jägerschnitzel (Pork Schnitzel with Creamy Mushroom Sauce), 78

Chicken Döner Kebab (Meat-Stuffed Bread Pockets), 105

Klößchen (Potato Dumplings), 117

Kartoffelpuffer (Potato Pancakes), 121

Spaghettieis (Spaghetti Ice Cream), 138

Spitzbuben (Jam-Filled Cookies), 161

ONE POT

Pflaumenmus (Plum Butter), 34

Spargelsuppe (White Asparagus Cream Soup), 45

Linsensuppe (Lentil Soup), 68

Milchreis (Rice Pudding), 96

Erbsbrei (Mashed Peas), 118

Käsefondue (Cheese Fondue), 166

QUICK

Obatzda (Bavarian Beer Cheese Spread), 41

Gebackener Camembert (Baked Camembert), 42

Spätzle (German Egg Noodles), 57

Sauerkraut (Fermented Cabbage), 60

Käsespätzle (Cheese Spätzle Noodles), 67

Linsensuppe (Lentil Soup), 68

Backfisch (Beer-Battered Cod), 74

Quark Dips, 87

Fleischsalat (Bologna Salad), 90

Pfannkuchen (Pancakes), 95

Saure Sahne Waffeln (Sour Cream Waffles), 99

Pommesgewürz (German Fry Seasoning), 107

Currywurst (Bratwurst with Curry Ketchup), 111

Spaghettieis (Spaghetti Ice Cream), 138

Rote Grütze (Berry Grits), 141

Käsekuchen im Glas (Raspberry Cheesecake in a Jar), 142

Apfelkuchen (Apple Cake), 144

Marmorkuchen (German Marble Cake), 148

Rotweinbirnenkuchen (Red Wine Pear Cake), 150

Erdbeerrolle (Sponge Cake with Strawberries and Cream Filling), 154

Vanillekipferl (Vanilla Bean Cookies), 158

Glühwein (Mulled Wine), 162

Käsefondue (Cheese Fondue), 166

VEGETARIAN

Brezeln (Pretzels), 39

Obatzda (Bavarian Beer Cheese Spread), 41

Gebackener Camembert (Baked Camembert), 42

Spargelsuppe (White Asparagus Cream Soup), 45

Mixed Pickles (Pickled Vegetables), 47

Gemischter Salat (German Mixed Salad), 48

Kartoffelklöße (Potato Dumplings), 51

Semmelknödel (Bread Dumplings), 52

Bratkartoffeln (Pan-Fried Potatoes), 55

Spätzle (German Egg Noodles), 57

Rotkohl (Braised Red Cabbage), 59

Sauerkraut (Fermented Cabbage), 60

Käsespätzle (Cheese Spätzle Noodles), 67

Linsensuppe (Lentil Soup), 68

Roggenmischbrot (Rye and Wheat Bread), 82

Körnerbrot (Seeded Bread), 85

Quark Dips, 87

Gewürzgurken (Sweet-and-Sour Pickles), 91

Pfannkuchen (Pancakes), 95

Milchreis (Rice Pudding), 96

Saure Sahne Waffeln (Sour Cream Waffles), 99

Dampfnudeln (Steamed Dumplings), 100

Pommesgewürz (German Fry Seasoning), 107

Klößchen (Mini Potato Dumplings), 117

Erbsbrei (Mashed Peas), 118

Glühwein (Mulled Wine), 162

Raclette (Tableside Cheese Meal), 163

Käsefondue (Cheese Fondue), 166

Scan the QR code for more information about Sophie and Dirndl Kitchen, deeper connections to the recipes in the book, free resources, and special offers!

Index

A

almond flour
  Franzbrötchen (Croissant-Style Cinnamon Rolls), 28–29
  Vanillekipferl (Vanilla Bean Cookies), 158
almonds: Apfelkuchen (Apple Cake), 144–145
anchovy paste: Königsberger Klopse (German Meatballs), 76–77
apples
  Apfelkuchen (Apple Cake), 144–145
  Käsefondue (Cheese Fondue), 166–167
  Rotkohl (Braised Red Cabbage), 59
applesauce
  Kartoffelpuffer (Potato Pancakes), 121
  Milchreis (Rice Pudding), 96
asparagus: Spargelsuppe (White Asparagus Cream Soup), 45

B

bacon
  Backfisch (Beer-Battered Cod), 74–75
  Bratkartoffeln (Pan-Fried Potatoes), 55
  Erbsbrei (Mashed Peas), 118–119
  Klößchen (Mini Potato Dumplings), 117
  Kohlrouladen (Stuffed Cabbage Rolls), 72–73
  Leberwurst (Liver Paté), 32–33
  Rinderrouladen (Beef Roulade), 70–71
  Rotkohl (Braised Red Cabbage), 59
  Zwiebelkuchen (Onion Pie), 122–123
beef
  Backfisch (Beer-Battered Cod), 74–75
  Chimichurri-Inspired Steak, 164–165
  Frikadellen (German Hamburgers), 108
  Kohlrouladen (Stuffed Cabbage Rolls), 72–73
  Königsberger Klopse (German Meatballs), 76–77
  Rinderrouladen (Beef Roulade), 70–71
  Sauerbraten (Sweet-and-Sour Beef Roast), 64–65
beer: Obatzda (Bavarian Beer Cheese Spread), 41
beets: Rohkostsalate (Raw Veggie Salad), 48–49
bell peppers
  Käsefondue (Cheese Fondue), 166–167
  Mixed Pickles (Pickled Veggies), 46
  Paprika Quark Dip (Quark Dip with Bell Pepper), 89
  Raclette (Tableside Cheese Meal), 163–165
Bergkäse cheese: Käsespätzle (Cheese Spätzle Noodles), 67
blackberries
  Milchreis (Rice Pudding), 96
  Rote Grütze (Berry Grits), 141
blueberries
  Blaubeer Quarkstrudel (Quark and Blueberry Strudel), 133–134
  Milchreis (Rice Pudding), 96
bologna: Fleischsalat (Bologna Salad), 90
brandy
  Jägerschnitzel (Pork Schnitzel with Creamy Mushroom Sauce), 78–79
  Jägersoße (Creamy Mushroom Sauce), 78–79
  Leberwurst (Liver Paté), 32–33
  Red Wine Jelly, 32–33
bratwurst: Currywurst (Bratwurst with Curry Ketchup), 111
breads. See also rolls
  Hefezopf (Yeast Braid), 130–131
  Körnerbrot (Seeded Bread), 85–86
  Pide (Turkish Bread), 105
  Roggenmischbrot (Rye and Wheat Bread), 82–83
  Sauerbraten (Sweet-and-Sour Beef Roast), 64–65
  Semmelknödel (Bread Dumplings), 52
Brie cheese: Obatzda (Bavarian Beer Cheese Spread), 41

C

cabbage
  Backfisch (Beer-Battered Cod), 74–75
  Chicken Döner Kebab (Meat-Stuffed Bread Pockets), 105–106
  Kohlrouladen (Stuffed Cabbage Rolls), 72–73
  Krautsalat (Coleslaw), 48–49
  Rotkohl (Braised Red Cabbage), 59
  Sauerkraut (Fermented Cabbage), 60
Camembert cheese
  Gebackener Camembert (Baked Camembert), 42
  Obatzda (Bavarian Beer Cheese Spread), 41
carrots
  Linsensuppe (Lentil Soup), 68
  Mixed Pickles (Pickled Veggies), 46
  Rinderrouladen (Beef Roulade), 70–71
  Rohkostsalate (Raw Veggie Salad), 48–49
  Sauerbraten (Sweet-and-Sour Beef Roast), 64–65
cauliflower: Mixed Pickles (Pickled Veggies), 46
celery
  Linsensuppe (Lentil Soup), 68
  Rinderrouladen (Beef Roulade), 70–71
  Sauerbraten (Sweet-and-Sour Beef Roast), 64–65
Cheddar cheese: Brezeln (Pretzels), 39–40
cherries
  Milchreis (Rice Pudding), 96
  Rote Grütze (Berry Grits), 141
  Schwarzwälder Kirschtorte (Black Forest Cherry Cake), 135–137
chicken
  Chicken Döner Kebab (Meat-Stuffed Bread Pockets), 105–106
  Flieten (Fried Chicken Wings), 112
  Leberwurst (Liver Paté), 32–33
chocolate
  Baumkuchen (Tree Cake), 126–127
  Marmorkuchen (German Marble Cake), 148–149
  Milchreis (Rice Pudding), 96
  Pfannkuchen (Pancakes), 95
  Rotweinbirnenkuchen (Red Wine Pear Cake), 150–151
  Schwarzwälder Kirschtorte (Black Forest Cherry Cake), 135–137
chocolate, white: Spaghettieis (Spaghetti Ice Cream), 138
cod: Backfisch (Beer-Battered Cod), 74–75
cognac: Glühwein (Mulled Wine), 162
cookies
  Spitzbuben (Jam-Filled Cookies), 161
  Vanillekipferl (Vanilla Bean Cookies), 158
corn: Raclette (Tableside Cheese Meal), 163–165
cranberry juice: Rote Grütze (Berry Grits), 141
cream cheese
  Dattel Curry Dip (Date and Curry Dip), 87
  Obatzda (Bavarian Beer Cheese Spread), 41
  Paprika Quark Dip (Quark Dip with Bell Pepper), 89
  Schnittlauchquark (Chive Quark Dip), 89
cucumbers
  Gewürzgurken (Sweet-and-Sour Pickles), 91
  Mixed Pickles (Pickled Veggies), 46
  Rohkostsalate (Raw Veggie Salad), 48–49

D

dates: Dattel Curry Dip (Date and Curry Quark Dip), 87

E

eggs
  Afternoon Coffee & Cake, 130–131
  Apfelkuchen (Apple Cake), 144–145
  Backfisch (Beer-Battered Cod), 74–75
  Baumkuchen (Tree Cake), 126–127
  Berliner (German Doughnuts), 23–24
  Blaubeer Quarkstrudel (Quark and Blueberry Strudel), 133–134
  Bratkartoffeln (Pan-Fried Potatoes), 55
  Dampfnudeln (Steamed Dumplings), 100–101
  Erdbeerrolle (Sponge Cake with Strawberries and Cream Filling), 154–155
  Franzbrötchen (Croissant-Style Cinnamon Rolls), 28–29
  Frikadellen (German Hamburgers), 108
  Frühstücksei, 15

Index **171**

Gebackener Camembert (Baked Camembert), 42
Jägerschnitzel (Pork Schnitzel with Creamy Mushroom Sauce), 78–79
Kartoffelklöße (Potato Dumplings), 51
Kartoffelpuffer (Potato Pancakes), 121
Kartoffelsalat (Potato Salad), 125
Käsekuchen im Glas (Raspberry Cheesecake in a Jar), 142
Klößchen (Mini Potato Dumplings), 117
Kohlrouladen (Stuffed Cabbage Rolls), 72–73
Königsberger Klopse (German Meatballs), 76–77
Körnerbrot (Seeded Bread), 85–86
Marmorkuchen (German Marble Cake), 148–149
Pfannkuchen (Pancakes), 95
Rhabarberstreusel (Rhubarb Streusel Cake), 146
Rotweinbirnenkuchen (Red Wine Pear Cake), 150–151
Saure Sahne Waffeln (Sour Cream Waffles), 99
Schwarzwälder Kirschtorte (Black Forest Cherry Cake), 135–137
Semmelknödel (Bread Dumplings), 52
Spargelsuppe (White Asparagus Cream Soup), 45
Spätzle (German Egg Noodles), 56
Spitzbuben (Jam-Filled Cookies), 161
Tante Heidruns Mandarinen-Schmand-Kuchen (Mandarin Orange Sour Cream Cake), 152–153
Zwiebelkuchen (Onion Pie), 122–123
Emmentaler cheese: Käsespätzle (Cheese Spätzle Noodles), 67

F
feta cheese: Chicken Döner Kebab (Meat-Stuffed Bread Pockets), 105–106
frisée: Gemischter Salat (Mixed Salad), 48–49

G
garlic
Chimichurri-Inspired Steak, 164–165
Creamy Garlic Sauce, 105–106
Frikadellen (German Hamburgers), 108
Jägerschnitzel (Pork Schnitzel with Creamy Mushroom Sauce), 78–79
Käsefondue (Cheese Fondue), 166–167
Lemon-Garlic Shrimp, 164–165
Mixed Pickles (Pickled Veggies), 46
Paprika Quark Dip (Quark Dip with Bell Pepper), 89
Raclette (Tableside Cheese Meal), 163–165
Sauerbraten (Sweet-and-Sour Beef Roast), 64–65
Schwenkbraten-Style Pork, 164–165
gelato: Spaghettieis (Spaghetti Ice Cream), 138
Gewürzgurken (Sweet-and-Sour Pickles)
Backfisch (Beer-Battered Cod), 74–75
Fleischsalat (Bologna Salad), 90
Kartoffelsalat (Potato Salad), 125
Käsefondue (Cheese Fondue), 166–167
Raclette (Tableside Cheese Meal), 163–165
recipe, 91

Rinderrouladen (Beef Roulade), 70–71
Gruyère cheese
Brezeln (Pretzels), 39–40
Käsespätzle (Cheese Spätzle Noodles), 67

H
ham
Käsefondue (Cheese Fondue), 166–167
Raclette (Tableside Cheese Meal), 163–165
hazelnuts: Müslibrötchen (Granola Rolls), 20–21
honey
Currywurst (Bratwurst with Curry Ketchup), 111
Kräuter Vinaigrette (Herbed Vinaigrette), 48–49
Krautsalat (Coleslaw), 48–49
Roggenmischbrot (Rye and Wheat Bread), 82–83
Rohkostsalate (Raw Veggie Salad), 48–49

I
ice cream
Rote Grütze (Berry Grits), 141
Saure Sahne Waffeln (Sour Cream Waffles), 99
Spaghettieis (Spaghetti Ice Cream), 138

J
jam
Berliner (German Doughnuts), 23–24
Pfannkuchen (Pancakes), 95
Rotkohl (Braised Red Cabbage), 59
Spitzbuben (Jam-Filled Cookies), 161
juniper berries: Sauerbraten (Sweet-and-Sour Beef Roast), 64–65

K
ketchup: Currywurst (Bratwurst with Curry Ketchup), 111
Kirschwasser
Käsefondue (Cheese Fondue), 166–167
Schwarzwälder Kirschtorte (Black Forest Cherry Cake), 135–137

L
lemons
Afternoon Coffee & Cake, 130–131
Baumkuchen (Tree Cake), 126–127
Blaubeer Quarkstrudel (Quark and Blueberry Strudel), 133–134
Caper Cream Sauce, 76–77
Erdbeerrolle (Sponge Cake with Strawberries and Cream Filling), 154–155
Glühwein (Mulled Wine), 162
Käsekuchen im Glas (Raspberry Cheesecake in a Jar), 142
Kräuter Vinaigrette (Herbed Vinaigrette), 48–49
Leberwurst (Liver Paté), 32–33
Lemon-Garlic Shrimp, 164–165
Marmorkuchen (German Marble Cake), 148–149
Pflaumenmus (Plum Butter), 34
Rhabarberstreusel (Rhubarb Streusel Cake), 146
Rohkostsalate (Raw Veggie Salad), 48–49

Spargelsuppe (White Asparagus Cream Soup), 45
Spitzbuben (Jam-Filled Cookies), 161
lentils: Linsensuppe (Lentil Soup), 68
lingonberry jam: Rotkohl (Braised Red Cabbage), 59
lye
Brezeln (Pretzels), 39–40
Laugenecken (Lye Pastries), 30–31

M
Mixed Pickles (Pickled Veggies)
Käsefondue (Cheese Fondue), 166–167
Raclette (Tableside Cheese Meal), 163–165
recipe, 46
mushrooms
Jägerschnitzel (Pork Schnitzel with Creamy Mushroom Sauce), 78–79
Jägersoße (Creamy Mushroom Sauce), 78–79
Raclette (Tableside Cheese Meal), 163–165

N
nutmeg
Semmelknödel (Bread Dumplings), 52
Spargelsuppe (White Asparagus Cream Soup), 45
Spätzle (German Egg Noodles), 56

O
oats: Müslibrötchen (Granola Rolls), 20–21
onions
Backfisch (Beer-Battered Cod), 74–75
Bratkartoffeln (Pan-Fried Potatoes), 55
Chicken Döner Kebab (Meat-Stuffed Bread Pockets), 105–106
Creamy Garlic Sauce, 105–106
Currywurst (Bratwurst with Curry Ketchup), 111
Erbsbrei (Mashed Peas), 118–119
Fleischsalat (Bologna Salad), 90
Frikadellen (German Hamburgers), 108
Kartoffelpuffer (Potato Pancakes), 121
Kartoffelsalat (Potato Salad), 125
Käsespätzle (Cheese Spätzle Noodles), 67
Klößchen (Mini Potato Dumplings), 117
Kohlrouladen (Stuffed Cabbage Rolls), 72–73
Königsberger Klopse (German Meatballs), 76–77
Linsensuppe (Lentil Soup), 68
Obatzda (Bavarian Beer Cheese Spread), 41
Raclette (Tableside Cheese Meal), 163–165
Rinderrouladen (Beef Roulade), 70–71
Rotkohl (Braised Red Cabbage), 59
Sauerbraten (Sweet-and-Sour Beef Roast), 64–65
Semmelknödel (Bread Dumplings), 52
Zwiebelkuchen (Onion Pie), 122–123
oranges
Glühwein (Mulled Wine), 162
Tante Heidruns Mandarinen-Schmand-Kuchen (Mandarin Orange Sour Cream Cake), 152–153

P

pears: Rotweinbirnenkuchen (Red Wine Pear Cake), 150–151
peas: Erbsbrei (Mashed Peas), 118–119
Pflaumenmus (Plum Butter)
    Dampfnudeln (Steamed Dumplings), 100–101
    Pfannkuchen (Pancakes), 95
    recipe, 34
pickles
    Fleischsalat (Bologna Salad), 90
    Kartoffelsalat (Potato Salad), 125
    Raclette (Tableside Cheese Meal), 163–165
pineapple: Raclette (Tableside Cheese Meal), 163–165
plums: Pflaumenmus (Plum Butter), 34
Plunderteig (German Croissant Dough)
    Franzbrötchen (Croissant-Style Cinnamon Rolls), 28–29
    Laugenecken (Lye Pastries), 30–31
    recipe, 25–26
pork
    Fleischsalat (Bologna Salad), 90
    Frikadellen (German Hamburgers), 108
    Jägerschnitzel (Pork Schnitzel with Creamy Mushroom Sauce), 78–79
    Königsberger Klopse (German Meatballs), 76–77
    Leberwurst (Liver Paté), 32–33
    Schwenkbraten-Style Pork, 164–165
potatoes
    Bratkartoffeln (Pan-Fried Potatoes), 55
    Erbsbrei (Mashed Peas), 118–119
    Kartoffelklöße (Potato Dumplings), 51
    Kartoffelpuffer (Potato Pancakes), 121
    Kartoffelsalat (Potato Salad), 125
    Käsefondue (Cheese Fondue), 166–167
    Klößchen (Mini Potato Dumplings), 117
    Linsensuppe (Lentil Soup), 68
    Pommesgewürz (German Fry Seasoning), 107
    Raclette (Tableside Cheese Meal), 163–165
pumpkin seeds
    Brezeln (Pretzels), 39–40
    Körnerbrot (Seeded Bread), 85–86
    Kürbiskernbrötchen (Pumpkin Seed Rolls), 18–19
    Laugenecken (Lye Pastries), 30–31
    Müslibrötchen (Granola Rolls), 20–21

Q

Quark
    Blaubeer Quarkstrudel (Quark and Blueberry Strudel), 133–134
    Dattel Curry Dip (Date and Curry Quark Dip), 87
    Käsekuchen im Glas (Raspberry Cheesecake in a Jar), 142
    Paprika Quark Dip (Quark Dip with Bell Pepper), 89
    Raclette (Tableside Cheese Meal), 163–165
    recipe, 12
    Schnittlauchquark (Chive Quark Dip), 89

R

raisins: Sauerbraten (Sweet-and-Sour Beef Roast), 64–65
raspberries
    Käsekuchen im Glas (Raspberry Cheesecake in a Jar), 142
    Milchreis (Rice Pudding), 96
    Rote Grütze (Berry Grits), 141
rhubarb: Rhabarberstreusel (Rhubarb Streusel Cake), 146
rice: Milchreis (Rice Pudding), 96
Roggenmischbrot (Rye and Wheat Bread)
    Käsefondue (Cheese Fondue), 166–167
    recipe, 82–83
rolls. See also breads
    Backfisch (Beer-Battered Cod), 74–75
    Franzbrötchen (Croissant-Style Cinnamon Rolls), 28–29
    Frikadellen (German Hamburgers), 108
    Kohlrouladen (Stuffed Cabbage Rolls), 72–73
    Königsberger Klopse (German Meatballs), 76–77
    Kürbiskernbrötchen (Pumpkin Seed Rolls), 18–19
    Müslibrötchen (Granola Rolls), 20–21
    Plunderteig (German Croissant Dough), 25–26
    Weizenbrötchen (White Rolls), 16–17
rum
    Blaubeer Quarkstrudel (Quark and Blueberry Strudel), 133–134
    Glühwein (Mulled Wine), 162
    Marmorkuchen (German Marble Cake), 148–149
    Rotweinbirnenkuchen (Red Wine Pear Cake), 150–151
rye flour
    Körnerbrot (Seeded Bread), 85–86
    Kürbiskernbrötchen (Pumpkin Seed Rolls), 18–19
    Müslibrötchen (Granola Rolls), 20–21
    Roggenmischbrot (Rye and Wheat Bread), 82–83

S

salami
    Käsefondue (Cheese Fondue), 166–167
    Raclette (Tableside Cheese Meal), 163–165
sambal oelek: Paprika Quark Dip (Quark Dip with Bell Pepper), 89
sauerkraut: Erbsbrei (Mashed Peas), 118–119
sausages
    Erbsbrei (Mashed Peas), 118–119
    Kartoffelsalat (Potato Salad), 125
    Linsensuppe (Lentil Soup), 68
schnapps: Glühwein (Mulled Wine), 162
sesame seeds
    Brezeln (Pretzels), 39–40
    Körnerbrot (Seeded Bread), 85–86
    Laugenecken (Lye Pastries), 30–31
shallots
    Dattel Curry Dip (Date and Curry Quark Dip), 87
    Gewürzgurken (Sweet-and-Sour Pickles), 91
    Leberwurst (Liver Paté), 32–33
    Mixed Pickles (Pickled Veggies), 46
shrimp: Lemon-Garlic Shrimp, 164–165
soy sauce: Currywurst (Bratwurst with Curry Ketchup), 111
Spätzle noodles: Käsespätzle (Cheese Spätzle Noodles), 67
strawberries
    Erdbeerrolle (Sponge Cake with Strawberries and Cream Filling), 154–155
    Milchreis (Rice Pudding), 96
    Rote Grütze (Berry Grits), 141
    Spaghettieis (Spaghetti Ice Cream), 138
sunflower seeds
    Brezeln (Pretzels), 39–40
    Körnerbrot (Seeded Bread), 85–86
    Laugenecken (Lye Pastries), 30–31
    Müslibrötchen (Granola Rolls), 20–21
Swiss cheese: Käsefondue (Cheese Fondue), 166–167

T

tomatoes
    Chicken Döner Kebab (Meat-Stuffed Bread Pockets), 105–106
    Currywurst (Bratwurst with Curry Ketchup), 111
    Käsefondue (Cheese Fondue), 166–167
    Linsensuppe (Lentil Soup), 68
    Raclette (Tableside Cheese Meal), 163–165
    Sauerbraten (Sweet-and-Sour Beef Roast), 64–65

V

vinaigrette: Kräuter Vinaigrette (Herbed Vinaigrette), 48–49

W

Weizenbrötchen (White Rolls)
    Backfisch (Beer-Battered Cod), 74–75
    Frikadellen (German Hamburgers), 108
    Kohlrouladen (Stuffed Cabbage Rolls), 72–73
    Königsberger Klopse (German Meatballs), 76–77
    Raclette (Tableside Cheese Meal), 163–165
    recipe, 16–17
white chocolate: Spaghettieis (Spaghetti Ice Cream), 138
wine
    Glühwein (Mulled Wine), 162
    Käsefondue (Cheese Fondue), 166–167
    Leberwurst (Liver Paté), 32–33
    Red Wine Jelly, 32–33
    Rinderrouladen (Beef Roulade), 70–71
    Rotweinbirnenkuchen (Red Wine Pear Cake), 150–151
    Sauerbraten (Sweet-and-Sour Beef Roast), 64–65
    Spargelsuppe (White Asparagus Cream Soup), 45

Y

yogurt
    Blaubeer Quarkstrudel (Quark and Blueberry Strudel), 133–134
    Chicken Döner Kebab (Meat-Stuffed Bread Pockets), 105–106
    Creamy Garlic Sauce, 105–106

Acknowledgments

I enjoyed the ease that I approached this book with, even as my final weeks to my deadline were approaching. The most difficult challenge was sorting my thoughts while getting them onto these pages. Oh, and that Baumkuchen recipe. I owe my kids and husband, Jason, a huge thank-you for allowing me the space to create, which wasn't always easy, and at times, required me to get out of the house and into different environments.

Jason, you tested my Rotwein-Birnen-Kuchen for me (again) when it was crunch time (twice in one day), and you did it with such positivity and with the kitchen towel over your shoulder. Man, that was distracting. Thank you for all your support during this amazing, stressful book-creation journey. I couldn't have done it without you. The kids' sweet hugs and kisses really helped me get to the finish line. You are my biggest motivation. Plus, you are my biggest reason to keep the German culture alive in our own home, with the food, the language, and celebrating German holidays, while living abroad. You inspire me so much.

Thank you to my German family for helping me out with recipes and new approaches and methods to try over the years. I miss you constantly and love you so much. I don't think I would have felt the ease without your support.

My Mama Ute, I know, is honored that she got to have a special place in my book with my rhubarb streusel cake, her favorite, and Käsefondue, her friendliest enemy.

I always have to think of my twin sister, Jeanne, when I am making my Laugenecken. They are our favorite German breakfast food. I miss you so much. Thank you so much for your beautiful, joyful soul. My dream is to one day live close to you again, so we can cook together whenever we want.

Whenever I was questioning whether writing a book is the right choice, I always thought of my Papa Sven. His entrepreneurial spirit had me trusting that anything is possible and that I can do hard things. His Mama, Oma Inge, still inspires me with her big cookbook collection and her love for creating beautiful, delicious food. And I always think of her when grating nutmeg.

Sitting at my Opa Elmar's house to write about my Oma Sieghilde's recipes and making her Klößchen in her kitchen with my mom was the best way to surround myself with my Oma's spirit. Many of my family's recipes ended up in this book, and I am so grateful and want to send a big thank you to all of them.

I am also so thankful for my American family who helped out with the kids during crunch time and always had an uplifting word for me when my energy was running low.

My friends were my biggest cheerleaders during this book-creation process and hyped me up when I was feeling overwhelmed and stressed. I didn't see much of them in the final weeks leading up to the deadline, but I was so thankful for every encouraging text. I am especially grateful for my friend Jess from Inquiring Chef, a fellow cookbook author who had just gone through the cookbook writing and publishing process for the first time as I was starting my own journey. She is such an inspiration for me and looking to her for support felt natural and comforting.

Thank you to my publisher for taking a chance on me and helping me to create the cookbook of my dreams. This book feels like my fourth baby and really everything I have always wanted in a cookbook. It was so hard selecting the recipes to go into this book. I feel so proud and grateful, and I just know this won't be my last cookbook.

And to all my blog readers and followers, you inspire me so much. It's the stories you constantly bring to me, of how my pretzels took you right back to Germany's best bakeries or

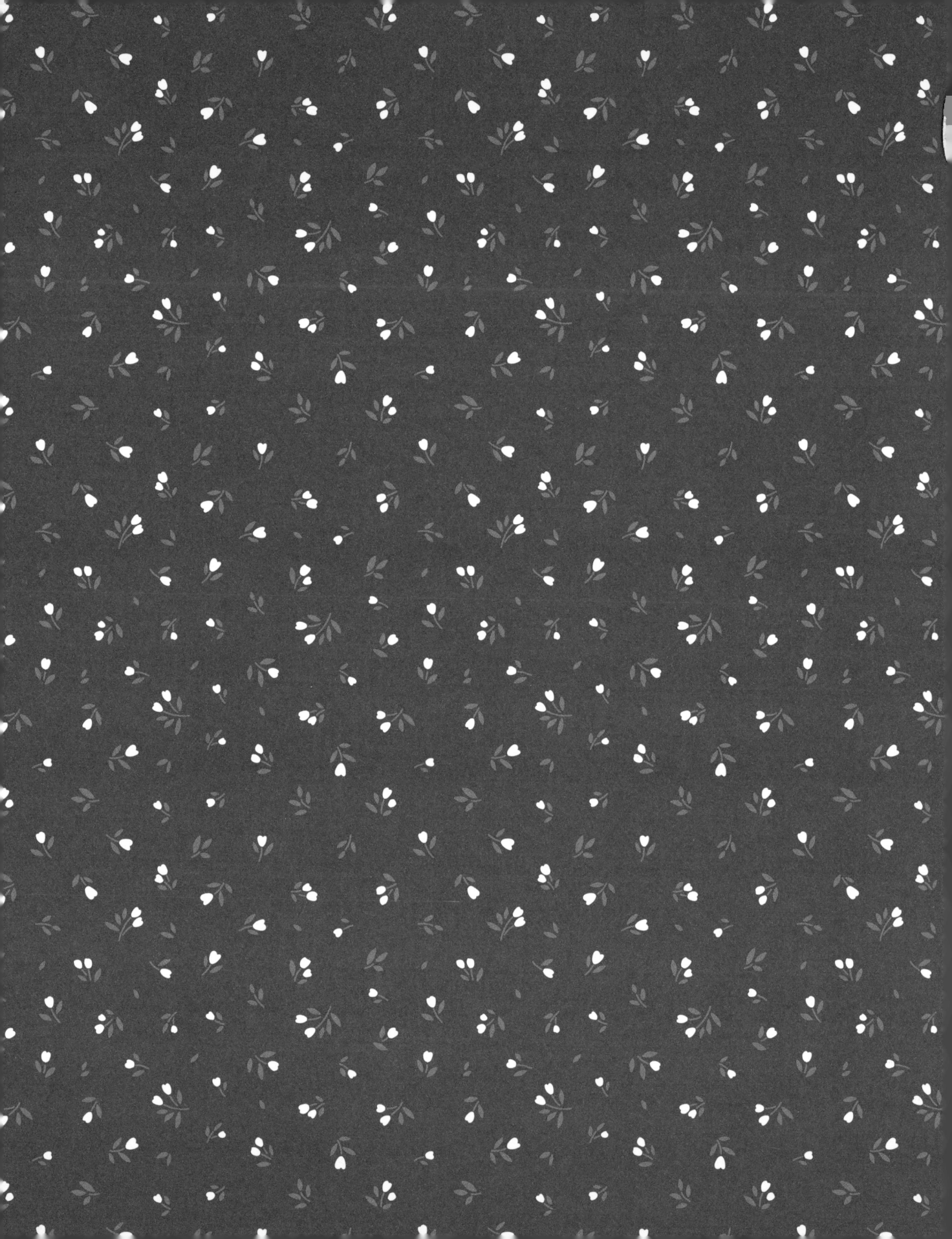

© 2025 by Quarto Publishing Group USA, Inc.
Text and Photography © 2025 by Sophie Sadler

First published in 2025 by Rock Point, an imprint of The Quarto Group,
142 West 36th Street, 4th Floor, New York, NY 10018, USA
(212) 779-4972 www.Quarto.com

EEA Representation, WTS Tax d.o.o.,
Žanova ulica 3, 4000 Kranj, Slovenia.
www.wts-tax.si

All rights reserved. No part of this book may be reproduced in any form without written permission of the copyright owners. All images included in this book are original works created by the artist credited on the copyright page, not generated by artificial intelligence, and have been reproduced with the knowledge and prior consent of the artist. The producer, publisher, and printer accept no responsibility for any infringement of copyright or otherwise arising from the contents of this publication. Every effort has been made to ensure the credits accurately comply with information supplied. We apologize for any inaccuracies that may have occurred and will resolve inaccurate or missing information in a subsequent reprinting of the book.

Rock Point titles are also available at discount for retail, wholesale, promotional and bulk purchase. For details, contact the Special Sales Manager by email at specialsales@quarto.com or by mail at The Quarto Group, Attn: Special Sales Manager, 100 Cummings Center Suite, 265D, Beverly, MA 01915, USA.

10 9 8 7 6 5 4 3 2 1

ISBN: 978-1-57715-482-2

Digital edition published in 2025
eISBN: 978-0-7603-9307-9

Library of Congress Cataloging-in-Publication Data

Names: Sadler, Sophie author
Title: German home kitchen : traditional recipes that capture the flavors of Germany / Sophie Sadler.
Description: New York, NY, USA : Rock Point, 2025. | Includes index. |
   Summary: "German Home Kitchen offers authentic yet easy-to-make recipes
   that bring the rich culinary traditions of Germany to your table"--
   Provided by publisher.
Identifiers: LCCN 2025009106 (print) | LCCN 2025009107 (ebook) | ISBN
   9781577154822 | ISBN 9780760393079 ebook
Subjects: LCSH: Cooking, German | Cooking--Germany | LCGFT: Cookbooks
Classification: LCC TX721 .S1255 2025 (print) | LCC TX721 (ebook) | DDC
   641.5943--dc23/eng/20250319
LC record available at https://lccn.loc.gov/2025009106
LC ebook record available at https://lccn.loc.gov/2025009107

Publisher: Rage Kindelsperger
Creative Director: Laura Drew
Managing Editor: Cara Donaldson
Editor: Kristy Mucci
Cover & Interior Design: Laura Klynstra

Printed in Huizhou, Guangdong, China TT072025

how my Zwiebelkuchen brought back memories of spending time in Germany during autumn. German food is all about finding the connection to Germany, but also to other like-minded individuals like you. You are here because you know you belong here. Stay as you are and don't ever give up on your dreams.

Finally, this book is for anyone missing Germany. I know that living abroad isn't easy and neither is recreating authentic German food experiences and keeping up with German traditions in a new country, like remembering to set your kids' boots outside on the night before December 6.

Prost to all of us cooking German food with and for our loved ones, one recipe at a time. My dream is to make German food approachable and accessible to everyone. And it all starts with you.

About the Author

Sophie Sadler grew up in and around Germany's oldest city, Trier, surrounded by mountains of vineyards and Roman ruins. She first visited the United States as an exchange student in 2005 and then moved to the United States in 2009 to attend the University of Kansas, where she graduated with a double major in marketing and finance, all while running a cupcake catering business out of her studio apartment.

Her Mama Ute's inventive cooking, her Oma Sieghilde's traditional German cooking, and her Oma Inge's detail-oriented, by-the-book cooking were her biggest influences when it came to inspiring and shaping her own cooking journey. She started her German food blog, *Dirndl Kitchen*, after figuring out some unique ways to make German food approachable and accessible to everyone, using simple ingredients and clear methods. Her hope is to inspire people to get in the kitchen and share authentic German cooking with those they love the most.

She lives in Kansas City, Missouri, with her best friend, biggest supporter, and husband, Jason, and her three little cheerleaders and loves, Zoë, Eloïse, and Maximilian. Ich habe euch unendlich lieb.

About the Author